Leadership in Communist China

Leadership in Communist China

John Wilson Lewis
Cornell University

CORNELL UNIVERSITY PRESS
Ithaca, New York

To
Jacquelyn

Preface

THE distinguishing characteristic of Chinese communism is the leadership doctrine by which the party elite rules China. The principles of party leadership examined here are primarily those derived by revolutionary Chinese Communist cadres under the leadership of Mao Tse-tung. Because of the sheer bulk of the material related to party leadership doctrine, I have emphasized the period of the rise and fall of "great leap" optimism—a period from 1958 to 1962, in which earlier doctrines fused in a dramatic culmination and met their most rigorous test. Although I have used refugee interviews to evaluate official pronouncements, the study on balance relates to party principles rather than to descriptive operation. Official principles, however, have placed exacting limits on Chinese realities and have been the key source of motivation and direction at all levels.

The book closes during a period of extreme uncertainty in China. The 700,000,000 Chinese face deepening economic and political crisis. In September, 1962, the Tenth Plenum of the party Central Committee brought changes to major party organs and further stress on economic retrenchment and on the recurring failures and mistakes of various leadership elements.

The thirteenth anniversary of the Chinese People's Republic also marks a period of mounting tension in Sino-Indian relations. The leadership doctrine that was born in the minds of guerrilla fighters and later base-area leaders bears a major responsibility for the magnitude of the chaos and the intensity of the modern Chinese tragedy. This probably does not mean that the continuing adherence to doctrine will destroy or drastically revise the Chinese leadership, although major modifications might well follow in the wake of Mao's death (Mao will be 70 in 1963). More likely, the doctrine itself will be subjected to fundamental modifications as Chinese and international realities prick the overage images of past revolutions. Signs abound that changes are already under way.

The Wade-Giles system of romanization has in the main been used in this study. Some names of individuals and place names which have an accepted, nonstandard spelling have been rendered according to common usage. One other slight change from the Library of Congress version of the Wade-Giles system is my use of "szu" instead of "ssu" in accordance with the best advice of language specialists. Unless otherwise indicated, the translation from the Chinese original is mine, and I am responsible for possible errors and misinterpretations. I have not considered it necessary to use Chinese characters in the study because in general the titles and phrases used reflect standard Chinese Communist terminology and present no recognition problems for students of the Chinese language.

This work owes whatever merit it may have to the training and guidance of H. Arthur Steiner, whose vital concern with rigorous scholarship and Chinese politics remains a genuine inspiration. Among a large number of others at the University of California, Los Angeles, who have given generously of their time and advice in the preparation of this study, I would like particularly to thank Thomas P. Jenkin.

I also wish to acknowledge with gratitude the contribution

of several individuals and institutions in the research and writing stages of this manuscript. For their assistance during my research in Taiwan and Hong Kong, I am deeply indebted to Robert and Jacqueline Goodnow, Arthur P. Wolf, and James Wrenn. The many Chinese who participated in the interviews or generously gave assistance and suggestions at various stages understandably wished to remain anonymous, but I would like to record publicly my sincere appreciation for their participation and invaluable assistance. A grant from the Ford Foundation supported my research in the Far East and the United States. Although the views expressed in this study are my own and not necessarily those of the Ford Foundation, I am deeply indebted to the Foundation for its financial and other assistance from 1958 to 1961. The personal advice and translation services of the U.S. Hong Kong Consulate General were of great value and are gratefully acknowledged.

Although it is inadequate recognition for the assistance I received, I wish to thank Howard L. Boorman, George Fischer, George McT. Kahin, G. William Skinner, and Allen S. Whiting for their important comments and suggestions on all or parts of the manuscript. For assistance in the preparation of the manuscript, I am indebted to the Faculty Research Grants Committee of Cornell University, to Yin-maw Kau, and to Marguerite R. Gigliello.

To my wife, Jacquelyn Lewis, I owe a very special debt for her unfailing encouragement throughout the years of research and writing and for listening to each revision of the manuscript with interest and insight.

Finally, I wish to acknowledge the permission of the following publishers and copyright holders to quote passages from their publications:

University of Washington Press to quote from *Mao's China: Party Reform Documents, 1942–1944,* translated by Boyd Compton.

The American Academy of Political and Social Science to quote from articles by H. Arthur Steiner and Chao Kuo-chün in *The Annals of the American Academy of Political and Social Science*, volume CCCXXI (January, 1959).

International Publishers to quote approximately 1,300 words from the four-volume *Selected Works* by Mao Tse-tung.

JOHN WILSON LEWIS

Ithaca, New York
October 1, 1962

Contents

Tables

Charts

Introduction

THIS is a study of the dynamics by which the Communist elite has sought to control and operate in Chinese society. The basic leadership theory and operational procedures of the Chinese Communist Party are the principal parts of these dynamics, which at first sight appear to be simply systems of command but in fact are designed to produce affirmative responses by the Chinese people and cadres to the goals of Chinese Communist policy. The techniques by which party leaders have attempted to initiate and direct the affirmative response of the general population are the principal subject of the present study.

The central leadership technique of the Chinese Communists has been to bring all Chinese into formal organizations of various kinds to advance and reinforce Communist actions and policies and to bring about rigidly structured relationships. The Communists hold that properly conceived "socialist" relationships between party leaders and the people and within the general population are founded on a permanent consensus which exists as a special quality of the working classes. Around this consensus the Communists have developed a new code of socialist morality to replace the traditional values of Chinese society and politics. They stipulate, or in their terms "prove," that the creative potential of the latent consensus has remained unfulfilled in China because of impediments within the pre-1949 society created by foreign and domestic exploiting classes and their agents. Some organizations have been used principally to suppress or control the "exploiters," while others have been employed to recast social relationships as allegedly required by the transformation of the Chinese society to socialist and Communist forms.

In constructing a socialist system which is total in its scope and content, the Chinese Communist Party had first to solve many problems related to the social orientation of party members and the Chinese people. Party leaders have appreciated the problems and difficulties of this task and have devised numerous practical measures to cope with the individual problems that have occurred in the course of implementing their policy goals. The hardship of tasks to be accomplished has been made to serve the party leadership by challenging party members and the general populace and by providing a basis for the evaluation of their performance. Party leaders have also utilized contrived forms of "struggle" and in general have endeavored to identify themselves with the Chinese people in a militant spirit in order to create a common ground of purpose and method in the solution of the complex problems that have arisen. Mutual involvement and common identity are among the conscious goals sought by leading party cadres as they seek to create the new social orientation of the lower-level cadres and the "broad masses."

The new relationships, which are being worked out in the main through organizational techniques, are more important than formal institutions. The proper organizational environment presumably accelerates the restructuring of the Chinese society by combining and maximizing the energies of the

Chinese people. Although organizations play a leading role in the restructuring process, "organization" in the Marxist-Leninist rationale belongs to the realm of "superstructure" and as such is temporary, expendable, and continuously subject to modifications. The prediction by the Communists that such organizations as the party and the state must eventually "wither away" will be fulfilled, the Communists hold, when the dialectical process creates a qualitatively new and permanently automatic set of relationships within the Chinese society. To hasten this millennial day, the direction of leadership and organization in Communist China has been toward a consistent expansion of organization to incorporate the greatest number of Chinese into the largest number of structured personal relationships. In such an organizational context, an emergence of a general consensus presumably signals the correct resolution of relationships, and this may partially explain the passion for unanimity in mainland China.[1] Mass organizations, communes, small study groups, work teams, and a variety of cultural and political organs overlap to coordinate and guide the total scope of the individual's activities.

Consistent with the "totalization" of organized relationships, the Communists have concurrently devoted considerable attention to systematizing the variety and complexities of leadership method into a single, unified whole. This effort has required a new vocabulary, some parts of which refer to actual techniques used by Communist cadres and some parts of which refer to the future era of communism. As is commonly recognized, the Communists argue the logical consistency of combining reality and mystique by recourse to the theory of dialectical union. This combination creates an aura of totality and inevitable purpose which lends support and gives direction to current leader-

[1] Edgar H. Schein *et al.*, *Coercive Persuasion: A Socio-psychological Analysis of the "Brainwashing" of American Civilian Prisoners by the Chinese Communists* (New York: W. W. Norton, 1961), chap. iii.

ship activities. In the leadership techniques of Communist China, the sense of unity facilitates cadre training, intellectual reform, and mass obedience irrespective of the internal logical flaws created by mixing the real world with Marxist fantasy.

The unification of leadership method within an all-encompassing organizational framework has been accompanied by the proliferation of on-the-spot techniques. All concrete forms of leadership action must fit the total entity and thus are given labels and a "place" in the over-all unified system. *Ad hoc* techniques as well as general "mass line" techniques have been given complex numerical and other identifications or such pretentious labels as the technique of "letting a hundred flowers blossom, a hundred schools of thought contend." One aspect of this present study is to examine the general integrating principles and rationale which underlie the vast variety of leadership techniques. This approach provides a foundation for judging many individual phenomena such as "thought remolding" and offers a means to isolate important leadership strategies and goals.

The reader may feel that too little attention has been devoted to Communist forms of coercion. There is no chapter on prisons, reform-through-labor camps, and the secret police, though each is handled in appropriate contexts. Coercion in the Communist mind falls into two general types—peaceful and violent. The first type which is applicable to "friendly" classes is a form of leadership manipulation within the range of leadership techniques examined. "Vanguard" leaders must zealously guide both the creation of the new socialist society and the liberation of the energy potential in the latent popular consensus. Thus conceived, leadership drive constitutes a form of "liberation"—not compulsion or force, though the threat of coercion may strengthen the leader's position. The second type of coercion requiring violence occurs outside of rec-

4

ognized leadership practice. This latter form of coercion applies to "enemy" classes and calls for suppression and elimination, quickly and ruthlessly. Obviously, the Communist Party deems itself the only body qualified to determine who is the "enemy" and in what degree. The unspoken threat of reclassification, moreover, remains an essential weapon in the arsenal of the leadership, though once the threat materializes, the "leader" is superseded by the prison warder or the firing squad. Communist officials have used brute terror as a primary weapon during the initial period of the consolidation of the regime, to a certain extent throughout the Korean War, and to a lesser degree during the rectification campaign of 1957–1958. Nevertheless, the Communist leaders emphatically deny the utility of terror for long-range leadership purposes and recognize that its use, however guarded, must give way to methods of persuasion to induce support. In effect, the initiation of violence on any enlarged scale even to resolve agricultural crises and unrest is an admission of leadership failure and a retreat into reaction.

The problem of Chinese Communist leadership is extensive and often perplexing. The vast source material on the party and its techniques of operation invites a variety of approaches in research. I have attempted to bring tentative answers to some of the central problems of leadership based on an examination of the written evidence of Chinese Communist policy statements and practices, as supplemented by interviews with forty-five Chinese refugees in Hong Kong in 1959–1961. Answers must remain tentative and uncertain because of distortions and omissions in the available documentation and limitations on the memories of the Chinese interviewed in Hong Kong. Moreover, the extensive scope of the problems of leadership and organization has led me to concentrate on the more significant leadership techniques and the contemporary (1958–1962) ideological and social framework within which the leadership personnel of the party function. Many specific details including biographies of individual leaders and historical developments have been given secondary emphasis.

Despite the limitations of the sources, it is still possible to make general statements and draw conclusions concerning Chinese Communist leadership doctrine which have a high degree of validity. The Chinese Communists have been in power more than thirteen years, and for the decade prior to their rise to power in 1949, they had maintained a government controlling more than ninety million Chinese in various "liberated" areas. The Chinese Communist Party celebrated its fortieth anniversary on July 1, 1961, and for a generation it has had a record unique among all Communist parties of stable, central leadership. Its principal leaders have held key positions for more than twenty-five years. The validity of general statements about Communist leadership in China can thus be examined in a variety of contexts over an extended period of time.

The examination of Communist leadership doctrine necessarily concerns itself more with the party elite than with non-party Chinese. This does not mean that the latter will not have a significant impact on the course of events in China. Given the preference of the elite for methods of consensus rather than of "commandism," the Chinese people should continue to play a major role in China's future development, though this role will probably be performed in accordance with elite prescriptions.

I

The Development of Communist Leadership Techniques in China

Factionalism and Mass Line in Early Party History

THE Communist Party of China was founded in Shanghai at its first congress in July, 1921.[1] Based on the organizational principles adopted at this congress and operating with anti-imperialist slogans and a united front line passed at the succeeding congresses, the Communist Party expanded to about 1,000

[1] On the founding of the party and subsequent party history, I have used primarily Yang Yu-chiung, *Chung-kuo cheng-tang shih* [History of China's Political Parties] (Shanghai: Shang-wu yin-shu kuan, n.d. [1936]); Shih Yün, ed., *Chung-kuo kung-ch'an tang ti ch'eng-li* [The Establishment of the Chinese Communist Party] (Peking: T'ung-su tu-wu ch'u-pan she, 1957); Hu Ch'iao-mu, *Chung-kuo kung-ch'an tang ti san-shih nien* [Thirty Years of the Communist Party of China] (Peking: Jen-min ch'u-pan she, 1951); Chung-kuo kung-ch'an tang chung-

members by 1925.[2] The Central Committee of the party under the leadership of Ch'en Tu-hsiu adhered to the directives of the Communist International (Comintern) and was guided by Comintern agents, though most of the provincial party organizations operated along independent local lines.

After the First Congress of the Kuomintang in 1924, the Kuomintang (Nationalist Party) organization, by then heavily indebted to Soviet support, became in essence identical to that of the Communists and was joined by members of the Chinese Communist Party. Because of the prestige of the Kuomintang leadership and that leadership's use of Comintern assistance, the Nationalist leadership under Sun Yat-sen and later Chiang Kai-shek dominated the united front with the Communists. After the death of Lenin in 1924, Communist organization in China

---

yang Hua-nan fen-chü hsüan-ch'uan pu [Communist Party of China, Central Committee, South China Regional Propaganda Department], ed., *Chung-kuo kung-ch'an tang shih hsüeh-hsi tzu-liao* [Study Materials on the History of the Communist Party of China] (Canton: Hua-nan jen-min ch'u-pan she, 1951), vols. I, II; Huang Ho, ed., *Chung-kuo kung-ch'an tang san-shih-wu nien chien shih* [A Short History of Thirty-five Years of the Communist Party of China] (Peking: T'ung-su tu-wu ch'u-pan she, 1957); Ho Kan-chih, *A History of the Modern Chinese Revolution* (Peking: Foreign Languages Press, 1959); Benjamin I. Schwartz, *Chinese Communism and the Rise of Mao* (Cambridge: Harvard University Press, 1951); Conrad Brandt, Benjamin Schwartz, and John K. Fairbank, *A Documentary History of Chinese Communism* (Cambridge: Harvard University Press, 1952); Harold R. Isaacs, *The Tragedy of the Chinese Revolution* (2d rev. ed.; Stanford: Stanford University Press, 1961); C. Martin Wilbur and Julie Lien-ying How, *Documents on Communism, Nationalism, and Soviet Advisers in China 1918–1927* (New York: Columbia University Press, 1956); Edgar Snow, *Red Star over China* (New York: Modern Library, 1944); and Tso-liang Hsiao, *Power Relations within the Chinese Communist Movement, 1930–1934* (Seattle: University of Washington Press, 1961).

[2] The place of meeting and dates of the eight party congresses (irregularly scheduled until the 1956 party Constitution) are: Shanghai (1921), Shanghai (1922), Canton (1923), Shanghai (1925), Wuhan (1927), Moscow (1928), Yenan (1945), and Peking (1956, 1958).

became subject to the influence of Stalin and the internecine Kremlin struggle for power. The Chinese Communists were required to obey Comintern directives issued to advantage Stalin in the Soviet power struggle. As a consequence of following unrealistic and misleading Comintern directives, the Chinese Communists were decimated in the 1927 struggle with the Kuomintang, and the united front was destroyed. After the chaotic period of the 1927 anti-Communist massacres,[3] abortive uprisings,[4] and the Kiangsi Soviet (1931–1934), Mao Tse-tung emerged the party leader of the shattered Communist forces during the Long March (1934–1935).

It is not necessary to sort through the major views of the primary groups within the Chinese Communist Party in the 1920's to gain a sense of the panorama of factionalism that then prevailed. Anarchism, pluralism, liberalism, and many other shades of opinion found advocates in the revolutionary journals and debates.[5] Party leader Ch'en Tu-hsiu was a respected intellectual who maintained the balance of factions under Comintern authority. After the Emergency Conference of August 7, 1927, when Ch'ü Ch'iu-pai replaced Ch'en as party secretary-general, the Communists who had survived the Kuomintang suppression were irrevocably committed to "party," but of these some—particularly Mao Tse-tung—sought to reconstruct the party organization that had brought them to the 1927 defeat.

[3] On April 12, 1927, Chiang Kai-shek staged an anti-Communist coup in Shanghai which was then carried to Nanking and Kwangtung Province. This was followed by the July 15 Wuhan anti-Communist Party suppression led by Wang Ching-wei. After these suppression campaigns, the Communist Party membership dropped from 57,900 to about 10,000.

[4] This refers to such Communist-supported uprisings as those at Nanchang (August 1, 1927), the "Autumn Harvest Insurrection" (September 5–18, 1927) in Hunan, the occupation of Swatow (September 25, 1927), and the Canton Commune (December 11–14, 1927).

[5] See, for example, Robert A. Scalapino and George T. Yu, *The Chinese Anarchist Movement* (Berkeley: Center for Chinese Studies, 1961).

Although the party had been organized nominally according to the principle of democratic centralism, organizational unity and operation had in fact been keyed to Soviet authority and the compromise of personal factions. Factionalism had been the hallmark of the pre-1927 political leadership in spite of the ideological trappings. The blow of the Kuomintang suppression, the purge of Ch'en Tu-hsiu, and contradictory and unrealistic Comintern policies brought discredit to the "code" of personal factionalism in the Chinese Communist Party and motivated the search by a few key Communists for alternative methods of political leadership.

Central Committee leaders after Ch'en's purge and before Mao's leadership was acknowledged (1935) failed to reintegrate the party, which increasingly was strained by internal policy dissension aggravated by Comintern manipulation.[6] Ch'ü Ch'iu-pai, Li Li-san, and the two Comintern-trained "returned students" (Ch'en Shao-yü and Ch'in Pang-hsien),[7] who led the Chinese Communist Party Central Committee between 1927 and 1935,[8] continued to operate according to the principle of leadership prestige and to issue doctrinaire commands. Contrary to this system of leadership, Mao Tse-tung in the 1920's was developing and utilizing techniques by which policy would be derived from, tested in, and integrated with the social sources of revolutionary power in China. His idea as evidenced in his original rural analyses was not to reverse the "policy-determining action" formula but to unite policy, ideology, and social practice in a continuous process, the basic idea of the "mass line."

During the 1920's, Mao was a stranger to most of the intra-

[6] Tso-liang Hsiao, *op. cit., passim.*

[7] These two "returned students" are better known as Wang Ming and Po Ku, respectively.

[8] Hsiang Chung-fa was the nominal leader of the party during the period of actual control by Li Li-san.

party factionalism that centered around Ch'en Tu-hsiu in the Central Committee. After attending the initial 1921 congress, Mao missed the Second and Fourth Communist Party congresses (1922 and 1925). Despite his membership in the Central Committee after the Third Congress (1923), Mao's primary arena of action remained in his native Hunan Province. Mao became Hunan party secretary in 1921, and the following year he was appointed chairman of the Hunan branch of the budding Chinese labor organization. In the labor organization, he participated in numerous strikes and renewed his acquaintance with Liu Shao-ch'i, member of the labor Secretariat (*Chung-kuo lao-tung tsu-ho shu-chi-pu*). Mao Tse-tung's primary commitment after 1925 was in the peasant movement,[9] but his success as a peasant organizer cannot be separated from his earlier achievements in worker organization, education, and strikes. Mao's 1927 judgment that "urban people and military accomplishments occupy only 30 per cent" in the over-all accomplishments of the democratic revolution (as opposed to 70 per cent for the village peasantry) was a tactical estimate based on rather substantial experience in both urban and rural organization.[10]

Mao related his daily contacts in worker-peasant organization and agitation to basic policy assessments. From his earliest writings to such post-1949 surveys as his preface to the *Socialist*

[9] After 1925, Mao successively held posts in the National Institute of Peasant Movement (the official translation of the *Nung-min yün-tung chiang-hsi hui*) in Canton (which coordinated the peasant organizations in advance of the Northern Expedition); in the Committee on the Peasant Movement in the Central Committee; and in the National Peasant Association in Wuhan.

[10] Mao Tse-tung, "Hu-nan nung-min yün-tung k'ao-ch'a pao-kao" [Report of an Investigation into the Peasant Movement in Hunan], *Nung-min yün-tung yü nung-ts'un tiao-ch'a* [The Peasant Movement and Village Investigations] (compiled and reprinted; Hong Kong: Hsin min-chu ch'u-pan she, 1949), p. 5.

Upsurge in China's Countryside (December, 1955),[11] Mao displayed a sense of close proximity to social realities. The survey technique popularized by Mao required on-the-spot investigation among a cross section of the ordinary Chinese in order to ascertain opinions, material conditions, and general support for alternative courses of action.[12] Mao understood first-hand both labor unions and peasant associations, and it is doubtful whether he had many illusions about the relevance of policy edicts emanating from the Central Committee in Shanghai or from the Comintern when he was engaged in the daily struggle in Hunan. Nevertheless, Mao did attempt to bring his ideas into conformity with Marxist-Leninist theory and equate his generalizations with Comintern doctrine. For example, he wrote the 1926 "Analysis of the Classes in Chinese Society" as a critique of the classes allied within the Kuomintang-Communist united front. By this skillful focusing on classes, Mao violated neither united front cooperation nor Marxist orthodoxy (see following paragraph) in stressing the role of the proletariat as the "most progressive class" and "the leading force in the revolutionary movement." [13] Yet, by this analysis of class forces in more doctrinaire terms, Mao was able to exploit his vantage point in Canton, where he witnessed during March, 1926,[14] the beginning of the power shift to the conservatives in the Kuomintang.

[11] *Chung-kuo nung-ts'un ti she-hui-chu-i kao-ch'ao* (Peking: Jen-min ch'u-pan she, 1956), vol. I.

[12] For example, see Mao Tse-tung, "Report of an Investigation into the Peasant Movement in Hunan" [March, 1927], *Selected Works* (New York: International Publishers, 1954–1956), I, 21–59, and Mao, "Preface and Postscript to 'Rural Survey'" [March 17 and April 19, 1941], *Selected Works*, IV, 7–11.

[13] Mao, "Analysis of the Classes in Chinese Society," *Selected Works*, I, 19–20.

[14] Ho Kan-chih, *op. cit.*, pp. 127–128, places Mao in Canton during part of 1925 and 1926. According to Edgar Snow, *op. cit.*, pp. 160–161,

Moreover, the orthodox "leading force" role Mao assigned to the proletariat in the alliance of revolutionary classes was not necessarily contradicted by his 1927 statement which assigned 70 per cent of the revolutionary accomplishment to the village peasantry. Lenin, among others, had frequently distinguished leading role from class participants. Majority peasant "accomplishment" was a fact of Chinese life, and, given the revolutionary character of China's peasantry, the Comintern's favorable appraisal of peasant movements in the "more backward states and nations in which feudal or patriarchal and patriarchal-peasant relations predominate" [15] had particular relevance in China. More important to this discussion than the much-debated orthodoxy of Mao's *Report of an Investigation into the Peasant Movement in Hunan* (March, 1927),[16] however, is the essential point Mao tried to make in the report. He wrote the *Hunan Report* after six months of dramatic successes in the Northern Expedition, much of which success was due to advance organization and propaganda work among the peasantry. Although the original version of the *Hunan Report* has since been edited to indicate the "key role" of the Communist Party,[17] Mao in fact avoided the question of party leadership and focused instead on the correct use of the peasant movement. As a ranking member in the peasant movement, the

---

Mao was "chief of the Agitprop department of the Kuomintang" and engaged in peasant work until he left Canton in the spring of 1926.

[15] V. I. Lenin, "Preliminary Draft of Theses on the National and Colonial Questions," *Selected Works* (Moscow: Foreign Languages Publishing House, 1952), II, pt. 2, 467–468.

[16] One phase of this debate is carried in the *China Quarterly*, nos. 1, 2, and 4 (1960).

[17] Mao, "Report of an Investigation," *Selected Works*, I, 31, 50, has added statements on the role of the Chinese Communist Party; the *Selected Works* omits the statement on 30 per cent–70 per cent accomplishment discussed above.

Kuomintang, and the Communist Party, he was appealing to the leaders of all "revolutionary parties" including the Kuomintang to remember that revolution was generated within the common Chinese people, not at the top. He said:

In a very short time . . . several hundred million peasants will rise like a tornado or tempest, a force so extraordinarily swift and violent that no power, however great, will be able to suppress it. . . . All revolutionary parties and all revolutionary comrades will stand before them to be tested, and to be accepted or rejected as they decide.[18]

Leadership Techniques during the "Low Ebb"

In Chinese Communist periodization of recent Chinese history, the years from 1924 to 1927 are called the "first revolutionary civil war." This war was "the first anti-imperialist and anti-feudal revolutionary war by the Chinese people under the leadership of the Chinese Communist Party," [19] Communist historians now assert, and was sustained by the cooperative efforts of the Communist Party and the Kuomintang. The "first revolutionary civil war" ended in the famous rupture between the two parties, and the Chinese Communist Party, close to complete annihilation from 1927 to 1930, remembers these three post-1927 years as the "low ebb of the Chinese revolution." [20] Mao Tse-tung in 1928 complained that the "revolutionary upsurge in the country as a whole is subsiding." [21] He described the attitude of the masses toward the Red Army as "cold and reserved" and the Kuomintang forces as strong and united. "We have to fight the enemy forces hard whoever they are," Mao

[18] *Ibid.*, pp. 21–22.   [19] Ho Kan-chih, *op. cit.*, p. 168.
[20] *Ibid.*, p. 172.
[21] The quotations from Mao in this paragraph are from his "The Struggle in the Chingkang Mountains" [November 25, 1928], *Selected Works*, I, 99.

wrote, "and scarcely any mutiny or uprising has taken place within the enemy forces." Mao summed up the tenor of the "low ebb" when he added: "We have an acute sense of loneliness and are every moment longing for the end of such a lonely life."

At the Emergency Conference of August 7, 1927, Ch'en Tu-hsiu was ousted as party secretary-general, and the delegates called for peasant uprisings during the autumn in Hunan, Hupei, Kiangsi, and Kwangtung. Mao Tse-tung was sent to Hunan to lead the "Autumn Harvest Insurrection," which lasted two weeks (September 5–18, 1927).[22] With the defeat of the uprising, Mao's forces retreated to Kiangsi Province, where Mao reorganized his troops into the Workers' and Peasants' Red Army and introduced the system of party representatives (*tang tai-piao*)[23] and the party "Front Committee" as the army's supreme leadership organ. After this reorganization, Mao's Red Army retreated into the Chingkang Mountains on the Hunan-Kiangsi border, where a "revolutionary base" was established in October, 1927. The following April, Chu Teh's troops which had participated in the Nanchang Uprising (August 1, 1927) joined forces with Mao in the Chingkang Mountains. Consolidated temporarily in the Chingkang stronghold, Mao in the fall of 1928 had time to cope with problems other than armed revolution and military survival. Among these other problems (which included strategy, government, land reform, and political control of the army), Mao dealt with the problem of leadership techniques of the Chinese Communist Party.

In his first writings in the Chingkang Mountains, Mao discussed party organization and leadership policy as critical deter-

[22] By isolating Mao's part in the establishment of the Chingkang base, his role has been unavoidably exaggerated. For a more general treatment, see Isaacs, *op. cit.*, Appendix.

[23] In 1929, the representatives were renamed political commissioners (*cheng-chih wei-yüan*); and in 1931, their titles were changed to political director (*cheng-chih ling-tao yüan*).

minants in the existence and development of Communist political power.[24] In subsequent reports, he paid particular attention to the party apparatus, to ideological orthodoxy, to propaganda and agitation, and to general methods for sustaining and promoting Communist power. Mao advocated a strong party to motivate and direct the latent revolutionary forces in an "upsurge" of China's revolutionary war.[25]

In "The Struggle in the Chingkang Mountains" (November 25, 1928), Mao indirectly referred to an inner-party struggle the outcome of which was to have a critical effect on leadership tactics and the course of the Communist revolution. In March, 1928, the Special Party Committee of Southern Hunan dispatched a representative to the Chingkang Mountains with instructions to criticize the Front Committee under Mao Tsetung "for leaning to the Right, for having not done enough burning and killing, and for having failed to carry out the policy of 'turning the petty bourgeoisie into proletarians and then forcing them into the revolution.' "[26] The Front Committee was abolished, and Mao was ordered to Southern Hunan. In April, after their defeat in Hunan, Mao and Chu Teh again retreated to the Chingkang Mountains, where they reluctantly carried out the policy of violence toward the petty bourgeoisie. "[T]hough we still did not do much burning and killing," Mao reported, confiscations and enforced contributions were sufficient to engender the hostility of the small bourgeoisie. The petty bourgeoisie were driven into the arms of the landed gentry. Between April and November, however, Mao and Chu Teh apparently induced the central leadership to reject this policy and to promote the support of the petty bourgeoisie. On November 6, 1928, the Front Committee was restored, and Mao

[24] Mao, "Why Can China's Red Political Power Exist?" [October 5, 1928], Selected Works, I, 67.

[25] Mao, "The Struggle," pp. 71–100.　　　[26] Ibid., pp. 99–100.

and Chu Teh resumed command. From that time to the post-1949 coalition of the four classes of the people, Mao Tse-tung followed a continuous, though flexible, policy of splitting the bourgeoisie by appealing to its less powerful members. This flexible policy not only cut into the Kuomintang support but also had a major objective in the Yenan period (1936–1949) of attracting bourgeois students and intellectuals. Years later, not only would Maoist writers laud the critical role of the 1928 policy switch in the final success of the Communist revolution, but they would also lay the blame for the erroneous policy directly on Stalin.[27]

According to Mao in 1928, the question of strengthening the party involved a unification of organization and leadership. Mao emphasized the techniques of party coverage of all parts of the apparatus, of interlocking directorates, of a strict chain of command, and of coordination and flexibility. The organizational hierarchy of the base area rested on the army company and on small area or production units as the primary levels for the party branch. Under the company branch, party groups were maintained for each squad. Mao reported that the 1928 ratio of party members to nonparty soldiers in the Red Army was about one to three and that the goal was one to one. The basic hierarchy outside the army was the party branch committee, the *ch'ü* (district) committee, and the *hsien* (county) committee. Mao emphasized the *hsien* level as the critical one for communications and cooperation under the coordinating leadership of a Special Committee for the Hunan-Kiangsi Border Area. Overlapping of personnel between a counterpart army committee and the Special Committee was common, and both these committees

---

[27] "On the Historical Experience of the Dictatorship of the Proletariat," editorial, *Jen-min jih-pao* [People's Daily], April 5, 1956, translated in *The Historical Experience of the Dictatorship of the Proletariat* (Peking: Foreign Languages Press, 1959), pp. 14–16.

were subordinate to the Front Committee, whose five members (led by Mao Tse-tung, Chu Teh, and T'an Chen-lin) were appointed by the party Central Committee.

In 1928, Mao also linked ideological problems directly to party solidarity and operation.[28] In particular, three problems—opportunism, localism, and careerism—were singled out by Mao as threats to united party action. To remedy these ideological defects, Mao advocated rectification through inner-party struggle and adherence to "objective facts." He insisted on education to eliminate cowardly opportunism and localism, the latter of which had allegedly reduced some party sessions to clan meetings. In addition to traditional clan localism in the Chingkang Mountains, Mao also attacked the parochial habit of antagonism between native inhabitants and settlers (k'o-chi-jen). Careerism, a third ideological error in party organization, endangered the party by bringing in large numbers of new members with improper motivation. These "careerists," Mao stated, stifled "good inner-Party education," and "as soon as the White terror came, the careerists became turncoats and led the counter-revolutionaries to arrest our comrades, and the Party organisations in the White areas mostly collapsed." [29]

After a series of defeats in the Chingkang Mountains and the retreat eastward in 1929 to the new "base area" on the Kiangsi-Fukien border, Mao systematically reviewed outstanding ideological errors ranging from "the purely military viewpoint" and "the non-organisational viewpoint" to "absolute equalitarianism" and "individualism." [30] Mao inferred that these major

[28] Mao, "The Struggle," pp. 93–96.   [29] Ibid., p. 96.

[30] Mao, "On the Rectification of Incorrect Ideas in the Party" [December, 1929], Selected Works, I, 105–115. This selection constitutes only the first part of Mao's nine-part resolution written for the famous Ninth Party Representatives' Conference of the Fourth Red Army held at Ku-t'ien, Fukien Province. For the full text see Mao Tse-tung, Chung-kuo kung-ch'an tang hung chün ti-szu chün ti-chiu tz'u tai-piao ta-hui chüeh-i-an [Resolution of the Ninth Party Representatives' Conference

ideological errors directly undermined the discipline and organizational purposes of the Red Army and Chinese Communist Party. As a leadership technique in handling these defects, Mao established the firm pattern of rectification which has become one hallmark of communism in China. This pattern was to clarify and highlight specific, labeled deviations; to exhort "subjective effort" and collective struggle to achieve the personal desire for self-remedy; to set forth clear rules and procedures for correction; to invoke criticism and self-criticism as well as organizational discipline; and to examine class background and experience for clues to ascertain the cause and seriousness of deviations. Mao held that incorrect thinking must be reformed by adhering to prescribed, organized methods.

One of these methods, education, was more than a simple corrective technique. Education shaped to propaganda could become a positive weapon in the revolutionary cause. Although Mao urged the transference of many leadership functions to the government, he explicitly reserved propaganda for the party and its organized "agitation teams." [31] In Mao's judgment political education profoundly determined the course of party and Red Army work and its success. "After receiving some political education," he said, "the Red Army soldiers have all become class-conscious and acquired a general knowledge about redistributing land, establishing political power, arming the workers and peasants, etc." [32] Given this political consciousness, Mao continued, the soldiers "know that they are fighting for themselves and for the working class and the peasantry. Hence they can endure the bitter struggle without complaint." Mao ordered his cadres to pay strict attention to the daily needs of the army, to

---

of the Fourth Red Army] (Hong Kong: Hsin min-chu ch'u-pan she, 1949). For a significant, recent article on the Ku-t'ien Conference, see *Jen-min jih-pao*, June 23, 1961.

[31] Mao, "The Struggle," p. 93; Mao, "On the Rectification," p. 107.
[32] Mao, "The Struggle," pp. 80–81.

share the same hardships as the common soldiers, and to make certain that all received equal treatment. Mao's intelligent manipulation of propaganda was never more clearly demonstrated than in the conduct toward captured Kuomintang troops. These troops were treated well and "informed" of the program and purposes of the Communist Party. Those who wished to return to the Kuomintang forces were given traveling expenses and then set free. Before their departure, the captured troops were feted at a "Farewell Party to New Brothers" during which they were called on to make speeches of gratitude to the Communists. From then on the Chinese Communist Party had potential friends in the Kuomintang army ranks.

Although Professor Hsiao Tso-liang in reviewing the basic documents of this period has concluded that Mao's power passed to the Central Committee led by the Russian-trained "returned students," [33] these 1929 views substantially outline Mao's basic leadership principles which survived his temporary decline in fortune to become the foundation of his method of operation after 1935. Mao systematized the organizational, ideological, and propaganda techniques into a "programme for the whole democratic revolution which takes into account the interests of the workers, the agrarian revolution and national liberation." [34] Mao's full 1929 report includes an extensive discussion of organization, educational materials and methods, propaganda, political training, and various problems within the army. In January, 1930, the policies of Mao Tse-tung and Chu Teh were defined as policies for "establishing base areas; building up political power according to plan; deepening the agrarian revolution; and expanding the people's armed forces by developing [the Red

[33] Tso-liang Hsiao, *op. cit.*, pp. 150–163.

[34] Mao, "The Struggle," p. 100. Although this quotation is part of a proposal to the Central Committee, there are good indications that Mao and Chu Teh in fact devised such a comprehensive plan on their own.

guards] in due order . . . and expanding political power by advancing in a series of waves." [35] Policies were to be carefully devised and consciously carried out according to the "objective situation," which Mao saw at that time in China as "desperately precarious." [36] He added: "China is littered all over with dry firewood which will soon be kindled into a conflagration." [37] The party, of course, was to be the incendiary.

In this 1927–1930 period, Mao and Chu Teh developed leadership techniques in response to the desperate military position of the party and the Red Army. The Communist Party was a minority organization largely discredited after the 1927 debacle yet dependent on the rural population for the support which it could not arbitrarily enforce. Desertions, betrayals, and apathy would have greeted openly dictatorial methods as evidenced in the early antagonistic policies toward the petty bourgeoisie. From the post-1927 position of superior armed force, the Kuomintang leaders were eager to exploit any Communist Party weakness, and realistic leadership techniques were required to forestall and minimize such weaknesses. Although the situation varied, the Communist numerical inferiority in the armed struggle persisted for nearly twenty years, and the Chinese Communist Party leaders were thus given sufficient time to systematize and test the "democratic, mass line" techniques of leadership adopted during the "low ebb." Between 1930 and 1949, administrative and leadership procedures were detailed, organizations were created, and habits of making and implementing policy were acquired. During the rectification campaign of 1942–1944, the image of the effective working style of the Chingkang Mountains area became the operational ideal necessary to perpetuate these procedures, organizations, and habits despite the fact that since 1949 they have been elaborated and

---

[35] Mao, "A Single Spark Can Start a Prairie Fire" [January 5, 1930], *Selected Works*, I, 117.

[36] *Ibid.*, p. 121.   [37] *Ibid.*

expanded to meet the requirements of total political authority.[38]

Although other Communists, both Chinese and Russian, had advocated popular support and the consistency of ideas and action, Mao was the first Chinese leader to develop in action a consistent line based not on authority but on the reciprocal and organized relationship between political leaders and the general Chinese population. The position Mao adopted after 1927 was that the party as leader of the revolution should not create artificial barriers in thought or behavior that would cut it off from the revolutionary "mass base." Mao set the responsibility for the elimination of such barriers squarely on the party and essentially set the outline for the "mass line." As the period of the Kiangsi Soviet was drawing to a close in 1934, Mao reminded the party cadres that their basic task was "to mobilise the broad masses to take part in the revolutionary war." [39] He advocated practical and specific methods of work to persuade the workers and peasants that "we represent their interests, that our life and theirs are intimately interwoven." By this time, Mao had made his point on "mass line" leadership. Party leadership meant to organize, educate, and integrate with the common people first, and a victorious wave, a "prairie fire," would follow. On this line of leadership, Mao became party leader on January 8, 1935.[40]

[38] A major theoretical discussion of this period is Mao Tse-tung, "Appendix: Resolution on Some Questions in the History of Our Party" [April 20, 1945], Selected Works, IV, 171–218. For a recent major article on the development of the leadership principles after 1930 and the role of the 1942–1944 rectification campaign, see Jen-min jih-pao, August 17, 1961.

[39] The quotations in this paragraph are from Mao Tse-tung, "Take Care of the Living Conditions of the Masses and Attend to the Methods of Work" [January 27, 1934], Selected Works, I, 147, 149. For comment on this speech, see Tso-liang Hsiao, op. cit., p. 273.

[40] Ta-kung pao [Impartial], July 2, 1961, in Survey of China Mainland Press [hereafter cited as SCMP], no. 2575 (1961), p. 7, gives this date for the election of Mao at the Tsunyi Conference.

The United Front and the Concept of Directness

Defeated in the Communist-controlled areas of southeast China which had been formally constituted as the Central Soviet Government on November 7, 1931,[41] the Communist forces in 1934 embarked on the "Long March" which brought them to northwest China in late 1935. With the arrival of the shattered remnants of the Red Army in the northwest "base area," the Chinese Communist organization (reduced to perhaps 10 per cent of its top pre-Long March strength) had the primary military task of holding the territorial bases in the Shensi-Kansu-Ningsia border region. In this task the party was probably saved by the Japanese movement into North China during the spring and summer of 1935, while the party and the Red Army were still on the Long March. Japanese troops in China diverted attention from the Communists and created a wave of patriotic emotion antagonistic to continued civil war. In a very meaningful sense, moreover, the Japanese—particularly after their full-scale 1937 invasion—made Communist mass line leadership strategies and techniques nationally relevant and popular.

The Japanese aggression revised the military picture for the Communists and also gave them a new basis for constructing an operative united front. According to Mao Tse-tung, this front would integrate "the activities of the Red Army with all the activities of the workers, peasants, students, the petty bourgeoisie and the national bourgeoisie of the whole country." [42] Such integration, however, would be different in character from the "one-sided" pre-1927 front with the Kuomintang wherein "the Communist Party made no effort to expand our own ranks (the

[41] Victor A. Yakhontoff, *The Chinese Soviets* (New York: Coward-McCann, 1934).
[42] Mao, "On the Tactics of Fighting Japanese Imperialism" [December 27, 1935], *Selected Works*, I, 163.

workers' and peasants' movement and the armed forces led by the Communist Party)." [43] Although Mao argued the necessity of the alliance with the petty bourgeoisie and the national bourgeoisie, he stipulated that the party's relationship to the workers and peasants would differ in kind from alliance with the bourgeoisie.[44]

The basis for distinguishing these kinds of "unity" was the reliability of the various classes within the front. Since Mao had predicated that relationship with the general population (or "masses" in Communist jargon [45]) was the foundation of successful policy, the less reliable elements would need to be differentiated from the more reliable in order to preserve that foundation. The united front must capture the widest support commensurate with safety. Therefore, Mao sought to create a united front which would particularly protect the interests of the workers and peasants and the basis of which would be the working classes.[46] Moreover, by arguing that the only justification for an alliance with the bourgeoisie was its opposition to Japanese imperialism, Mao implicitly affirmed the transitory nature of alliances with "secondary-status" classes.[47] He assumed that the alliance necessitated by the anti-Japanese struggle would eventually yield to the unified relationship of party and worker-peasant masses. If for no other reason, he would argue the limited role of the front with the bourgeoisie, because the bourgeoisie were a temporary historical phenomenon. Alliance with bourgeois classes constituted a restricted form of class struggle that must vanish with the elimination of all classes. Mao's

[43] Ibid., p. 168.   [44] Ibid., p. 172.

[45] The use of "masses" in this study is for convenience only. By "masses" (ch'ün-chung) the Communists mean to imply collectivity and some internal consistencies and consensus within a social group defined by economic and political criteria. Chinese have, of course, both individuality and striking personal differences, which are not conveyed in the term "masses."

[46] Mao, "On the Tactics," p. 172.   [47] Ibid., pp. 170–172.

point, stated differently, was that the party-proletarian (and peasant) relationship was that of vanguard to masses and a question of direct unity. As the Communists were by definition not the vanguard of the bourgeoisie, unity (in the sense of identity) and directness with them were impossible.

Cooperation with bourgeois allies theoretically supplanted overt class struggle. Communists equated this cooperation with a controlled form of class struggle, a compromise between mass line directness and class antagonism. In 1949, the party leadership made the principle of alliance "consultation" the theoretical foundation of the Chinese People's Political Consultative Conference and expanded the definition of allies to include democratic parties, democrats without party affiliations, national minorities, intellectuals, religious groups, and overseas Chinese. These "allies" belonging to the periphery of the "people" after 1949 became the primary targets of a "benevolent" struggle for which there was no safe defense. The precarious position of these marginal "people" has engendered a calculated uncertainty in their minds which has been a major weapon to induce their "self-reform."

Cooperation and consultation were viewed, therefore, as temporary but useful substitutes for more reliable forms of mass line unity. Moreover, the party always premised cooperation on the "wider interests" of the people. These interests were made identical to the interests of the "majority" of the worker and peasant masses for whom the party operated as spokesman.[48] Cooperation functions according to the requirement that bourgeois allies subordinate themselves to the needs of the worker-peasant masses led by the Communist Party. Although this party

[48] Mao, "The Role of the Chinese Communist Party in the National War" [October 12, 1938], *Selected Works*, II, 247–248, 251. This selection is pt. VII of Mao's famous Report of the Sixth Enlarged Plenum of the Party Central Committee entitled *The New Stage*. For the full report, see Mao, *Lun hsin chieh-tuan* (Hong Kong: Hsin min-chu ch'u-pan she, 1949).

role was subdued from time to time when cooperation with the Kuomintang was in its active stages, the essential feature of party leadership for the united front was clarified more than twenty years before the antirightist movement of 1957 caught the democratic party leaders denouncing the leading role of the Communist Party.

In Yenan, the Communists adapted the united front to the border region government. When the Shensi-Kansu-Ningsia Border Region Assembly was formed in January, 1939, the united front was brought within the official, governmental framework.[49] The purpose was "to change the united front policy into a mass policy for the whole region" in order to "educate" the people and "penetrate" into the workers and peasants. Integrated with government, united front consultation assumed authoritative status and became a positive mechanism to condition and educate both the working classes and allies and to exercise direct political leadership over worker-peasant representatives.[50] Indirect consultation with allies was coupled with the direct unity of party and working class representatives.

In 1940, Mao placed the united front concept in the central position of the projected "new democracy."[51] Although he differentiated the classes which would jointly rule China into

[49] See Lin Po-ch'ü, "Shan-Kan-Ning pien-ch'ü cheng-fu tui pien-ch'ü ti-i chieh ts'an-i-hui ti kung-tso pao-kao" [Work Report of the Shensi-Kansu-Ningsia Border Region Government to the First Border Region Assembly], in Chung-kuo k'o-hsüeh yüan li-shih yen-chiu so ti-san so [Chinese Academy of Sciences, Historical Research Institute, Third Office], ed., *Shan-Kan-Ning pien-ch'ü ts'an-i-hui wen-hsien hui-chi* [Collected Documents of the Shensi-Kansu-Ningsia Border Region Assemblies] (Peking: K'o-hsüeh ch'u-pan she, 1958), pp. 13–17.

[50] *Ibid.;* "Shan-Kan-Ning pien-ch'ü hsüan-chü t'iao-li" [Shensi-Kansu-Ningsia Border Region Election Laws], in Chung-kuo k'o-hsüeh, *op. cit.,* pp. 53–54.

[51] Mao Tse-tung, "On New Democracy" [January, 1940], *Selected Works,* III, 116–121.

"already awakened" and "on the point of awakening," no compensations for such distinctions were evident in the "state system" (*kuo-t'i*) of the joint dictatorship or the "political structure" (*cheng-t'i*) of people's congresses organized according to the principle of democratic centralism.[52] Mao voiced distrust for the bourgeoisie [53] but made no apparent provisions for controlling them in the transitional "new democratic" government. Presumably few bourgeoisie would be elected to the congresses, and their power would diminish "naturally" under "the proletariat as the leading force." [54]

At the time of the establishment in 1949 of the Chinese People's Political Consultative Conference (CPPCC), however, the system of people's congresses was significantly postponed, and the party leaders temporarily invested the CPPCC with the formal functions and powers of the National People's Congress. The Chinese Communist Party, however, held actual power through its leaders acting in official capacities in the Central People's Government and the People's Liberation Army. When the elections for local congresses were held in 1953–1954 and the National People's Congress approved the new constitution in 1954, the CPPCC remained as a symbolic expression of the united front separate from the new hierarchy of congresses. The 1935 united front in theory had been devised to manipulate "marginal" groups of Chinese sympathetic to the struggle against Japan. In "On New Democracy" (January, 1940), the united front became central to the state system (joint dictatorship of classes) and appropriate for the political structure of democratic centralism. In 1949, the united front was still theoretically central in the state structure and only a temporary substitute for

[52] *Ibid.*, pp. 118–119, 120–121. See H. Arthur Steiner, "Constitutionalism in Communist China," *American Political Science Review*, XLIX (March, 1955), 1–21, esp. 7–13.
[53] Mao, "On New Democracy," p. 118.   [54] *Ibid.*

the political structure. The 1954 united front was peripheral in the state structure and unsuitable for the political structure.[55]

These contrasts highlight the transformations which have taken place in the objectives for the united front. According to Marxism-Leninism, organizational forms reflect the fundamental condition of classes within the state. The linkage of state organization to the four major classes of the people (workers, peasants, petty bourgeoisie, and national bourgeoisie) was evident in 1949, when Communist Party leaders reemphasized the direct and indirect distinctions within the united front, which Mao had first clarified in 1935, and did not form the CPPCC according to democratic centralism. Tung Pi-wu, for example, stipulated that the CPPCC was a "dual" mechanism which contained workers and peasants (direct unity) and allies (indirect alliance) and which would eventually have its elements of directness given to a National People's Congress.[56] This congress, formed in 1954, was to express the "unity of vanguard and masses" organized on the basis of democratic centralism.[57] The Organic Law of the CPPCC did not specify the organizational principle of the CPPCC but called it the organization of the united front to

[55] For a recent Chinese Communist Party commentary on the history of the united front, see Li Wei-han, "The United Front—A Constitution of the Chinese People for Winning Victory" (in Chinese), *Hung-ch'i*, no. 11, June 1, 1961, pp. 1–11. *Hung-ch'i* or *Red Flag* is a fortnightly journal of the Central Committee of the Chinese Communist Party and is identified according to the new Chinese orthography as *Hongqi*. See also Li Wei-han, "The Characteristics of the Chinese People's Democratic United Front" (in Chinese), *Hung-ch'i*, no. 12, June 16, 1961, pp. 5–26, and Li Wei-han, "The Struggle for Proletarian Leadership in the Period of the New Democratic Revolution" (in Chinese), *Hung-ch'i*, no. 3–4, February 10, 1962, pp. 5–37.

[56] Tung Pi-wu, "Kuan-yü chung-yang jen-min cheng-fu tsu-chih-fa ti pao-kao" [Report on the Organic Law of the Central People's Government], *Jen-min ta hsien-chang hsüeh-hsi shou-ts'e* [Study Handbook on the People's Great Constitution] (Shanghai: Chung-kuo k'o-hsüeh kung-szu, 1949), pp. 28–29.

[57] *Ibid.*, p. 29.

rally all democratic classes and nationalities for the common effort.[58] By inference, however, because the CPPCC failed to meet the standards of democratic centralism,[59] the CPPCC was not organized according to democratic centralism but according to democratic dictatorship. This judgment is consistent with Mao's exposition of the "people's democratic dictatorship" in 1949 [60] and is further borne out by Article 5 of the Organic Law, which prescribed threats and expulsion for disagreeing individual and organizational members rather than the method of democratic centralism, "unity-criticism-unity."

Thus, two kinds of class relationship are seen to involve different kinds of organization and leadership method which may coexist temporarily despite their basic dissimilarities. After the establishment of the National People's Congress in 1954, for example, the CPPCC was retained "to play its part in mobilizing and rallying the whole people" [61] without authoritative functions and distinct from the system of people's congresses. At that time the political structure became "direct" in spite of the persistence of the "indirect" CPPCC in the state structure. Not until China becomes a classless society will it be theoretically possible to synthesize a completely direct political and state structure on the basis of democratic centralism alone (see Chapter VIII).

The progress toward directness undergirds the operation of all organization. In 1951, Tung Pi-wu called for the indirect

[58] Organic Law of the CPPCC, Art. 1.

[59] These standards included the election of congresses and a people's government.

[60] Mao Tse-tung, "On People's Democratic Dictatorship" [June 30, 1949], *Selected Works* (Peking: Foreign Languages Press, 1961), IV, 421–422. This volume of Mao's works corresponds to the fourth Chinese volume published in 1960. Although this volume comes after four previous volumes of Mao's *Selected Works* published in London and New York (and therefore should be vol. V), the Peking Foreign Languages Press has chosen to ignore these previous editions in the West.

[61] Constitution of the People's Republic of China, preamble.

implementation and enforcement of party policies.[62] The party, Tung said, should issue general directives to the government administration, "but the party does not directly conduct the affairs of state." This clear distinction between party leadership and the state administrative apparatus deteriorated, however, between 1951 and 1957. In his 1957 "Report on the Work of the Government" Chou En-lai, for example, said: "Some people have criticized the lack of a clear division of function between the Party and the government. . . . In directly issuing political calls and announcing policy-making decisions to the masses, the Party, far from hampering the work of the government, renders it great help." [63] Chou listed the joint actions taken by party and government organizations such as publication of decisions and field inspections. The growth of direct party administration in policy implementation proceeded to new dimensions when the Central Committee issued the Resolution on the Establishment of People's Communes in Rural Areas (August 29, 1958). Since that time, the party has openly dealt with rural (and urban) communes on matters of scope, form, and details of administration.

Degrees of directness in the general state organization operate at all levels according to the principle of democratic centralism. These degrees should not be confused with indirect united front structure, which is different in kind. Direct organization exists because of the "vanguard mass" relationship. The indirectness of the united front type, on the other hand, is based on the incompatibility of classes and the need for the artificial bridge of "consultation." As spelled out by Li Wei-han in 1956, "Political consultation [in the democratic united front] does not negate class contradictions." [64] The united front, Li said, is a "weapon

[62] *Jen-min jih-pao*, January 30, 1952.
[63] *Hsinhua News Agency Release*, June 28, 1957, supplement, p. 19.
[64] "Speech of Comrade Li Wei-han," *Eighth National Congress of the Communist Party of China* (Peking: Foreign Languages Press, 1956), II, 361.

and a special form of class struggle." [65] It was expected that the united front would "promote socialist unanimity in politics and ideology," [66] so that it could be completely replaced by the organizational patterns of democratic centralism. The development from indirectness, to directness in degrees, then to complete directness, is the political lesson of the Communist united front. Indirect leadership is based on consultation to maximize the contribution of the marginal classes. Direct leadership is based on the mass line to mobilize the working-class masses and utilize all their creative energies. In both cases the leader is the Chinese Communist Party, though in the first its method is that of modified state coercion (democratic dictatorship), while in the second its method is mass line unity and criticism (democratic centralism).

Effect of the Party Role on Leadership and Organization

Prior to the turning point in 1949, Mao reexamined the party's role and set the themes to "turn the army into a working force" [67] and to continue to "carry the revolution through to the end." [68] At the crucial second plenary session of the Seventh Central Committee in March, 1949, Mao announced the post-victory goals of economic restoration, production development, and industrialization for the construction of a "great socialist state." [69] Mao reminded the party that continuous revolution

[65] *Ibid.*, p. 352.   [66] *Ibid.*, p. 365.

[67] Mao, "Turn the Army into a Working Force" [February 8, 1949], *Selected Works*, IV (Peking), 337–339.

[68] Mao, "Carry the Revolution Through to the End" [December 30, 1948], *Selected Works*, IV (Peking), 299–307.

[69] Mao, "Report to the Second Plenary Session of the Seventh Central Committee," *Selected Works*, IV (Peking), 373.

would require cooperation with non-Communists and non-party cadres. "The Chinese revolution is great," he reported, "but the road after the revolution will be longer, the work greater and more arduous." [70] All Communist Party members were warned to continue an excellent style of work and to utilize criticism and self-criticism. Four months later, in "On People's Democratic Dictatorship," Mao said: "We shall soon put aside some of the things we know well and be compelled to do things we don't know well." [71] He called on the party members to "overcome difficulties" and "learn what we do not know." [72]

As seen in retrospect, the redirection of the party to undertake the post-1949 "continuous revolution" and economic construction affected the party organization and leadership in several important ways. These include the rapid growth in the party membership, the reassessment of personnel capabilities and cadre training in the light of new state tasks, and the adaptation of proved aspects of inner-party organization to extraparty situations as a major technique to fill the organizational gap after 1949. These changes were necessitated by the Communist economic and social policies and the personnel requirements to run the vast political, economic, social, and military enterprise of China. All these changes, including the redirection of economic and social goals after 1949, directly stemmed from the basic change of the party's role. In victory the party was no longer a contender for power but was in absolute control, with minor exceptions, of all state power on the China mainland.

Because the Communist Party after 1949 was no longer in competition for state power, the attitude of its leadership drastically changed. The party organization which had promoted civil war and chaos was suddenly the champion of law and order even if some of the legal techniques employed, such as the peo-

[70] *Ibid.*, p. 374.   [71] *Selected Works*, IV (Peking), 422.
[72] *Ibid.*, p. 423.

ple's tribunals, were hardly created for the purpose of impartial justice. As early as 1948, Mao called for "different tactics for carrying out the land law in different areas." [73] Mao based the different tactics on the length of experience of the area under party control [74] and opposed excessive haste and "doing everything as the masses want it done." [75] He advocated an orderly reform which would proceed in stages after careful preparation.[76] Peasants were warned against "indiscriminate" beatings and killings, and the Communist leaders labeled all "excessive" actions as a "product of the feudal society." [77] The hated landlords suddenly became hated in degrees, and treatment was to be varied among big, middle, and small landlords and between those who were "local tyrants" and those who were not.[78] The main target became counterrevolutionaries—which meant simply those who had sided with the Kuomintang. To restore industry in the cities, Communist cadres were ordered to distinguish between the "feudal exploitation" practiced by landlords and rich peasants and the industrial and commercial enterprises run by them.

In general, the party called on two decades of tactical practicality and organizational flexibility to adjust to the new situation of absolute authority after 1949. No longer contending for

[73] Mao, "Different Tactics for Carrying Out the Land Law in Different Areas" [February 3, 1948], Selected Works, IV (Peking), 193.

[74] Ibid., pp. 193–194.

[75] Mao, "Correct the 'Left' Errors in Land Reform Propaganda" [February 11, 1948], Selected Works, IV (Peking), 198.

[76] Mao, "Essential Points in Land Reform in the New Liberated Areas" [February 15, 1948], Selected Works, IV (Peking), 201–202.

[77] Ibid., p. 202; Jen Pi-shih, "T'u-ti kai-ko chung ti chi-ko wen-t'i" [Several Problems in Agrarian Reform], T'u-kai cheng-tang tien-hsing ching-yen [Model Experiences of Agrarian Reform and Party Rectification] (Hong Kong: Chung-kuo ch'u-pan she, 1948), pp. 55–58. Cf. Mao Tse-tung's 1927 attitude in "Report of an Investigation into the Peasant Movement in Hunan." Then, of course, he was frankly sympathetic to peasant excesses.

[78] Mao, "Essential Points," pp. 201–202.

power, the party changed to the utilization and consolidation of state power on a grand scale for economic, social, and political purposes. Unlike the utilization of power during the Yenan period, the use of power by the Chinese Communist Party after 1949 was free of the need to account for a competitor. The new role as sole ruling party of China created a whole range of domestic and international opportunities for the party leadership. Faced with the challenge of these opportunities, the Communists enthusiastically responded with a feeling of coming into a destiny which was their right and for which they had been preparing for more than twenty years.

II

Basic Chinese Communist Philosophy and Ideology Applied to the Leadership Elite

General Aspects of Chinese Communist Ideology

THE prevailing intellectual climate of Communist China blends extremes of philosophy, sophistication, and emotion. Simple, self-evident statements attain the sanctity of dialectical truth. Adaptations from Marxist classics are heralded as original contributions of Mao Tse-tung. Exhortation to accept a mixture of profound and obvious doctrines complements bold leadership principles and tactical expertise. Binding the acceptable climate of opinion to moral exhortation and organizational skills produces an avenue to adjust to Communist programs. The very simplicity and

35

obvious coherence of slogans and policies strengthen the appeals of Chinese communism.

When applied to the members of the elite, basic Chinese Communist philosophy and ideology which structure and give content to the climate of mind become an effective instrument of training. The fabric of the Chinese Communist mind woven in the training process has diverse threads. Hegelianism and Russian Marxism-Leninism combine with Chinese precepts and preferences, and Chinese interpretations attain a certain distinctiveness more from selectivity in application than from originality in thought. Comparative analysis of the broader patterns of Marxist-Leninist ideology and dialectical method as borrowed from Hegel would seriously damage the Chinese assertion of their theoretical originality,[1] but lack of ideological innovation does not detract from the unique Chinese amalgam chosen from its Marxist heritage. The revolutionary years taught the Chinese to place high value on ideological commitment and voluntary conformity to ensure reliability in the stress of combat and deprivation. At the same time, the modest intellectual level of most party recruits required a special Chinese formulation which became noted for its remarkable directness, its disarming simplicity, and its endless variety of concrete examples.

Indoctrination in Communist philosophy and ideology follows a continuous, accumulative pattern for those who have chosen to believe. Among other things, Chinese Communist ideology and philosophy constitute an educational process which elevates the system of training above simple discipline. When successful, the training process remolds the character of the individual so that proper responses in party situations become automatic if not intuitive. Such responsiveness theoretically is feasible irrespective of the original motives of members for join-

[1] Arthur A. Cohen, "How Original Is 'Maoism'?" *Problems of Communism*, X, no. 6 (November–December, 1961), 34–42.

ing the Chinese Communist Party organizations. The romantic and the ambitious, the astute and the "backward," undergo intensive retraining to attain, if possible, a common "advanced" character, a keen class point of view, and a "proletarian standpoint." To train the party member or cadre, to bring him to the level of class consciousness where his proletarian standpoint places him at the "vanguard" of the working-class Chinese and where he is thus qualified to determine the status and fate of all others, is a basic purpose of Communist leadership training.

In practice, this purpose represents an aspiration which materializes only in a tiny elite. Nevertheless, a sufficient amount of ideological maturity results in all trainees to justify the extraordinary training effort. Those who fail to attain the elite can still be expected to perform at least partly in accordance with the highest standards of socialist morality. For the core elite which epitomizes this morality, however, the person theoretically attains a special "party character" and qualifies as a "proletarian individualist." This proletarian individualist can be trusted on his own. He does what Mao Tse-tung would do if Mao could be all over China at the same time. He thinks the same way, uses the same method of leadership, assigns the same priorities, speaks the same ideological language, and is equally dedicated.

The sections which follow analyze the progressive molding of this "proletarian individualist." The analysis adheres to the Chinese Communist description of their ideology on the assumption that Chinese communism can be understood as a belief system on its own terms. Excessive secondary comment and interpretation would mar the clarity of both the dynamics and the logical deficiencies of the thought. This approach, however, requires special attention on the part of the reader who must adapt to a different pattern of thought and belief using somewhat misleading vocabulary and wholly different standards for

37

judging validity. Moreover, for the sake of brevity, such "warning signs" as "theoretically," "presumed," or "the Communists hold" have been used only occasionally to remind the reader of the ideological medium in which he is operating.

Moral Character and the Dialectical Process of Knowledge

Character. For training the cadre and party member, Chinese Communist theory begins with the individual and, thus conceived, provides a comprehensive theory of learning to ensure the thorough remolding of each individual. Mao Tse-tung has said that "as long as there are people, every kind of miracle can be performed." [2] In Mao's writings, man is not an abstract unit, and basic Communist goals in China concern 700,000,000 individuals with their relationships and their "concrete problems." [3]

The key to the analysis of the person and his problems is, in Communist terminology, "character." [4] The decisive element

[2] Mao Tse-tung, "The Bankruptcy of the Idealist Conception of History" [September 16, 1949], *Selected Works* (Peking: Foreign Languages Press, 1961), IV, 454.

[3] See Li Kuang-ts'an, *Lun ch'ing-nien ti ko-ming hsiu-yang* [On the Revolutionary Cultivation of Youth] (4th ed.; Tientsin: Chih-shih shu-tien, 1950); Chung-kuo hsin min-chu-chu-i ch'ing-nien t'uan Hua-tung kung-tso wei-yüan-hui hsüan-ch'uan pu [China New Democratic Youth League, East China Work Committee, Propaganda Department], ed., *An-chao tang yüan piao-chun tuan-lien tzu-chi* [Train Yourself According to the Standard of the Party Member] (rev. 10th ed.; Shanghai: Hua-tung ch'ing-nien ch'u-pan she, 1952); and *Szu-hsiang kai-tsao wen-hsüan* [Selected Essays on Ideological Reform] (Peking: Kuang-ming jih-pao she, 1951, 1952).

[4] Chung-kuo hsin min-chu-chu-i ch'ing-nien t'uan Hua-tung kung-tso wei-yüan-hui hsüan-ch'uan pu [translated in preceding note], ed., *Hsüeh-hsi kung-ch'an tang yüan ti yu-hsiu p'in-chih* [Study the

entering into character is the quality which permits the individual to accept his role in a society moving toward proletarian collectivism and which permits him to become fully identified with the working class. From this point of view, the character or nature of the individual is malleable and changeable. Members of the Chinese Communist Party, especially its cadres, are assumed to possess this character in unusual degree, but even for them the processes of leadership training and education are designed to heighten "party character." [5]

Linking change of character to dialectical materialism, character is also seen as the reflection in the person of his perception of and place in class society. The class contradictions of society are manifested in the character of each individual. Persons with contradictory class characters compete in class struggle, and in each individual in a class society the variety of contradictory elements in his character reflect the basic class conflict. Resolution of these contradictions through the identification and fostering of proletarian class qualities and the purging of bourgeois qualities leads to the new social individual, the new Communist man.

Elements of the Marxist-Leninist learning process. Resolution of contradictions, including contradictions of character, depends in the first instance on understanding them or, in Communist terminology, on cognition of them.[6] Cognition describes the

Excellent Character of the Communist Party Member] (4th ed.; Shanghai: Hua-tung ch'ing-nien ch'u-pan she, 1953).

[5] An August, 1961, speech by Ch'en Yi elaborated the distinctions between the character leading to the ordinary specialist and the character productive of the political specialist or cadre. For text of speech, see *Jen-min shou-ts'e 1961* [People's Handbook 1961] (Peking: Ta-kung pao she, 1961), pp. 319–321.

[6] This discussion is based on Mao Tse-tung, *On Practice* [July, 1937] (rev. trans.; Peking: Foreign Languages Press, 1958), and Mao, *On Contradiction* [August, 1937] (rev. trans.; Peking: Foreign Languages Press, 1958). The historian and the philosopher face the crucial task of establishing the dates and merits of these essays. Many students of

dialectical process of knowledge. This epistemological process aims to reduce leadership to practical precepts and steps which may be followed and which may be employed by the elite in grooming its lower echelons and communicating its policies. The elements of Marxist-Leninist epistemology have been briefly elaborated by Mao Tse-tung in *On Practice* and *On Contradiction*.

The Marxist-Leninist process of knowledge is conceived to be totally dependent on "objective reality" (or "objective being").[7] Objective reality is at base material, and knowledge is therefore a reflection of the material world. The essential make-up of the material world is a combination of natural phenomena and human relationships. "Man in the process of knowing, chiefly through his activity in material production," Mao has said, "gradually understands nature's phenomena, characteristics, laws and the relations between himself and nature."[8] In a class society, the Communists hold that production activity is further complicated by class relations which result from productive activity. In a class society, through productive activity and class struggle, man "also gradually understands in varying degrees certain human relations."[9] Social practice, which combines production and class struggle, plus "secondary" scientific,

---

Chinese communism seriously doubt that these essays existed in the present form prior to their appearance in print in the early 1950's. For a discussion of these problems, see Cohen, *op. cit.*, pp. 35–36, and H. Arthur Steiner, "'On the Record' with Mao and His Regime," *Journal of Asian Studies,* XVII, no. 2 (February, 1958), 215–223.

[7] An important recent article discussing the Communist Chinese interpretation of matter and consciousness is in *Jen-min jih-pao* [People's Daily], November 1, 1961. In this same issue there also appears an article on the brain and consciousness. On general epistemology, I have also used two important articles by Wu Ch'iang and Wang Jo-shui in *Jen-min jih-pao,* June 2 and June 4, 1961.

[8] Mao, *On Practice*, p. 1.   [9] *Ibid.*

artistic, and social pursuits,[10] is the only source of knowledge and the "criterion of truth."

Man's knowledge, Mao Tse-tung said, "develops step by step from a lower to a higher level, that is from the superficial to the profound, and from the one-sided to the many-sided." [11] Mao held that "productive activity to meet the needs of material life . . . is the primary source of man's knowledge." [12] Until the emergence of the modern proletariat and large-scale industry, Mao asserted, knowledge was limited by the distortions of "exploiting classes" and small-scale production. The rise of the proletariat and modern industry has enabled man to "acquire a comprehensive, historical understanding of the development of society and turn this understanding into a science, the science of Marxism." [13] By this definition of progressive, comprehensive knowledge, the proletariat's vanguard has *ipso facto* the most profound knowledge to which others can only aspire through diligent productive activity and which they must obey out of respect for the higher truth.

According to Mao, the process of knowledge has three stages: perception, conception, and verification. Perception fundamentally begins in production, but it may also occur through social practice in any part of objective being, because knowledge also consists in "knowing in varying degrees the various kinds of human relations through political and cultural life, both being closely connected with material life." [14] Perception is an impression through the sense organs and is "only the appearance of various things, their separate aspects, their external relations." [15] Perceptual knowledge is basic, however, to all other forms of

[10] *Ibid.*, pp. 1–2. "Secondary" means that the activity relates to those parts of objective being which belong to the "superstructure" and are a reflection of the economic base.

[11] *Ibid.*, p. 2.   [12] *Ibid.*, p. 1.   [13] *Ibid.*, p. 2.
[14] *Ibid.*, p. 2.   [15] *Ibid.*, p. 4.

knowledge. If a person continues his active, repeated involvement in those areas where he has acquired perception, "a sudden change or leap takes place in the process of knowing, resulting in the forming of concepts." [16] Conception, the second stage in the process, is grasping the essence of things, "their totality and their internal relations." [17] Conception is qualitatively different from perception in that it employs "the method of judgment and inference" by which logical conclusions can be drawn.[18]

Conceptual or rational knowledge reflects "a thing fully in its totality" and gradually builds up "a system of concepts and theories." [19] The prerequisite for this development is continued social practice. But, Mao added, social practice in essence is of a singular kind, to "change reality." [20] Thus, in *On Practice*, Mao said that "if you want to acquire knowledge you must take part in the practice of changing reality." [21] To Marx, there was knowledge of the reality of change; to Mao, the change of reality was knowledge. All "genuine" knowledge, according to Mao, was derived from the participation in social practice by some person at some time. Valid social practice was defined as "taking part personally in the practical struggle to change reality." [22] Aspiration to true knowledge precluded the armchair revolutionary, and Mao discredited the philosophy and ideology of those who stood aside from guided "social practice."

The third stage of knowledge is actively to change "the world by applying the knowledge" of the "objective laws" and concepts acquired in the second stage.[23] "Knowledge," Mao wrote, "begins with practice, reaches the theoretical level through practice, and then returns to practice." [24] This third stage is to bring theory and the objective world into consonance. Theories are tested and developed, and the cycle of knowing is renewed. When this advanced knowledge is checked against the "universal

[16] *Ibid.*, pp. 4–5.   [17] *Ibid.*, p. 5.   [18] *Ibid.*
[19] *Ibid.*, pp. 13–14.   [20] *Ibid.*, p. 8.   [21] *Ibid.*   [22] *Ibid.*
[23] *Ibid.*, p. 15.   [24] *Ibid.*

truth" of Marxism-Leninism, the result is verified knowledge.

According to Mao, the verification process is "to discover truth through practice, and through further practice to verify and develop truth." [25] But even this verified knowledge must be considered tentative. The whole of objective being is changing and developing. Because objective being "advances and develops through its internal contradictions and struggles, the process of knowing it must also advance and develop accordingly." [26] "Verified" knowledge must be continuously tested and revised in order to keep it from lagging behind actual events. What may be "objectively true" today may be "objectively false" tomorrow for "man's knowledge of the particular process at each given stage of development is only relatively true." [27] In this repeated testing over a period of time, two developments take place in addition to the continuation of the three-stage cycle of knowing. One development is the advancement in the "universal truth" of Marxism-Leninism which "has in no way summed up all knowledge of truth, but is ceaselessly opening up, through practice, the road to the knowledge of truth." [28]

The concept of right and wrong. The second development must be inferred indirectly from Mao's analysis in *On Practice.*[29] The validity of this inference rests on Mao's statements that verification must be directed and that knowledge without proletarian social practice is not knowledge. In short, a concept of right and wrong is interposed by the party elite to guide the uninitiated in how they must acquire knowledge. Although Mao

---

[25] *Ibid.,* p. 21.   [26] *Ibid.,* p. 18.   [27] *Ibid.,* p. 20.
[28] *Ibid.*

[29] Since the appearance of *On Practice* in 1950, the Chinese Communist philosophers have made explicit and elaborated their definition of morality. In this discussion I have used particularly articles on moral judgments and ethics in *Kuang-ming jih-pao* [Bright Daily], December 6, December 14, and December 15, 1961, as translated in *U.S. Joint Publications Research Service,* no. 12472 (1962), pp. 1–9, and no. 12524 (1962), pp. 46–55.

never explicitly states this concept, without a clear awareness of its intrusion into the epistemological process the continuity in the theory of leadership indoctrination is broken. The theory of dialectical materialism, Mao stated, has a class nature and openly serves the proletariat.[30] The reason for this is that the emergence of the proletariat has made possible both "a comprehensive, historical understanding of society" and the scientific method for acquiring knowledge. A "proletarian" who faithfully follows the three-stage method for acquiring knowledge and studies the "universal truth" of Marxism-Leninism consciously adopts the perspective of the elite on objective reality. This perspective enables him to distinguish "right" from "wrong." A moral quality is added to his character. Marxist-Leninists view this emergent moral sense as a special potentiality within the proletariat. Having this moral quality places a unique burden on the working class, particularly its most-advanced section, the Chinese Communist Party. "At the present stage of social development," Mao said, "the responsibility for correctly understanding and changing the world has, by historical necessity, fallen upon the shoulders of the proletariat and its party." [31]

The moral quality of the proletariat always depends on adherence to the dialectical process of knowledge. Morality assumes the continuing correctness with which knowledge is pursued. Correct cognition must be based on "objective reality," and cognition not based on this objectivity is not knowledge but subjective fantasy.[32] Knowledge is "a correct reflection of objective reality and error is a distortion of objective reality." [33] Mao said in 1957: "Sometimes, because our arrangements do not correspond to objective reality, contradictions arise and the

---

[30] Mao, *On Practice*, p. 3.   [31] *Ibid.*, p. 21.

[32] *Hung-ch'i* [Red Flag], no. 2, January 16, 1960, p. 9.

[33] Po Ching, *T'an-t'an "ts'o-wu"* [Talk about "Mistakes"] (Peking: Hsüeh-hsi tsa-chih she, 1957), p. 8.

balance is upset; this is what we call making a mistake." [34] Given the proletariat's ability to recognize and correct its mistakes, the subjective activity of the working class is seen to maintain the moral quality. One critical mission of the party members and cadres, therefore, is to publicize and rectify mistakes.

The Marxist-Leninist world outlook. What a person perceives and conceptualizes in the process of knowledge is objective reality, which is materialist in essence. While acquiring knowledge, moreover, a person forms a set of attitudes, a point of view, which reflects the reality perceived. According to Marxist-Leninists, the moral qualities of the proletariat are special points of view derived from the proletariat's unique ability to follow the process of knowledge faithfully and to learn from the universal truth of Marxism-Leninism. In general, however, points of view are the attitudes manifested by the individual as the result of the totality of his knowledge. Because the proletariat enables the process of knowledge to become comprehensive and moral, the person who wishes to achieve the moral quality must identify with the proletarian collective. The moral character is therefore defined in terms of its tendency to promote proletarian unity and to submerge the individual in the collectivity of the working masses. In 1959, *People's Daily* enumerated the elements of the moral character as love of country; love of labor; love of the collective body; honesty, sincerity, and loyalty; and diligent, thrifty, and plain living.[35]

There are many kinds of points of view, each kind reflecting a different content or type of knowledge. But all types of knowledge are interrelated through the common denominator of

[34] Mao Tse-tung, *On the Correct Handling of Contradictions among the People* [February 27, 1957] (Peking: Foreign Languages Press, 1957), p. 26.
[35] *Jen-min jih-pao*, July 18, 1959.

the materialist base. Moreover, all types of knowledge (and points of view) emanate from practice, and the fundamental modes of practice correspond to the essential production relations and class relations of the economic base. The comprehensive content of knowledge which corresponds to the totality of objective being and especially to the economic base is reflected in a similarly comprehensive point of view or "world outlook" (*yü-chou kuan* or *shih-chieh kuan*). Citing Lenin's "On Dialectics," Mao Tse-tung in *On Contradiction* wrote that at base there were only two kinds of world outlook: dialectical materialism and idealism.[36] The latter outlook of "vulgar evolutionism consists in adopting an isolated, static, and one-sided view of the world." [37] The world outlook of dialectical materialism, on the other hand, studies "the development of a thing from the inside, from its relationship to other things." [38] That moral point of view which expresses the basic interrelationship of all types (or comprehensive content) of materialist knowledge and clearly acknowledges the integrating function of the proletarian class is called the Marxian or proletarian world outlook.

Marxist-Leninists contend that the proletarian world outlook equips the leading members of the proletariat to comprehend the totality of objective being and the direction of its movement. Moreover, as stated by Lin Piao in 1959, "the Party character cannot be successfully tempered and strengthened without a change in world outlook." [39] As in all other "knowing," the studying to achieve the proletarian world outlook must concurrently take the form of practice to change reality. The form of practice or subjective activity at this stage is called revolutionary activity. According to T'ao Chu, "One of the greatest

[36] Mao Tse-tung, *On Contradiction*, p. 2.   [37] *Ibid.*, p. 3.
[38] *Ibid.*, p. 4.
[39] Lin Piao, "March Ahead under the Red Flag of the Party's General Line and Mao Tse-tung's Military Thinking," *Ten Glorious Years* (Peking: Foreign Languages Press, 1960), p. 88.

characteristics of the Communists is that they have a strong subjective desire to transform the world, display their subjectivity
as far as possible with respect for objective reality, and never
show themselves helpless in the face of objective reality." [40]
Aspiration to the proletarian elite not only requires guided
study, specialized practice, and moral judgments but also entails
an enthusiastic and conscious role in the Communist-led revolution. The revolutionary activity of the proletariat, Mao said, had
two basic purposes: "to remould their [the proletariat's] faculty
of knowing as well as [to remould] the relations between the
subjective world and the objective world." [41] Such a remolding
process, he added, "includes the opponents of remoulding, who
must undergo a stage of compulsory remoulding before they
can pass to a stage of voluntary remoulding."

Contradictions, Standpoint, and Struggle

Contradictions. When the party novice attains the Marxian
world outlook, he may feel that he has proceeded a significant
distance in the purification and heightening of his thinking. The
leadership quickly disabuses him of this idea. His remolding and
testing for the elite has only begun. The learning process continues as before with an ever-deeper commitment to revolutionary
practice. For a few select, however, a breakthrough comes by
an intuitive "leap" or an immediate awareness of the true nature
and purpose of reality. This awareness begins another tortuous
path to the inner sanctum of the vanguard.

By continuously remolding their thinking and by engaging in
revolutionary practice, Communists contend that the essential
nature of total reality will become evident to the most en-
lightened. This essential nature is contradictory. In the Marxist-
Leninist view, the world "teems with contradictions": life and

[40] *Jen-min jih-pao,* June 18, 1959.   [41] Mao, *On Practice,* p. 21.

death, plus and minus, action and reaction, positive and negative, combination and dissociation, class struggle, offense and
defense, and war and peace. As Mao has said, contradictions are
both universal and particular. Contradictions exist "in the process of development of all things and . . . in the process of
development of each thing a movement of opposites exists from
beginning to end." [42]

The universality and particularity of contradictions, Mao said,
supports the view that everything must be looked at from two
angles: the whole and the parts. Superficiality occurs when a
person "denies the necessity of deeply probing into and minutely
studying the characteristics of the contradiction, but would proceed to solve the contradiction (to answer a question, to settle
a dispute, to perform a task, or to direct a military operation)
after only a cursory glance from a distance." [43] Looking at the
whole and each of its aspects, Mao added, "we must notice not
only the special features of the interconnections and conditions
of each aspect, but also the special features of every stage in the
process of development." [44]

In addition to the fundamental universality and particularity
of contradictions, Marxists hold that three other characteristics
of contradictions are crucial: (1) contradictions are the basic
cause of development; (2) complex contradictions contain one
"principal" contradiction; and (3) the aspects of a contradiction
have "identity and struggle."

(1) *Contradictory development.* "The basic cause of development of a thing," Mao asserted, "is not external but internal and
lies in its internal contradictions." [45] These contradictions are
the primary cause of all development and take two basic forms:
"relative rest and conspicuous change." [46] The Marxist-Leninist
"proof" that contradictions determine all development need not
concern us here, for in the final analysis Communist proof gives

[42] Mao, *On Contradiction,* p. 9.   [43] *Ibid.,* p. 22.   [44] *Ibid.*
[45] *Ibid.,* p. 4.   [46] *Ibid.,* p. 48.

way to simple stipulation. Communist deductions from this theory of determinant cause are important, however, and the notion of "relative rest and conspicuous change" is particularly significant.

The addition or subtraction of elements through contradictory struggle is assumed to follow from the universal presence of contradictions. Quantitative change proceeds within all things, though the appearance of things at the first stage of quantitative transformation is one of calm and inactivity. For example, a society undergoing incipient industrialization appears unaffected and in a state of "relative rest." But at some point the quantitative additions (or subtractions) drastically revise the nature of the thing undergoing change. Industrialization, in our example, creates poverty, rural-urban imbalance, classes, strikes and thence a proletarian revolution. Conspicuous, qualitative change takes place. "When it [the contradiction] assumes the second form," Mao said, "it has already reached a certain culminating point of the quantitative change of the first form, caused the dissolution of the entity, produced a qualitative change, and consequently appears as conspicuous change." [47]

For each thing, that period from the beginning of quantitative change to the sudden transformation or conspicuous change is considered an essentially homogeneous unit during which basic judgments correctly formed at the outset apply. In Marxism-Leninism, these units are considered "stages" neatly dividing the parade of dialectical history. While a contradictory development is moving from pure quantity to the conspicuous "qualitative leap," the basic contradiction of the process and the "nature" of the process "will not disappear until the process is completed." [48] Thus, a line of action correctly devised for a given stage will (or should) remain valid until the advent of conspicuous change, when the contradiction within that process is resolved. Other lines proposed prematurely or in opposition to

[47] *Ibid.*, pp. 48–49.   [48] *Ibid.*, p. 22.

the "correct" line run afoul not merely of the will of the leadership but also of historical necessity.

(2) *Principal contradictions.* In a complex thing such as Chinese society, many contradictions exist. But, according to Mao Tse-tung, among these many contradictions, "one is necessarily the principal contradiction whose existence and growth determines or influences the others." [49] There is only one principal contradiction "playing the leading and decisive role while the rest are secondary or subordinate." [50] Unlike the stages of lesser contradictions, a "stage" associated with a principal contradiction stands as a major period in the historical process. Thus, in addition to the variety of lines to solve the multitude of particular contradictions, there must be one "general line" to solve the principal contradiction of each "period." The basic role of the leadership at each point in the historical process is to grasp and solve the principal contradiction by devising a general line. For example, in the anti-Japanese war, to resolve the contradiction between Japanese imperialism and Chinese survival, the party propounded the general line of the united front, and in 1952 the Central Committee of the Chinese Communist Party put forward the general line for the period of transition to socialism to solve the principal contradiction between economic backwardness and socialist industrial aspiration. As discussed in the following chapter, the present general line is the general line of socialist construction.

(3) *Identity and struggle of contradictions.* The theory of contradictions basically holds that an identity exists between the two aspects of a contradiction and that these two aspects are united or "coexist in an entity." [51] To be contradictory, opposite aspects must "condition each other's existence." Mao cited such examples as rulers to ruled, life to death, imperialists to colonies, and proletariat to bourgeoisie. "The fact is," he

[49] *Ibid.*, p. 31.   [50] *Ibid.*, p. 33.   [51] *Ibid.*, p. 40.

50

said, "a contradictory aspect cannot exist all by itself." [52] But, existing as opposites, the contradictory aspects have a special quality, the ability of one aspect "to transfer itself to the position of its opposite." [53] This transformation results from the struggle that takes place between the opposites during the stage of development. Struggle between ruler and ruled, for example, causes the ruler to change place with the ruled. This may be called a "dialectical reversal" which takes place when struggle develops to the point of intense antagonism.[54] Not all contradictions are antagonistic, however, and as Mao pointed out in 1957, nonantagonistic contradictions may be resolved peacefully without undergoing a dialectical reversal of the present ruling Communists and the ruled bourgeoisie so long as party members follow the correct line of action.[55]

Szu-hsiang. For the aspirant to the proletarian elite, who initially comprehends these complexities and ramifications of contradictions, a sense of awe is engendered for the leaders who have opened the way for such compelling insight. His awe becomes (or is expected to become) new resolution to obey those who have entrusted this unique dialectical tool to him. He turns with new vigor to a special kind of contradiction that now confronts him in the path of his training and development. This is the contradiction, heretofore subdued, between theory and practice.

In the process of training party members and cadres, the principal contradiction that emerges from the dialectical development of their knowledge is the contradiction between theory and practice. Up to the point of insight into the nature of contradictions in objective reality, quantitative additions to the

[52] *Ibid.*, p. 41.   [53] *Ibid.*, p. 42.
[54] *Ibid.*, pp. 50–53. The term "dialectical reversal" is mine. For a recent discussion see *Jen-min jih-pao*, June 4, 1961.
[55] Mao, *On the Correct Handling*, pp. 7–27, 64–65.

knowledge of the trainee have developed increasing antagonism between his theoretical knowledge and his practice. This antagonism becomes acute during revolutionary practice, and the two aspects become transformed into their opposites—practice becomes new revolutionary theory and theory becomes the guide to revolutionary action.

Theory and practice are bound as a unity of opposites. One cannot exist without the other. Social practice and resultant revolutionary theory are absolutely combined to become the principal, contradictory source in the development of knowledge. The Chinese Communists call this critical combination of theory (*li-lun*) and practice (*shih-chien*) by the term *szu-hsiang*. *Szu-hsiang* is strictly translated as "thought" though often loosely as "ideology." *Szu-hsiang* incorporates both the cognitive elements leading to the Marxian world outlook and the active techniques for identifying, heightening, and purifying that outlook. In the course of the growth of *szu-hsiang*, two interrelated developments are seen to take place. The first is an advancement in knowledge with a greater awareness of the laws and direction of movement of total objective being. This awareness becomes acute when the concept of contradictions is grasped by the Communist student during the high point of his revolutionary practice.

The second development in *szu-hsiang* is emotional rather than intellectual and reflects the intensification of antagonism manifested in revolutionary practice. At some point in the revolutionary process of thought (*szu-hsiang*), the laws of movement and the heightened antagonism theoretically will reveal the sharp cleavage between the proletariat and the bourgeoisie, and the individual's moral sense will become enraged. Some will see this cleavage and will become angered earlier than others because of the keen advancement in their "level of thought." In order to resolve this acute moral and emotional contradiction, those with the highest level of thought, the Communists hold, will consciously and eagerly elect to "stand on the proletarian field" (*chan tsai wu-ch'an-chieh-chi ti li-ch'ang shang*). This choice of "standpoint" will recast for the person choosing it the entire process of knowledge and his moral character. Standing on the proletarian field, the individual's character undergoes a "qualitative leap." That individual is a new person. He is on the threshold of the vanguard.

Standpoint. Standpoint (*li-ch'ang*) marks the boundary line between the proletarian vanguard and the general population. In theory, standpoint distinguishes the Communist elite by establishing advanced intellectual attainment as the central criterion for leadership selection.

The importance of philosophy consists in the fact that the philosophy of dialectical materialism provides men with a correct way of thinking [Lu Ting-yi wrote in 1958]. The essential distinction between men lies not in differences of "disposition" or personality, but, first of all, in their different class standpoints and, in addition, their ways of thinking.[56]

Standpoint also marks the character that is completely identified with the proletarian collective. "Our standpoint," Mao said in 1942, "is that of the proletariat and the broad masses of the people. For members of the Communist Party this means that they must adopt the standpoint of the Party and adhere to Party spirit and Party politics." [57] To indoctrinate a party member or cadre, to advance him to the point where his standpoint places him above all others and where he is thus qualified to determine the status and the fate of all others, is, to repeat the statement made at the outset of this chapter, the basic purpose behind leadership training.

[56] Lu Ting-yi, *Education Must Be Combined with Productive Labour* [September 1, 1958] (Peking: Foreign Languages Press, 1958), pp. 5–6.
[57] Mao Tse-tung, "Talks at the Yenan Forum on Art and Literature," *Selected Works* (New York: International Publishers, 1954–1956), IV, 64.

The question of standpoint allows no leeway. It is "a basic one and a question of principle." [58] The choice of the proletarian standpoint separates the world into black and white. If I have the proletarian standpoint and you the bourgeois, says one writer, "towards the same thing, you say 'What a mess!' and I say 'Very good!' There is absolutely no common speech." [59] This kind of clarity is typical, the Communists hold, "when the class struggle is extremely sharp and tense." [60] People are then forced to choose either the proletarian or the bourgeois standpoint. "It is nearly impermissible to have an undecided bystander, undecided elbowroom . . . and even temporary overlapping groups are not possible." [61] When this clear crisis point arrives in the mind of the Communist novice, he stands with emotions welling within him and declares to his applauding comrades that he henceforth stands on the side of the proletariat.

"Armed" with the proletarian standpoint, Communists become qualified to analyze the classes of China.[62] Class analysis is the foundation of the Communist mass line method. Clarity of standpoint combines "objective" determinants of class with "levels" of thought and enables the Marxist-Leninist to identify backward elements, class allies, progressives, activists, and po-

[58] Ma Ling-yün, "T'an li-ch'ang wen-t'i" [Talk about the Problem of Standpoint], in Chang Yu-yü et al., Hsüeh-hsi Mao Tse-tung ti szu-hsiang fang-fa ho kung-tso fang-fa [Study Mao Tse-tung's Method of Thought and Method of Work] (Peking: Chung-kuo ch'ing-nien ch'u-pan she, 1958), p. 41.

[59] Ibid. This example is based on Mao Tse-tung, Report of an Investigation into the Peasant Movement in Hunan [March, 1927] (Peking: Foreign Languages Press, 1953), pp. 6–8, though at that time Mao had not clarified the concept of "standpoint." In the English translation, the last sentence mentions "stand" (p. 8), but this does not appear in the original Chinese.

[60] Ma Ling-yün, loc. cit.   [61] Ibid.

[62] Li Hung-lin, "Chieh-chi fen-hsi ti fang-fa" [The Method of Class Analysis], in Chang Yu-yü, op. cit., pp. 54–55. A typical, but important, article which relates class analysis to the changing social structure of China is in Kuang-ming jih-pao, August 4, 1961.

tential Youth League or Communist Party members. Class analysis as the technique to separate the reliable from the unreliable, friends from enemy, is a single thread running through the works of Mao Tse-tung. The first essay in Mao's *Selected Works* is "Analysis of the Classes in Chinese Society" (1926); the second is the famous 1927 report on the Hunan peasant movement. More recently, standpoint determined the thesis of *On the Correct Handling of Contradictions among the People* (1957). The dividing line between enemy and people, antagonistic and nonantagonistic, becomes plainly evident to those whose standpoint is correct. The class analysis that determined the four classes belonging to the "people" in *On People's Democratic Dictatorship* (1949), the fundamental statement by Mao on the projected state and program, rested solely on the basic question of standpoint.

Proletarian standpoint is thus a precondition for full admission to the Communist Party elite and is assumed to control the minimal action of the party members. Simple, open declaration of the proletarian standpoint, however, does not end the process of perfecting and heightening still further the levels of thought (*szu-hsiang*). A new set of more exacting standards inevitably follows the decision to "stand on the proletarian field." Judgments are built up to determine the "genuineness" and "clarity" of standpoint. These standards can be applied only after there has been a basic decision to adopt the proletarian standpoint, but when they are applied they reopen the question of the initial commitment itself, as part of the process of raising the level of deliberate revolutionary consciousness. Party members are exhorted to determine "whom one listens to" and to watch the way one consistently acts.[63] "That is to say," commented one party official (Wang Jen-chung), "we have to satisfy ourselves

[63] This example is based on Mao's discussion in 1938 of how to judge cadres: Mao Tse-tung, *The Role of the Chinese Communist Party in the National War* (Peking: Foreign Languages Press, 1956), p. 13.

that one can stand the long test of the great storm of the class struggle." [64]

Struggle. As defined, standpoint cannot be static, and thus no person can ever say that he has achieved final certainty. Marxism-Leninism places stress on the continuation of uncertainty and goes as far as to give the idea of continuous struggle a permanent place in the organizational life of the party as well as in the program for grooming a new generation of leaders. Continuous struggle is called "raising the level of consciousness." This struggle after the election to "stand on the proletarian field" when combined with the guided process of knowledge preceding the choice of standpoint broadly describes long-range leadership training in Communist China. The advanced ideological method of Chinese communism is in essence unremitting involvement in "struggle," [65] and by this struggle the established elite provides for the motivation and directed activity of its lower echelons.

To refer to the language of contradictions, standpoint resolves a basic ideological contradiction in the relationship of the individual to the proletarian collective. After choosing the proletarian standpoint, the person compares himself, his capacities, hopes, and desires with the total working-class movement and interests as stated by the party. In his new sense of awe, he theoretically should feel small, uncertain, and apprehensive.[66] The party anticipates, however, that many will fail to live up to this theoretical expectation and has devised numerous

[64] *Chung-kuo ch'ing-nien* [China Youth], no. 10, May 16, 1960, translated in *Selections from China Mainland Magazines* [hereafter cited as *SCMM*] (Hong Kong: American Consulate General), no. 220 (1960), p. 21.

[65] Chang Yu-yü, *op. cit., passim.*

[66] This is based on *Wo tsen-yang ch'eng-wei kuang-jung ti kung-ch'an tang yüan* [How I Became a Glorious Communist Party Member] (Hankow: Chung-nan jen-min ch'u-pan she, 1953), *passim,* and Wu Yün-to, *Pa i-ch'ieh hsien-kei tang* [Give Everything to the Party] (3d ed.; Peking: Kung-jen ch'u-pan she, 1954), pp. 70–74.

practical tests—including long-term assignments to menial tasks
—to determine who merits further advancement in the ranks of
the vanguard. In theory, the person who truly merits consideration for such advancement will feel tense and uncertain. To
resolve his tension caused by this new contradictory gap between his insignificance and the great masses, he consciously
dedicates himself again and again to struggle to the end of his
life without counting the personal cost.[67]

Mao Tse-tung as early as 1937 approvingly noted the occur-
rence of tension and struggle within the party. He said:

Opposition and struggle between different ideas constantly occur
within the Party, reflecting contradictions between the classes and
between the old and new in society. If in the Party there were
no contradictions and no ideological struggles to solve them, the
life of the Party would come to an end.[68]

The way to solve these contradictions, Mao said, was to use
criticism and self-criticism. Based on Mao's affirmative appraisal
of struggle for party members, Liu Shao-ch'i in 1941 wrote
On Inner-Party Struggle,[69] which has become the textbook on
controlled struggle.

Liu began this essay with Mao's proposition that "inner-
party struggles are a reflection of the class struggle outside the
party"[70] and insisted that they "consist principally of ideological struggles."[71] In effect, Liu was warning party comrades
that inner-party debates should be handled on the highest level
of ideology (*szu-hsiang*) to prevent the degeneration of struggles into factional name calling and trivia, on the one hand, and

[67] On entering the party, the new member pledges: "I voluntarily
enter the Chinese Communist Party. I will actively work, make great
effort to study and unsparingly sacrifice my all. I swear to struggle to
the end of my life for the final realization of communism."

[68] Mao, *On Contradiction*, p. 11.

[69] Liu Shao-ch'i, *Lun tang-nei tou-cheng* (reprint; Hong Kong: Cheng-
pao she, 1947).

[70] *Ibid.*, p. 2.   [71] *Ibid.*, p. 3.

to avoid legitimate opposition to agreed policies and methods of implementation, on the other. Struggles conducted on the ideological level could dissipate the emotions of discontent while leaving party unity—and leadership authority—intact.

Liu further argued that struggle should take place within the organizational context and have as a primary objective the enhancing of mutual solidarity. For these reasons struggle not only was consistent with discipline and centralism but was absolutely essential to their operation. To make such a guided struggle effective, Liu insisted on the necessity of raising the ideological level of party members and inferred that the suppression of criticism and self-criticism or the rise of excessive struggle was tantamount to serious ideological deviation. The proper form of struggle was neither mechanical nor excessive but followed a theoretical median of correctness. Because the preservation of this correctness remained essential to the organizational solidarity of the party, Liu rejected the practice of special "struggle meetings" and insisted instead on an uninterrupted flow of struggle in daily party activities.

In contrast to "unprincipled" struggle, which ran counter to the foregoing stipulations and became antagonistic to party and proletarian interests, Liu enumerated seven major points on how to conduct inner-party struggle. In general, these points incorporated the arguments above and stressed the basic line of membership responsibility for undertaking correct ideological struggles in a spirit of solidarity and organizational discipline. The emphasis was on self-confession (self-criticism) and comradeship rather than on accusation and individual grievance.

Party struggles have intensified dramatically during periods of rectification campaigns within the party—such as 1942–1944, 1947–1948, 1950–1953, and 1957–1958—and the literature was particularly forceful in arguing the need for correct struggle during the 1957–1958 rectification campaign. At that time the techniques of inner-party struggle were extended to numerous nonparty organizations and situations. Thus, the element of struggle supposedly embodied in the principle of consultation was made analogous to inner-party struggle because of the attainment of socialism in enterprises formerly run by bourgeois "class allies." Following the new character of the economic base, party leaders revamped struggle for bourgeois intellectuals in the policy of "letting a hundred flowers blossom, a hundred schools of thought contend." [72] As was to be expected, the extension of the technique of struggle beyond the confines of the party involved not only the use of criticism and self-criticism but also the complete rationale for Marxist-Leninist epistemology and the proletarian standpoint. In a typical article on the revival of the "hundred flowers" movement in 1961, for example, the following line was argued: "Marxism-Leninism brought about a fundamental change in philosophy and the social sciences. In these fields, if one does not consciously take the Marxist-Leninist stand and apply the Marxist-Leninist viewpoint and method, it would be next to impossible really to solve any question of substance." [73]

We do not have to search very far to discover the ubiquitousness of the concept of struggle in the thinking of the Chinese Communist elite. Struggle is one hallmark of the Chinese Communist mind. Struggle—affirming the operation of "objective" dialectical forces—precedes and determines all progress. Resolution and unity remain empty without the dynamic of struggle. As early as 1945, Mao wrote: "What is work? Work is struggle. There are difficulties and problems in those places for us to overcome and solve. We go there to work and struggle to overcome these difficulties." [74] In 1960, cadres departing for the communes and "lower-level" work were told that "strug-

---

[72] Mao, *On the Correct Handling*, pp. 48–59.
[73] *Hung-ch'i*, no. 5, March 1, 1961, pp. 3–4.
[74] Mao, "On the Chungking Negotiations" [October 17, 1945], *Selected Works*, IV (Peking), 58.

gle is happiness." [75] The important point was not victory, for "happiness can be found not only in victory of struggle but also in struggle itself." [76] In the course of this struggle, cadres would find true freedom, for "freedom is the understanding of the objective necessity." [77]

Struggle has the avowed purpose of complete, personal tension [78] and must be continuously intensified. Active struggle jars the complacent, stifles complaint, and motivates lower-level cadres to ensure that the masses "work more, better, faster and more economically." In announcing the new general line in 1958, Liu Shao-ch'i explained that tension "is simply normal revolutionary activity to which we should give our heartiest approval. This kind of 'tension' is nothing to be afraid of." [79] In a 1959 explanation of the new struggle, Communist youth were told that "as far as an individual is concerned, the participation in political campaigns, the unfolding of ideological struggles, and the review and criticism of one's own mistakes would bring mental agony." [80] In these struggles, the individual "would suffer loss of sleep and appetite because of nervousness." But in the end the struggle of remolding would come automatically, almost with a sense of relief.

But provided he goes through the ideological struggle to enhance his consciousness, he will be able to realize his mistakes, and is bound to acquire another state of mind. He will feel that while the bitter sea had no bounds yesterday, the shore is near at hand today, and there is a bright future for him.[81]

---

[75] *Jen-min jih-pao*, November 12, 1960.   [76] *Ibid.*

[77] *Hung-ch'i*, no. 17, September 1, 1960, p. 22.

[78] *Chung-kuo ch'ing-nien*, no. 22, 1959, translated in *Extracts from China Mainland Magazines* [hereafter cited as *ECMM*] (Hong Kong: American Consulate General), no. 205 (1960), p. 27.

[79] Liu Shao-ch'i, "Report on the Work of the Central Committee," *Second Session of the Eighth National Congress of the Communist Party of China* (Peking: Foreign Languages Press, 1958), p. 44.

[80] *Chung-kuo ch'ing-nien, loc. cit.*   [81] *Ibid.*

Jen-sheng kuan

The course of ideological training for party members and cadres has an over-all direction of movement which begins in the first stages of perception and culminates in ideological struggle. This training, which spans a lifetime, cannot be separated into intellectual study and revolutionary practice, for the two are mutually supporting and proceed simultaneously toward the goal of strengthening the proletarian vanguard. In the Chinese Communist *Weltanschauung*, the element of goal transcends the maturation of individual cadres or Chinese Communist Party members, however, and permeates objective being itself. The concept of purpose in the ideology expresses itself as a "view of life," or *jen-sheng kuan*.[82] When the integrating or "holistic" aspect implicit in *jen-sheng kuan* is examined, the term "general viewpoint" (*ch'üan-chü kuan-tien*) frequently substitutes for *jen-sheng kuan*.

For the Chinese Communist Party, *jen-sheng kuan* is measured in individual cases according to the ability of the member to profit from his ideological reflection and revolutionary activity. *Jen-sheng kuan* unites and directs the "method, viewpoint, and stand" of the correct party member. Regulated by a theoretical norm of objective purpose, individual Communists can only aspire to the highest aim, but always expect to fall short

[82] Yü Ming-huang, *Hsin jen-sheng kuan* [The New View of Life] (Hong Kong: Hsin chih-shih shu-tien, 1948); Ch'en Chih-yüan, *Ko-ming jen-sheng kuan* [Revolutionary View of Life] (Shanghai: Chan-wang ts'ung-k'an, 1951); Chung-kuo hsin min-chu-chu-i ch'ing-nien t'uan Hua-tung kung-tso wei-yüan-hui hsüan-ch'uan pu [China New Democratic Youth League, East China Work Committee, Propaganda Department], ed., *Kung-ch'an-chu-i jen-sheng kuan* [The Communist View of Life] (rev. 14th ed.; Shanghai: Hua-tung ch'ing-nien ch'u-pan she, 1952). For an important recent article by Sha Ying on "general viewpoint," see *Jen-min jih-pao*, January 3, 1962.

and thus require, as we have seen, a continuous struggle and remolding. Although the Chinese Communist Party "view of life" distinguishes itself sharply from the bourgeois and pre-revolutionary patterns of Chinese life by infusing objective reality with proletarian morality and revolutionary activism, the theory of "forces" acting according to fate or a rigid teleology have significant precedents within the Chinese tradition. Certainly, the concept of measuring individual attainment against theoretical life purposes would have—with reservations on the application of certain Communist objectives—appealed to the Confucian mind. What is new is the preoccupation with change and with revolutionary violence.

Theoretically, standpoint clearly differentiates the Communist "view of life" from all other *jen-sheng kuan*. Because of its point of origin in proletarian standpoint, *jen-sheng kuan* pertains only to the "people." To have the bourgeois or rightist standpoint is by definition to have no "purpose," to have an antipurpose, and to be a counterrevolutionary against the tide of history's purpose. *Jen-sheng kuan* is the nature of direction in life or, in the usual Chinese Communist phraseology, "one's road." That *jen-sheng kuan* which strictly adheres to the road beginning at the proletarian standpoint is deemed "moral," and the person who travels such a road has the supreme moral character. Although the Communist treatment of *jen-sheng kuan* is often inconsistent and artificial, one constant theme is that there is only one moral road, the party's road.

The proletarian and party essence of Communist *jen-sheng kuan* is most graphically portrayed in attacks by party leaders on individualism. Mao Tse-tung first explained the evil of individualism for the party when he was fighting for survival in the Chingkang Mountains in 1929. He then condemned such manifestations of individualism as vindictive retaliation, cliquism, the search for personal pleasure, and passivity in education and work.[83] Individualism depicts the self-seeking that belongs to the road of the bourgeoisie. It epitomizes the culmination of the idealistic world outlook, the bourgeois standpoint, and the counterrevolutionary attitude in general. "In short," Lin Piao said in 1959, "individualism is the source of all evils." [84]

Mao elaborated the kinds of individualism which were considered particularly corrosive to Communist *jen-sheng kuan* in *Combat Liberalism* (1937). In Mao's lexicon, liberalism and individualism are virtually interchangeable. Typical expressions of "liberalism" to which Mao objected were the family-type attitude toward mistaken comrades with whom relationship was close, the trait of saying "nothing to people's faces, but to gossip behind their backs," the cautious personal concern "in order to save one's own skin," and the use of struggle and dispute for personal reasons.[85] Four years later in *On Inner-Party Struggle*, Liu Shao-ch'i, echoing Mao, singled out liberalism as the most insidious threat to correct struggle and party solidarity and a direct cause of leadership deviations.[86] Communist leaders have consistently argued against that kind of liberalism which assigns values to the individual or groups smaller than the working class. To the extent that individualist ideas have survived in the party, Mao, for example, has insisted on waging a relentless ideological struggle to preserve party solidarity and discipline and to destroy passivity and opportunism.

For those potential revolutionaries who have begun at the nonproletarian standpoint, the Communist instructions are clear:

[83] Mao Tse-tung, *On the Rectification of Incorrect Ideas in the Party* [December, 1929] (Peking: Foreign Languages Press, 1953), pp. 13–15.
[84] Lin Piao, *op. cit.*, p. 87.
[85] Mao Tse-tung, *Combat Liberalism* (Peking: Foreign Languages Press, 1954), pp. 1–4.
[86] Liu Shao-ch'i, *Lun tang-nei tou-cheng*, pp. 16–17.

"Confess your error and repent." [87] If you do not confess and repent, the Communists warn, "then a 'thousand generations will hate you.' " [88] But after the revolutionary has gone through this repenting process, after he has been aroused to action "in the fire of the mass movement," [89] he is propelled into endless tension and struggle which brings "joy" because of his proletarian identification and his faith in the Communist future. In the course of the progress toward that future, he is taught that there is only one acceptable purpose for a true revolutionary: Be a docile tool of the party. "To be a docile tool of the party," said a *People's Daily* article in 1960, "is a noble quality peculiar to the proletariat and is a concentrated expression of the resolute and pure class character of the proletariat." [90] Leaving nothing to doubt, Liu Shao-ch'i said in 1939: "The supremacy of the party's interest is the highest principle in our party members' thinking and action." [91]

The Communist *jen-sheng kuan* thus subordinates in all possible ways the interests of the individual to that of the party-

[87] Yü Ming-huang, *op. cit.*, p. 3.   [88] *Ibid.*

[89] Yü Kuang-yüan, "Ko-ming ch'ing-nien ying-kai nu-li chien-li kung-ch'an-chu-i jen-sheng kuan" [Revolutionary Youth Should Strive to Establish the Communist View of Life], in Ch'ing-nien t'uan Su-nan ch'ü kung-wei hsüan-ch'uan pu [(New Democratic) Youth League, Su-nan Work Committee, Propaganda Department], ed., *Yao i cheng-ch'üeh ti t'ai-tu tui-tai ju tang wen-t'i* [Have the Correct Attitude toward Entering the Party] (reprint; Wu-hsi: Su-nan jen-min ch'u-pan she, 1952), p. 1.

[90] *Jen-min jih-pao*, January 14, 1960.

[91] Liu Shao-ch'i, "On the Cultivation of the Communist Party Member" (in Chinese), *Hung-ch'i*, no. 15–16, August 1, 1962, p. 19. This is a revised version of Liu Shao-ch'i, *Lun kung-ch'an tang yüan ti hsiu-yang* (reprint; Hong Kong: Hsin min-chu ch'u-pan she, 1949), p. 51. The new edition was used because of its greater emphasis on subordination to the party. This work is better known by the English-translation title *How to Be a Good Communist*. The earlier version in Chinese gives August 7, 1939, as the date of the lectures, but the 1962 revision states that the lectures were given in July, 1939.

led collective. Mao in *Combat Liberalism* called on members to be "frank, faithful and active" and to "adhere to correct principles and wage a tireless struggle . . . so as to consolidate the collective life of the Party." [92] Only the person more concerned about the party and the masses than himself could be considered a Communist.[93] Nevertheless, in this new *jen-sheng kuan* appear requirements for a proletarian-type individualism to contrast with bourgeois individualism. The first is "moral," and the second is "immoral." The trained proletarian individualist can be given difficult assignments beyond the confines of direct party supervision. Outside the party, he can be expected to do what the highest leaders would do if they occupied his position. He thinks and acts as they would and is equally committed to the realization of communism.

When he has been so trained, the rigidity of mind allows delegation of complete implementing responsibility to him. His training is the key to the directness, to the flexibility, and to the decentralization of organization. Within the party organization, at each stage in the leadership training and especially during struggle the inconsistencies of thought, action, purpose, and belief are obliterated and the total collectivization (or integration of the individual into the collective) of the trainee comes closer to the Marxian ideal. In the final analysis, the Chinese Communist Party seeks to lead the 700,000,000 Chinese by making it psychologically [94] impossible for each Chinese not to depend on the party for guidance. This is a fundamental and conscious objective of Communist leadership in China. The outlines of this objective are clearly visible in elite manipulation of basic Marxist-Leninist philosophy and ideology for cadre and

[92] P. 5.   [93] *Ibid.*, p. 6.

[94] See *Jen-min jih-pao*, July 6, 1959, and May 21, 1961, and *Kuang-ming jih-pao*, July 18, 1961, for Chinese Communist discussions of psychology. On educational psychology, see also *Kuang-ming jih-pao*, March 9 and 13, 1962, and *Jen-min jih-pao*, March 13, 1962.

party-member indoctrination, but current inner-party forms are not bound by organizational limits. They are the prototype of tomorrow's China.

Ideology in Perspective

The typical Chinese cadre facing the daily round of chores and endless demands on his time may honestly believe that a new mental state would strikingly improve his limited capacity to cope with life's problems. That belief alone would cause him to invest some energy in study and "thought remolding" and to pay some attention to the nature of his "road" in struggle. This psychic readiness would correspond to the prevailing atmosphere of exhortation generated by the leadership elite. Not all cadres will pay heed to this exhortation, however; not all will accommodate their lives to the level of struggle and mental discipline demanded. China remains a vast, diverse state, and responses to central policy vary across a wide spectrum. Nonetheless, the pressures to conform and to display individual conformity by action places a "constant" on the character of the Chinese cadres that is remarkably uniform in practice. Beneath the surface there must surely be diversity and disagreement, but the inculcation of the mind of the ideologue fashions an imposing mien that for practical purposes erases significant discrepancies.

Chinese Communist ideology fosters personality patterns which manifest several key traits. The typical Chinese cadre reveals his exposure to Communist doctrine by his quick appraisal of situations and people. There is a correct niche for everything. The appraisal is undertaken in a serious, almost pompous, manner and with constant recourse to the basic categories of Marxism-Leninism. Cadre "struggle" manifests itself in the unrelenting search for contradictions. Cadres probe each event for its underlying contradiction; nothing ever is completely satisfactory or quite successful. Potential enemies constantly threaten even though their number always remains small. Ideology provides the cadre with ready explanations and a vast inventory of techniques, slogans, and labels. Marxist-Leninist doctrine tempts the cadre to substitute name calling and jargon for more careful study and analysis. Most significant for policy, party members and cadres readily assume from the ideology that the objective world corresponds to their perception of it, and leading cadres confidently make policies in the belief that they alone understand domestic and international realities.

Ceaselessly criticizing others, the cadres and party members are reared in a climate of sin. Ideology warns that behind the mask of overt obedience lurks the contradiction of latent deviation. The slightest error may presage an avalanche of criticism for hidden "bourgeois" motives and even greater errors. In time, all must expect to be exposed for errors which even now remain hidden to them. Ideology stipulates that right prevails in the party and in the objective process. Only the subjective failures of party members and cadres deny the party and the "people" just victories. An individual must be blamed for every failure. Those fully attuned to ideology respond to struggle and criticism in a sense of gratitude and willing repentance. Contritely, they beg forgiveness and express joy at the least favor bestowed by the party. Ever after, they confess new dimensions of their errors which are usually traced to the experiences of childhood. Those who reject the criticism, on the other hand, may be cast from the party. The purged are then vilified for the most heinous offenses and are repudiated as the source of failure in entire periods or organizations. As a balance to the pervasive iniquity of individuals, however, the ideology also emphasizes the essential correctness of the cadre's mission and the moral justification of his struggle. According to Liu Shao-ch'i, even if the party member is subjected to various attacks for the sake of upholding the truth, even if the opposition and rebuff of the great majority of the people force him into temporary isolation (glorious isolation), and even if on this account his life be endangered, he will still be able to stem the tide and uphold truth and will never resign himself to drifting with the tide.[95]

Thus ideology combines the notion of "correct mission" with the concept of faulty man and emphasizes the negative aspect of present conditions while striking an unusually optimistic note concerning the future.

Didactic ideology serves leadership by limiting the expectations of new leadership cadres. The investment in human resources in Communist China has remained unusually free—in comparison to many developing countries—of the psychological by-products of elite education, by-products which distort efficient and maximum utilization of subordinate cadres. Theoretically at least, indoctrination prepares cadres and party members not only to accept party-determined life careers but also to engage in any assigned task in an enthusiastic and realistic spirit. Moreover, through the operation of the training process dull, withdrawn trainees disqualify themselves, and the system provides both the purger and the purged with ample justification for casting out the failure.

Once acquired, the Communist state of mind presumably undergirds and necessitates leadership action. In the following chapter, the close affinity between dialectical cognition and the mass line will be established. The mass line structures mental activity into a leadership process and gives content to the required revolutionary practice underlying progressive thought. The amalgam of leadership psychology and leadership practice constitutes the essential focus of Chinese leadership theory. Derived by Chinese Communist Party leaders in the revolutionary war years, this amalgam, once articulated, gave those leaders

[95] Liu, *Lun kung-ch'an tang yüan ti hsiu-yang*, p. 53.

a faith in the correctness of their guidance, an effective measure for group solidarity and personal commitment, and a uniform operational code for cadres scattered in isolated guerrilla areas. During the years after 1949, however, the Chinese Communist leaders also had to cope with the possibility that the amalgam not only had origins in revolutionary war—origins beyond the experience of new, youthful cadres—but was dependent on an intimate, personal knowledge of that war. Without such knowledge, many young Chinese—if one can generalize the statements of refugees in Hong Kong—question the relevancy of the ideology and of the politically motivated cadre in the new, industrializing China.

III

Mass Line as a Concept of Leadership

Mass Line Method

THE mass line is the basic working method by which Communist cadres seek to initiate and promote a unified relationship between themselves and the Chinese population and thus to bring about the support and active participation of the people. This method includes the two techniques of "from the masses, to the masses," and "the linking of the general with the specific," [1] the basic formulization given by Mao Tse-tung in "On Methods of Leadership" (June 1, 1943). More recently,

[1] Mao Tse-tung, "On Methods of Leadership," *Selected Works* (New York: International Publishers, 1954–1956), IV, 111, 113. A more accurate translation of the Chinese title is "Some Problems of Leadership Method." For typical articles on the mass line, see *Jen-min jih-pao* [People's Daily], June 29, 1959; *Kuang-ming jih-pao* [Bright Daily], August 4, 1961; *Hung-ch'i* [Red Flag], no. 14, July 16, 1961, pp. 1–8; and *Hung ch'i,* no. 6, March 16, 1962, pp. 1–7.

Teng Hsiao-p'ing, Chinese Communist Party secretary-general, summed up the mass line as a Communist method of work

to integrate the leadership with the masses, to pursue the mass line in all fields of work, to mobilize the masses boldly, to develop energetic mass movements under the guidance of the leadership, to sum up the views and pool the wisdom of the masses and rely on the strength of the masses to carry out the policies of the Party.[2]

The success of the revolution, Chou En-lai stated in 1959, "is inseparably connected with the fact that the Party has persisted in the Marxist-Leninist working method of the mass line." [3] The primary elements of this method were the leadership of the party combined with broad mass movements.

As outlined in the discussion of "directness" in Chapter I, the mass line incorporates Communist tactics and techniques applicable to workers and peasants. Cadres must consciously employ these tactics and techniques to activate and direct the working-class masses according to tasks assigned by the Chinese Communist Party leaders. The mass line method of leadership prescribes techniques to maximize participation and enthusiasm of the Chinese people and to dissipate their possible antagonism toward party officials. To achieve the greatest motivation of the population with the least hostility has necessitated a wide variety of propaganda, training, and guiding techniques such as debates, rallies, small-group studies, and campaigns of emulation and "self-reform." [4] The mass line places particular emphasis on the points of direct contact between the Chinese people and cadres in order that supervision and guidance may be

[2] Teng Hsiao-p'ing, "The Great Unity of the Chinese People and the Great Unity of the Peoples of the World," *Ten Glorious Years* (Peking: Foreign Languages Press, 1960), p. 91.
[3] Chou En-lai, "A Great Decade," *Ten Glorious Years*, pp. 56–57.
[4] For a comprehensive study of these techniques, see Franklin W. Houn, *To Change a Nation: Propaganda and Indoctrination in Communist China* (New York: Free Press, 1961).

concrete and flexible. Although the method requires a high degree of alert response to developments within the masses and at the levels of actual work, it in no way stipulates that party leaders should allow the common Chinese workers and peasants to dictate the party's course of action.

From the conceptual viewpoint, Mao's method of the mass line has four progressive stages: perception, summarization, authorization, and implementation.[5] That these stages exactly parallel the epistemological process of perception, conception, and verification reinforces the assertion in the previous chapter that the Communist state of mind has important practical significance. In the first stage of "perception," the cadres operate within the worker-peasant masses, studying their "scattered and unsystematic views" and knowledge in order to identify problems, to coordinate views and knowledge, and to determine areas of strength and weakness for party operation. Then cadres sum up tested and scattered views and information into reports.[6] The highest committee responsible for the area covered by the reports receives the cadre reports with comments from lower echelons and if necessary issues authoritative directives or instructions.[7] These general directives are then sent back through the apparatus to be explained and popularized among the masses "until the masses embrace the ideas as their own, stand up for them and translate them into action by way of testing their correctness."[8] This process is continuously repeated in a steady integration, reassessment, and implementation of decisions. Problem identification-investigation-preliminary

[5] This conceptual outline is based on Mao's "On Methods of Leadership," pp. 111–117.

[6] See Mao, "On Setting Up a System of Reports" [January 7, 1948], *Selected Works* (Peking: Foreign Languages Press, 1961), IV, 177–179. See above, p. 29, n. 60.

[7] See Mao, "On Strengthening the Party Committee System" [September 20, 1948], *Selected Works*, IV (Peking), 267–268.

[8] Mao, "On Methods of Leadership," p. 113.

decision-testing-revision-report-authoritative decision-implemen-
tation-supervision-new problem comprises the life cycle of the
action affecting a particular policy operation.

The general flow of this process emphasizes direct, open
channels of communication to the lowest levels of information
and opinion. Further, since the process is continuous in one
operation, and in addition is integrated with others, a high value
is placed on regularized procedures for the routine collection
and assembly of information, systems for preliminary testing,
permanent committees of specialists for the routine evaluation
and decision, and the training of personnel in direct, practical
techniques of information collection, propaganda, and supervision. Mao Tse-tung has written that correct leadership comes
from the synthesis of material, reports, and views of the different localities which have been derived from repeated investigation and study.[9] More specifically, Mao said: "Some documents,
after having been drafted, are withheld from circulation for a
time because certain questions in them need to be clarified and
it is necessary to consult the lower levels first." [10] The cadre is
to be a pupil first, then a teacher, and is not to pretend to have
knowledge without concrete study and reconsideration of data.[11]

Under the mass line, the Communist concept of leadership
method is one of continuous, organized interaction between
cadres and members of the worker-peasant class. The resolution of problems, as a function of that interaction, never ends.
All "solutions" are temporary; review is consistent and uninterrupted. No problem is even temporarily resolved until projected action is brought within the scope of organizational tech-

[9] Mao, "Methods of Work of Party Committees" [March 13, 1949],
Selected Works, IV (Peking), 378–379.

[10] *Ibid.,* p. 378.

[11] *Ibid.* The specific aspect of cadre training related to this aspect
of the mass line is called "investigation and research" (*tiao-ch'a yen-
chiu*). According to *Kuang-ming jih-pao,* August 4, 1961, "investigation
and research are inseparable from the mass line." See below, Chapter V.

niques for implementation and review. This is a key aspect of the Communist concept of leadership.

To return to the four-stage conceptualized operation of the mass line method, the process from the masses to the party center and back variously emphasizes flexibility and participation under general guidance, on the one hand, and supervision and centralized rigidity, on the other. It is in this sense that Liu Shao-ch'i's 1945 statement on flexibility and rigidity takes on meaning: "While our Party must be rigid in matters of principle, it must possess a high degree of flexibility in the application of principles to concrete tasks." [12] Since flexibility and rigidity vary in importance at successive stages in an operation, the Communists have devised elements of organization to assign patterns of flexibility and rigidity in advance, or, in their terms, to "link the general with the specific." Flexibility allows modifications to be made for concrete conditions at the stages of perception and implementation. This adaptability encourages participation and inventiveness to achieve support and to improve the chances for success in implementation. This flexibility, however, occurs within a rigid general framework and decreases sharply during the stages of summarization and authorization. In general, leading cadres have absolute flexibility at all stages, though their participation in the process is more active during summarization and authorization. Working-level cadres have flexibility during perception and implementation, but the latitude of their action is more rigidly defined during implementation. Working cadres follow rigid procedures in summarization and have only a minor role in authorization. The common Chinese may participate with some flexibility during perception but thereafter must proceed within increasingly narrow limits.

By bringing workers and peasants into their concept of the

[12] Liu Shao-ch'i, *On the Party* (2d ed.; Peking: Foreign Languages Press, 1950), p. 150.

leadership process, the Communists can minimize the application of overt party power when that concept is correctly implemented. Leadership in Marxist-Leninist theory is not a matter of power but of correct relationship. The working masses are in principle assumed to hold all power. The party, as the vanguard of the working class, exercises leadership as its principal function in the mass line process. It devises the organizational guides, initiates and maintains new advances in technique, and makes certain that the ordinary Chinese play their part within the leadership operation. As the "bourgeois rightists" found out in 1957, to oppose party leadership is to oppose the working masses and the "destiny" of China.[13] The leadership method of the mass line is designed to unleash the creative power of the masses to solve problems, create a big leap forward in construction, bring prosperity, and usher in communism. Greater control by the party is considered equivalent to greater control by the working class. The party controls by leading and the masses "control" by participating, and in this theory the "vanguard" cannot have interests differing from those of the masses. When this is understood, the apparent contradiction of "democratic centralism" is also understood.

Recent slogans regarding party leadership can be explained in these terms. The party leads in everything because the working class masses "lead" China. As Lu Ting-yi reminded the "rightists" in 1957: "The Chinese people summarised their long experiences in one sentence: 'Without the Communist Party, there is no New China.'"[14] The two causes of this mass demand for party leadership, the Communists hold, are the relationship and the guidance which have been forged within the mass line method. The Communists speak of the mass line

---

[13] See Lu Ting-yi, "The Basic Difference between the Bourgeois Rightists and Us," in *Hsinhua News Agency Release*, July, 1957, item 071123, pp. 94–96.
[14] *Ibid.*, p. 96.

relationship in terms of "ties of blood" and assert: "The mass of the people look upon them [the party members] as their dearest, closest friends and comrades, treating them as affectionately as they would their own brothers and sisters." [15] With respect to the second cause of the theoretical mass demand for party leadership, the act of guiding, the party's vanguard role is regarded by Communists as a "sacred duty . . . to achieve the great goal of socialism and communism in China." [16] The ability of the Chinese Communist Party to ascertain correct direction and to employ effectively the process of leadership substantiates the party's vanguard claim. Once the right by successful performance has been firmly established, as the Communists assert it has been, it then becomes the party's duty to consolidate its leading position still further by ideological and policy direction. The ideological and political bolstering of party leadership coincides with Mao's general dictum that ideology and politics are the "soul and commander" of all work under the post-1958 slogan "politics in command." The party ensures its leadership organizationally by bringing all other organizations under its policy control and the direct supervision of its cadres.

Conceptual Implications of the Mass Line

The primary Communist argument for the mass line is the well-known rationale for the theory of the vanguard: the masses are the creators of history. The working-class masses are the "most far-sighted, most selfless and most thoroughly

[15] Liu Lan-t'ao, "The Communist Party of China Is the High Command of the Chinese People in Building Socialism," *Ten Glorious Years*, pp. 284–285. This article is the basic source for this paragraph.
[16] *Ibid.*, p. 285.

revolutionary." [17] The relation of the Communist Party to the masses is the clearest standard which differentiates that party from other parties.[18] This relationship is in theory sought by the masses themselves, because in their political awakening they realize the necessity for liberation under their most-advanced section, their vanguard. Under the direction of the vanguard, the masses reciprocally encourage and sustain the organization of the vanguard, the Communist Party. In 1945, Mao capsulized this mass support for the party: "The people want liberation and therefore entrust power to those who can represent them and work faithfully for them, that is, to us Communists." [19] Because of its unique knowledge and training gained in the historical process of the class struggle, the party has been able to equip itself with basic theory and the organizational means required to liberate and lead the masses. "We completely understand," Liu Shao-ch'i said in 1945, "the decisive function of the vanguard of the masses which rises up in the entire process of the mass liberation struggle." [20]

The essential aspect of this vanguard function, Liu asserted, was the development of the proper relationship between party cadres and the Chinese masses.[21] Liu presented three criteria for the promotion of this relationship: (1) the party must repre-

[17] Mao Tse-tung, "On People's Democratic Dictatorship" [June 30, 1949], *Selected Works,* IV (Peking), 421.

[18] The outline of this argument is taken from Chung-hua ch'üan-kuo tsung kung-hui kan-pu hsüeh-hsiao Ma-k'o-szu-Lieh-ning-chu-i chiao-yen shih [All-China Federation of Trade Unions, Cadre School, Marxist-Leninist Institute], ed., *Lun ch'ün-chung lu-hsien* [On the Mass Line] (1st enlarged 3d ed.; Peking: Kung-jen ch'u-pan she, 1957).

[19] Mao, "The Situation and Our Policy after the Victory in the War of Resistance against Japan" [August 13, 1945], *Selected Works,* IV (Peking), 16.

[20] Liu Shao-ch'i, *Kuan-yü hsiu-kai tang chang ti pao-kao* [Report on the Revision of the Party Constitution] (reprint; Hong Kong: Chung-kuo ch'u-pan she, 1948), p. 25. This report is better known by the English-translation title *On the Party.*

[21] *Ibid.,* pp. 25–26.

sent the interests of the masses; (2) the masses must be treated with the correct attitude; and (3) the masses must be led with the correct method.[22] These three criteria were addressed to the party cadres, because the responsibility for defining and maintaining the relationship belonged to the leaders, not the led. Failure to abide by these criteria, Liu warned, not only would incapacitate the party in fulfilling the tasks of mass liberation but would also bring the danger of mortal destruction by the enemy. Duty and survival were at stake.

The principal party deviations from the mass line, to which all cadres must be alert, were enumerated in the 1945 Communist Party Constitution as "tailism," "commandism," "isolationism," "bureaucratism," and "warlordism."[23] In his report on the Constitution, Liu Shao-ch'i condemned these specific ways in which the cadres might separate themselves from nonparty Chinese and thus violate the basic standards of leadership relationship. "Tailism" was defined as the erroneous practice of blindly following untutored popular demands; the other four deviations were forms of practice too far removed from the people. "Commandism" and "bureaucratism," the most serious deviations, are phenomena common to officious, arrogant bureaucrats and will be described in the following section. "Isolationism" is the failure to enlist the participation of nonparty elements or, as Mao said in 1938, "to think that only we ourselves are good and everyone else is of no use."[24] "Warlordism," an important deviation of the People's Liberation Army during the civil war, has since 1949 given way to more critical civil "sins" such as "sectarianism" and "subjectivism," which will also be discussed in the next section on the mass line

[22] *Ibid.*

[23] See H. Arthur Steiner, "Current 'Mass Line' Tactics in Communist China," *American Political Science Review*, XLV (June, 1951), 422–436, esp. 427–435.

[24] Mao Tse-tung, *The Role of the Chinese Communist Party in the National War* (Peking: Foreign Languages Press, 1956), p. 6.

working style. In general, moreover, mass line deviations have fallen into "right" and "left" categories.[25] The elaborate scheme for identifying different types of general ideological transgressions, which are illustrated differently in individual situations, permits cadres to recognize their errors and approach the solution correctly. A continuous evaluation of new situations and exposure of incorrect cadre methods become regularized in order to maintain the correct standard of relationship with the Chinese people. Without a correct standard for dealing with nonparty Chinese, policy decisions may cease to be concrete and realistic and may even become inoperative.

In maintaining a correct line, "from the masses, and to the masses," it is necessary to establish close contact "not only between the Party and the masses outside the Party (the class and the people), but first of all between the leading bodies of the Party and the masses within the Party (the cadres and the membership)." [26] Mao Tse-tung further asserted in 1945 that the organizational building of the party as a model for the mass line required conformity to the principle of democratic centralism, which involved organizational unity and the conduct of inner-party struggles to maintain the "truth." Organizational relationships within the party (democratic centralism) thus may serve as the model for relationships between the party and the Chinese people (mass line). Organizational deviations from democratic centralism within the party challenged correct mass line relationships, and at base, Mao held, these and other deviations "stemmed invariably from the ideological violation of Marxist-Leninist dialectical materialism and historical materialism, from subjectivism, formalism, doctrinairism and empiricism." [27] In overcoming ideological deviations, Mao said that

[25] See Mao Tse-tung, "Appendix: Resolution on Some Questions in the History of Our Party" [April 20, 1945], *Selected Works*, IV, 171–218.

[26] *Ibid.*, p. 205.   [27] *Ibid.*, p. 210.

the party must "develop criticism and self-criticism, carry on persuasion and education with patience, make a concrete analysis of the features of the mistakes and point out their dangers, explain their historical and ideological source and the way to rectify them." [28]

In the main, Mao linked the rectification of deviations to the central role of struggle in the organizational life of the party. Party struggle, as discussed in the foregoing chapter, aims "to educate the Party and the comrades who have committed mistakes." [29] Education and struggle, Liu Shao-ch'i wrote in 1941, "cannot be viewed separately. Struggle is a kind of education and education is a kind of struggle." [30] Deviations, struggle, and education are parts of a normal and necessary process within the context of organization. Liu denied that inner-party struggle was a "contradiction in organization or in form," because struggle proper takes place within and helps to heighten the framework of party unity. Stated differently, "party"—as the Communists conceive their organization in the abstract—epitomizes unity, the ideal synthesis, while inner-party struggles are a dialectical method to achieve that unity in fact.[31] The

[28] *Ibid.*, p. 216.
[29] Liu Shao-ch'i, *Lun tang-nei tou-cheng* [On Inner-Party Struggle] (reprint; Hong Kong: Cheng-pao she, 1947), p. 20.
[30] *Ibid.*
[31] *Ibid.*, p. 21. For an excellent example of inner-party struggle and the reasons why such struggle and democratic centralism must not, from the party viewpoint, be confused with a contradiction, see *Hsin min-chu-chu-i lun hsüeh-hsi tzu-liao* [Study Materials on New Democracy] (Canton: Kuang-chou-ch'ü kao-teng hsüeh-hsiao cheng-chih k'o tsung chiao-hsüeh wei-yüan-hui and Kuang-tung jen-min ch'u-pan she, 1951), p. 128. Liu Shao-ch'i in 1954 spoke of apparent contradictions between democracy and centralism and insisted that this missed the point since only democracy compatible with centralism or vice versa was the "true" principle. See *Documents of the First Session of the First National People's Congress of the People's Republic of China* (Peking: Foreign Languages Press, 1955), pp. 44–47. For an additional discussion on democratic centralism in the context of the period of "communism," see

principle of the party's organizational unity is democratic centralism, which at times appears to be an inherent contradiction owing to the presence of ideological contradictions and which must be continuously "synthesized" through struggle as reinforced by a "united, iron discipline." Despite the appearance of contradiction, however, mistaken democracy ("individualism," "tailism," "adventurism") and excessive centralism ("commandism," "bureaucratism," "warlordism") are held to reflect basic ideological errors arising from class contradictions outside the party, rather than contradictions within party organization.

By constantly applying criticism and self-criticism to prevent or correct deviations from proper ideological practice, ideal relationships of the mass line theoretically are created in the organizational life of the party. In correcting mistakes, criticism and self-criticism become unifying forces. Party members are thus educated to participate "democratically" in the process of rectification so that they can distinguish "right from wrong," eliminate impure attitudes, and improve leadership and working style. According to *Southern Daily*, "criticism and self-criticism can expose and correct in good time different acts which deviate from the Party line and [are] in violation of the discipline of the Party, intensify the education of Party members in Party spirit, and advance the Party's members' conception of organization and discipline." [32] In the rectification campaign of 1957, moreover, the technique of criticism and self-criticism was extended to all organizations and "non-Party people who wish to participate." [33] This extension of "direct" techniques, as described in Chapter I, has accompanied the general expansion

below, Chapter VIII. For a different point of view, see H. F. Schurmann, "Organisational Principles of the Chinese Communists," *China Quarterly*, no. 2 (April–June, 1960), pp. 47–58.

[32] *Nan-fang jih-pao*, November 26, 1960, in *SCMP*, no. 2416 (1961), p. 6.

[33] Text of rectification directive in *Hsinhua News Agency Release*, May, 1957, item 043055, pp. 10–12.

of the working-class designation to coincide with "the people." This more comprehensive "directness" reflects alleged changes in the class character of the economic base in 1955–1956. Having witnessed the rapid completion of agricultural collectivization and the socialization of businesses and industries by that time, Mao Tse-tung wrote: "In settling matters of an ideological nature or controversial issues among the people, we can only use democratic methods, methods of discussion, of criticism, of persuasion and education." [34] As early as 1956, at the outset of the "hundred flowers" movement for "blooming and contending" among intellectuals [35] and in commentaries on the downgrading of Stalin and on the Soviet handling of the Hungarian revolt,[36] criticism and struggle were the prescribed corrective techniques to be used among all the "people." Liu Shao-ch'i in 1958 spoke of ordinary Chinese who openly criticized leading personnel and each other by name in order to rectify deviations and "contradictions." [37]

Thus, the mass line defines the basically correct relationships between cadres and the "people" and—by its connection with democratic centralism—between leading party cadres and party members. Deviations from these relationships have been categorized and well publicized to permit effective criticism and struggle in the interests of educating the cadres and general population and promoting still further their solidarity. Resist-

[34] Mao Tse-tung, *On the Correct Handling of Contradictions among the People* (Peking: Foreign Languages Press, 1957), p. 16.

[35] See, for example, Chou En-lai, *Report on the Question of Intellectuals* [January 14, 1956] (Peking: Foreign Languages Press, 1956), pp. 29–31, and Lu Ting-yi, *"Let Flowers of Many Kinds Blossom, Diverse Schools of Thought Contend!"* [May 26, 1956] (Peking: Foreign Languages Press, 1957), sec. III.

[36] See the reprinted *Jen-min jih-pao* editorials of April 5 and December 29, 1956, in *The Historical Experience of the Dictatorship of the Proletariat* (Peking: Foreign Languages Press, 1959).

[37] *Second Session of the Eighth National Congress of the Communist Party of China* (Peking: Foreign Languages Press, 1958), p. 25.

ance or apathy by the common Chinese toward the "correct" relationship, however, is expected for several reasons. The masses, the Communists hold, are not as farseeing as the vanguard; the masses are more contaminated by reactionary ideologies and counterrevolutionary elements; and incorrect leadership conduct by the cadres may prevent the arousing of the populace and even antagonize it. To the extent that the ideological level of the working-class elements falls short of the desired intensity, the belief of the leadership in its unique mission and difficult responsibility is further heightened. In 1934, Mao Tse-tung wrote: "We should make the broad masses realise that we represent their interests, that our life and theirs are intimately interwoven." [38] The ordinary Chinese, Mao implied, have neither the duty to create the mass line relationship nor the right to reject it. They cannot turn against the vanguard because they cannot reverse the tide of their own historical movement which creates the vanguard.

Style of Work

Party literature abounds with descriptions of the mass line style of work. In 1938, Mao compared the differences between a style of work which would gain popular support and one which would repel such support. He argued that

such things as selfishness and self-interest, inactiveness and negligence in work, corruption, degeneration and vainglory are most contemptible; while the spirit of impartiality, of active and hard work, of self-denial in the interest of the public and of complete absorption in arduous work, commands respect.[39]

[38] Mao, "Take Care of the Living Conditions of the Masses and Attend to the Methods of Work," *Selected Works*, I, 149.
[39] Mao, *The Role of the Chinese Communist Party in the National War*, p. 5.

Service, responsibility, consultation, and common sacrifice are among the repeated themes of correct style.[40] In addition, Mao in 1942 compared style of work to military precision and preparation and stated: "Once our Party's style in work becomes completely right, the people of the whole country will follow us." [41] As elusive and yet as meaningful as the military concepts of morale and battle fitness, style of work describes the quality and degree of preparation to be exhibited by the cadres in their daily contacts with nonparty Chinese.

The Communist style of work is primarily determined by cadre attitudes and training, the concrete forms of daily work, and the response of the people to Communist performance. The mass line in party work, Teng Hsiao-p'ing wrote in 1956,

demands that the Party leadership should conduct themselves with modesty and prudence. Arrogance, arbitrariness, rashness, and habits of pretending to be clever, of not consulting the masses, of forcing one's opinions on others, of persisting in errors to keep up one's prestige—all these are utterly incompatible with the Party's mass line.[42]

The training of the Communist to perform with an effective mass line style primarily hinges on a progressive understanding by the trainee which comes from theoretical study and effective daily practice. To be divorced from objective reality is the error of "subjectivism," and to fail to create unity and solidarity within the party and masses is the error of "sectarianism." [43] The training of the cadre must combine Marxist-Leninist pre-

[40] Teng Hsiao-p'ing, "Report on the Revision of the Constitution," *Eighth National Congress of the Communist Party of China* (Peking: Foreign Languages Press, 1956), I, 176–177.

[41] Mao, "Rectify the Party's Style in Work," *Selected Works*, IV, 28–29.

[42] Teng Hsiao-p'ing, "Report on the Revision," p. 179.

[43] Mao, "Rectify the Party's Style," pp. 28–45. Mao's earliest ideas on subjectivism are found in "On the Rectification of Incorrect Ideas in the Party" [December, 1929], *Selected Works*, I, 112.

cepts with specific and concrete daily work to overcome these errors and thus instill the habit of the mass line style of work.

The concrete forms of daily work by which style is judged are closely bound to attitude and training. Concrete forms express themselves in action rather than in states of mind, though the two presumably interact fully. The primary mistakes in concrete behavior are usually defined as "bureaucratism" and "commandism." "Commandism" is the offense of issuing direct orders, or passing on higher orders, without preparing the masses to understand and accept them. "Bureaucratism" is the mistaken style of office-minded cadres who act officiously without informing themselves adequately about the concrete situations with which they deal and who think that sorting papers from "in" to "out" baskets is equivalent to the discharge of leadership responsibilities. In 1934, Mao denounced bureaucratic tendencies to propose tasks and issue orders but not to get out in the field to apply practical, specific guidance to each job.[44] In the 1957 campaign to rectify the working style of the party, the Central Committee initiated the *hsia-fang* (lit.: to go to the lower levels) movement for party and government cadres and required them to engage in physical labor at the production levels as part of a permanent system.[45] The *hsia-fang* objective was to have "no staff member who is completely removed from production," so that it would be "easier to avoid and overcome many bureaucratic, sectarian and subjective errors." [46]

How the common Chinese respond to Communist leadership performance is also a specific determinant or criterion for the mass line style of work. Because the party by its own proclamation is the leading force of the people "for carrying

[44] Mao, "Take Care of the Living Conditions," pp. 151–152.

[45] *Hsinhua News Agency Release*, May, 1957, item 043055, pp. 11–12. See below, Chapter VII, for a complete discussion of the *hsia-fang* movement.

[46] *Ibid.*, item 051421, pp. 120–121.

out their given historical mission in a given historical period," [47] the style of work of the party as a tool for that purpose should correspond with the popular will and interests. With the Communist emphasis on mass enthusiasm, mass participation, production records, and overfulfillment of quotas, the party leaders assume that cadre success is directly measured by the welfare and morale of the Chinese people. Chou En-lai, for example, has said:

This correct leadership by the Party has enabled the masses both to maintain their revolutionary enthusiasm . . . and to raise the level of their consciousness. . . . It is because of this that every call of the Party . . . has been warmly supported by the mass of the people. It is also because of this that . . . industrial and agricultural production has been on the rise constantly.[48]

Party manuals clearly declare that the working style of lower-level cadres will be judged by their success in "educating and organizing the masses, continuously raising the level of mass consciousness, organizational, technical, and cultural level," and by the degree of mass unity and activism.[49] Yet cadres must not forsake their primary mission of leading. They cannot, without becoming guilty of "tailism," appease the ordinary peasants and workers by yielding to mass pressures for actions which the leadership considers inappropriate in a particular stage or situation. The mass line is not properly followed if the cadres simply strive to become popular with the Chinese people. The mass line relationship cannot be governed by the un-tutored response of nonparty Chinese alone; its effectiveness is measured by the total "objective situation" which must support all leadership action.

[47] Teng Hsiao-p'ing, "Report on the Revision," pp. 177–178.
[48] Chou En-lai, "A Great Decade," Ten Glorious Years, p. 56.
[49] Kung-hui hsiao-tsu chang kung-tso [The Work of the Labor Union Small-Group Leader] (trial ed.; Peking: Kung-jen ch'u-pan she, 1954), p. 1.

The Party's Line, Dialectically Considered

In the theory of the mass line, the party's ability to make correct estimates of the current situation and to assign and carry out tasks in the light of such estimates plays a crucial part in sustaining and justifying the mass line leadership method. Practically every speech and report by a Communist leader could be subtitled: "The Present Situation and Our Tasks." This over-all estimate of the present situation is called a party line. But what is the relationship between the party line and the mass line? For practical purposes, without party lines there can be no mass line, since the party must devise the general tasks for cadres to carry out and supervise among the masses. Some party lines, however, emanate from the people, though others are clearly conceived by the party leaders first and then transmitted to the nonparty Chinese. But in all cases the mass line process is the assumed theoretical source of the party lines. That is, the party leaders are assumed to speak for the people irrespective of whether they have consulted the people or not.[50] It is the mystique of mass party identity which provides the consistent relationship between the party and mass lines. Only occasionally does the mystique coincide with empirical reality.

Thus the party cadres are theoretically the "most capable of focalizing the will of the masses, understanding their aspirations, and representing their interests."[51] Party leaders determine the specific lines of action derived from estimates of

[50] The theoretical validity of such initiative is implied in Communist Chinese assertions that "when the people's republic was established, the government and the people essentially became one" (*Hung-ch'i*, no. 14, July 16, 1961, p. 1). On the other hand, the party insists that members must seek to become the "true representatives of the masses" by cultivating an identity of interests with them and a sense of service (*Hung-ch'i*, no. 6, March 16, 1962, pp. 1–7).

[51] *Jen-min jih-pao*, November 11, 1959.

popular interests and needs, as these become known during operations within the general populace (or on behalf of the people) in theoretical conformity with the mass line. When so determined, the party line is considered to be practical and realistic.[52] Party "lines" therefore reflect "the supreme interests" and concretely express, in concept at least, "the volition and desires of the overwhelming majority of the people." [53]

According to the Communist argument, these lines are "things drawn from the masses for the masses, and are not subjectively concocted by some people." [54] By this reasoning, the mass line method and style create and reinforce party lines. The proper implementation of a line calls for the successful completion of individual tasks encompassed by the line.[55] These tasks or "policies" link the general scope of the line to the specific, concrete situation. Thus the policies of the party "are meant to serve as an instrument for the fulfillment of its tasks and also as an important standard for assessing whether a task has been fulfilled satisfactorily or otherwise," while the party's style of work describes the manner of operation and individual appreciation of Marxist-Leninist working methods. In sum, the party asserts that within the scope of the party line "the close combination of these three—tasks, policies and styles of work—represents the unity of Marxist-Leninist epistemology and methodology and of theory and practice." [56]

Broadly stated, any party line may be conceived as a device by which the ideology and strategy of the revolutionary movement are harmonized with tactical necessity and political expediency. Professor H. Arthur Steiner has listed the five following characteristics common to all party lines:

They deal with specific problems and issues which may be national, regional, or local in incidence; they give conscious expression of

---

[52] *Hung-ch'i*, no. 22, November 16, 1960, pp. 22–34.
[53] *Jen-min jih-pao*, November 11, 1959.   [54] *Ibid.*
[55] *Ibid.*, February 7, 1961.   [56] *Ibid.*

the purpose or intention of the leadership; they incorporate specific action directives . . . ; they seek to maintain ideological compatibility between the several party lines in effect at a given time and to distinguish lines applicable at a particular "stage of the revolution" from lines enforced under other circumstances; and, they usually enlarge rather than contract the scope of political and administrative action.[57]

He adds that a party line resolves differences and establishes orthodoxy and correctness, that it is used for indoctrination and discipline, that it facilitates guided movement toward objectives, and that it sustains the infallibility of the Communist leader.

Each party line is conceived as containing a permanent element of "truth," which has been discovered by the wise leadership. Party leaders insist that the "success or failure of the revolutionary enterprise is determined by whether or not the lines and guidelines are correct but can never be determined by certain individual shortcomings in work style and work method." [58] Although party lines are created and reinforced by party cadres through the effective utilization of the mass line method and style, the element of "truth" incorporated in a line determines whether or not it is "correct." The Communists transcend the style and work method of mass line operation to create "correct" lines by reliance on the theory of contradictory reality and the interaction of the economic base and the political superstructure.

The law of unity of opposites is one of the primary "laws" of dialectical materialism.[59] According to this law, "contradictions" (which were introduced in the previous chapter) are

[57] H. Arthur Steiner, "Ideology and Politics in Communist China," *Annals of the American Academy of Political and Social Science*, CCCXXI (January, 1959), 33–34.

[58] *Jen-min jih-pao*, November 11, 1959.

[59] This follows Mao Tse-tung's general argument in "On Contradiction" [August, 1937], *Selected Works*, II, 13–53.

universal and exist in the development of all things and in the particular form of each thing. All things are different because of particular contradictions, but conversely all things may be considered to have a common denominator because of the universality of contradictions. In the development of such a complex thing as human society, many contradictions exist, but "among these, one is necessarily the principal contradiction whose existence and development determine and influence the existence and development of other contradictions." [60] Contradictions in human society may or may not be capable of nonviolent resolution, or, as usually expressed, they may or may not be antagonistic. Moreover, "based on the concrete development of things, some contradictions, originally non-antagonistic, develop and become antagonistic, while some contradictions, originally antagonistic, develop and become non-antagonistic." [61] In a "socialist" society such as contemporary mainland China, Chinese Communists consider the major contradictions to be nonantagonistic (capable of "democratic" resolution) and basically those "between the relations of production and the productive forces, and between the superstructure and the economic base"—not between classes.[62]

Contradictions, viewed in the previous chapter as the basic cause of all development, are, in the logic of dialectical materialism, the only motive force for social progress.[63] According to *People's Daily*,

if the party and state leadership is able to discover contradictions and, on its initiative, adopt a correct guideline and method to resolve the contradictions in time, then the resistance and irreconcilability in all fields can be eliminated, all positive factors can be

[60] *Ibid.*, p. 35.   [61] *Ibid.*, p. 50.

[62] Mao, *On the Correct Handling*, pp. 22–23.

[63] *Jen-min jih-pao*, June 14, 1960; see also Yui [Yü] Kuang-yüan, "The Role of Politics in Speeding Up the Development of Socialist Economy," *World Marxist Review*, III, no. 8 (August, 1960), 66, and *Jen-min jih-pao*, February 25, 1960.

mobilized, and the enthusiasm and creativeness of the people can be brought into full play to ensure high-rate development of the socialist cause.[64]

Since contradictions in bourgeois society theoretically are antagonistic (cannot be resolved without violence), these societies, the Communists hold, lack the positive motive force of non-antagonistic contradictions as the central mechanism for progress. Herein lies the source of Communist confidence in "great leap" programs and of their optimistic belief in the long-term superiority of communism over capitalism. By the logic of contradictions, "properly used" contradictions in the working-class society must further socialist construction and the transition to the Communist millennium.

Correct use of nonantagonistic contradictions depends on a proper political and ideological assessment of them. The Communists assign both politics and ideology to the category of "superstructure." They follow Lenin's analysis, however, that though the superstructure is determined by the economic base, superstructural politics and ideology can in turn guide the development of that economic base. More particularly, since in theory the contradictions between the superstructure and the economic base, and between production relations and productive forces, constitute the basic contradictions in socialist society, the Chinese Communists have asserted that a primary role of politics is to resolve correctly these economic contradictions.[65] They add:

What is needed is to make full use of this political superstructure in order, in keeping with the requirements of the rapid development of the productive forces, consciously and in good time to regulate, transform and change the production relations, remove obstacles in the way of social productive forces and thus assist their rapid development.[66]

[64] *Jen-min jih-pao*, June 14, 1960.
[65] Yui Kuang-yüan, *op. cit.*, p. 66.   [66] *Ibid.*

91

The political resolution of contradictions consists of ordering and manipulating all material and social relationships so that the latent motive force of the contradictions may be fully employed. Policy resolution therefore is a strategic estimate of "objective contradictions." This estimate, which remains valid during the life cycle of a contradiction, is "correct" when it stems from contradictory reality and has been tested in mass line practice and conforms to Marxism-Leninism, as interpreted by the responsible leadership. Communists call these estimates the party line.

As the world teems with contradictions, so the party must devise an endless variety of lines, and, in practice, innumerable party lines operate at the same time. Party lines apply to such varied subjects as organization, leadership, industry, planting, hog raising, party building, international relations, bank savings, commune administration, and every other conceivable aspect of a total social system. In the general dialectical sense the mass line itself may be viewed as a party line resolving the nonantagonistic contradiction between leadership and participation or between leaders and the people. Since this nonantagonistic contradiction assumes the character of a "principal contradiction" for the operation of party leaders, all other party lines must conform to the mass line method for the correct resolution of contradictions. This statement thus provides the dialectical dimension to answer the question asked earlier concerning the relationship of the mass line and the party line. The general procedures to give effect to these lines are the relevant party policies. Theoretically, lines persist throughout the full cycle of a contradiction from "relative rest" to "conspicuous change." Policies change with each new phase of the contradiction and are thus more specific and more temporary than the over-all party line. In the operation of the mass line method, it is the party's policies which most frequently result from the mass line "stages" of perception, summarization, and authorization and which are "handed to the masses" and are "translated into action" during implementation.

At an enlarged meeting of the Political Bureau of the Chinese Communist Party on April 25, 1956, Mao Tse-tung delivered a report on ten important sets of relationships wherein contradictions provided the key to China's development. These critical relationships as summarized by Liu Shao-ch'i were:

(1) The relations between industry and agriculture and between heavy industry and light industry.
(2) The relations between coastal industry and inland industry.
(3) The relations between economic construction and defense construction.
(4) The relations between the State, cooperatives, and individuals.
(5) The relations between the central and local authorities.
(6) The relations between the Han nationality and minority nationalities.
(7) The relations between the Party and non-party people.
(8) The relations between revolution and counter-revolution.
(9) The relations between right and wrong inside and outside the Party.
(10) International relations.[67]

Mao reportedly conceived of these sets of relations as basically contradictory.[68] For the proper handling of the contradictions in the economic relations, he proposed a set of policies for the simultaneous development ("walking on two legs") of industry and agriculture, heavy and light industry, national and local industry, and large, medium, and small enterprises and for the simultaneous use of modern and indigenous methods under a combination of centralization of powers and decentralization.

[67] See *Second Session of the Eighth National Congress*, pp. 36–37, and *Jen-min jih-pao*, June 14, 1960.
[68] *Jen-min jih-pao*, June 14, 1960.

In February, 1957, in *On the Correct Handling of Contradictions among the People*, Mao elaborated those relationships which pertained to the people.

The party lines on "simultaneous development" as well as all other lines and policies between 1952 and 1958 were given within the context of a "general line" for the period of transition to socialism. The Central Committee announced this line in late 1952 in order to synthesize all party lines and policies into a general statement of the then current purpose and motivation.[69] The present general line for socialist construction was popularized in May, 1958, at the second session of the Eighth National Congress of the Chinese Communist Party. This line, which was introduced in the previous chapter as the essential formula for solving the principal contradiction of a given historical period, is: "To build socialism by exerting our utmost efforts, and pressing ahead consistently to achieve greater, faster, better and more economical results." [70] The general line for socialist construction, Liu Shao-ch'i reported, "is the application and development of its [the party's] mass line in socialist construction." [71] As a synthesis of all other lines, this general line sets the context for the chief task of planning which is "to resolve this main contradiction between imbalance and balance, between disproportions and proportions in economic development." [72] The general line is a formula for integrating the objective possibility of the economic base with the subjective activity of the masses led by the party. In this way, the Communists hold that the party solves "the various problems of the Chinese revolution and construction by flexibly applying

[69] Liu Shao-ch'i described the successive general lines in the party's history in "The Victory of Marxism-Leninism in China" [September 14, 1959], *Ten Glorious Years*, pp. 1–34.

[70] *Second Session of the Eighth National Congress*, pp. 33–51.

[71] *Ibid.*, p. 51.

[72] Wang Kuang-wei, "The Big Leap in China's Economy," *World Marxist Review*, III, no. 6 (July, 1960), 49.

the general principles of Marxism-Leninism in the light of the concrete conditions of China." [73]

Political leadership of the socialist system according to the general line and the lines and policies subsumed under it provides the advanced preparation and control necessary in theory, at least, for rapid, unhindered development of otherwise "natural" forces. These forces are dramatically manifested in China's economic growth. The Communists refer to the "poor and blank" condition of the old society and the enormous potential of 700,000,000 people with new tools, new skills, and new sources of raw material. The Chinese Communist Party proudly lauds the country's new bridges, factories, communes, "big leap" production figures, and schools as the visible evidence that the party's lines are properly unleashing the potential of China's social contradictions.

These material advances are displayed to "prove" the practical importance of the mass line and party lines in action. But, according to the Marxist-Leninist epistemological theory discussed in the foregoing chapter, practice and action are also inseparable from theory and intellectual growth. The less tangible counterpart of material development in following the party's lines and policies is the alleged transformation that concurrently takes place in the human mind. Adherence to the party line theoretically creates conditions of understanding beyond the fulfillment of specific programs. Those who work for the implementation of party policies purportedly achieve by virtue of their obedient activity a more profound knowledge of the basic operation of the historical process and the underlying material base. In discussing the mass line and party policies in 1961, *People's Daily* wrote: "A work assignment cannot be described as properly accomplished if its completion is not accompanied by a heightening of the consciousness of the masses." [74]

[73] Liu Shao-ch'i, "The Victory of Marxism-Leninism," p. 33.
[74] *Jen-min jih-pao*, January 14, 1961.

"Social practice alone is the criterion of truth," Mao wrote in *On Practice* (1937).[75] "To make practice the point of departure is the first and basic feature of the theory of knowledge of dialectical materialism."[76] The kinds of activity which Mao specifically mentioned were productive activity, class struggle, and political struggle in addition to scientific and artistic pursuits. Knowledge begins in the social practice of class. For cadres, knowledge follows the four stages of mass line operation: perception, summary, authorization, and implementation. Knowledge is changed from mere perception to rational proposals of the party leaders who base their decisions on cadre reports. These rational proposals are the party lines which "deepen" the initial knowledge gained by the cadre's perception. These lines are insufficient, however, until they have become specific guides to action or policies. "The policies of the party represent the setting out of the party's programs, lines, and guiding principles into regulations," *People's Daily* stated in 1960.[77] Cadres must implement these policies to maintain the flow of knowledge, not merely to complete a given task. "The process of knowing," Mao wrote in *On Practice*, ". . . can be considered completed if the man, through practice, can realize his preconceived aim, if he can, more or less completely, transform these preconceived ideas, theories, plans or programmes into facts."[78] On the one hand, the implementation of policies releases the activism of the masses through the resolution of social contradictions, and, on the other, the implementation in revolutionary practice raises the level of understanding. The issue of enforced obedience to party dicta is never raised, for discipline must come from the inner desire to see the "liberation" of the masses from their backward-

[75] Mao, *On Practice* (rev. trans.; Peking: Foreign Languages Press, 1958), p. 3.
[76] *Ibid.*, pp. 3–4.   [77] *Jen-min jih-pao*, October 31, 1960.
[78] P. 17.

ness and to gain an added insight into the creative mechanism of objective reality.

The earnest and careful handling of the policies of the party therefore involves both a duty [79] and an opportunity. Struggle brings the perception of problems, lines raise this perception to rational appraisals of the general situation, and policies detail the carrying out of these lines in revolutionary action. Thought and action are unified from beginning to end. The cadres are duty-bound to follow rigidly the dictates of the unified process in order to maintain their leadership quality. The faithful execution of each step of the process, however, involves the opportunity to increase the certainty and clarity of political and technical knowledge in a reciprocal system of advancement. According to Liu Shao-ch'i's famous 1957 slogan, all must be "red and expert." [80] Within the mass line operation, the party cadres are to increase their technical ability while technical personnel learn politics. Party leaders must operate within the population, and workers and peasants are expected to participate in and seek to improve party programs. The realization of these "advantages" provided by the opportunity to carry out party policies gradually reduces the sense of constraint and eliminates the apparent contradiction between duty and opportunity. In the fulfillment of party policies, therefore, the latent consensus of the working class theoretically is given real content and meaning.

[79] On this point of policy implementation as a basic guarantee of victory, see *An-hui jih-pao* [Anhwei Daily], September 30, 1959, in *SCMP*, no. 2133 (1959), pp. 27-34.

[80] "Liu Shao-ch'i t'ung-chih t'an 'yu hung yu chuan'" [Comrade Liu Shao-ch'i Talks on "Red and Expert"], *Lun yu hung yu chuan* [On Red and Expert] (Peking: Chung-kuo ch'ing-nien ch'u-pan she, 1958), pp. 3-4.

Key Aspects of the Mass Line Concept

The synthesis of the ideal mind and the ideal leadership method epitomizes the Chinese Communists' perception of their revolutionary experience. The total synthesis, the Communists assert, reflects and affirms "laws" of objective reality, including laws of leadership operation. The ideal synthesis, moreover, takes practical form only through a well-trained elite body whose members—having an advanced ideological consciousness —comprehend the union of revolutionary theory and revolutionary practice. The type of leadership training conforms to the concrete steps of mass line techniques under the direction of senior cadres. Detailed and concrete, the mass line stages form the practical—indeed, the party leaders insist, the only—bridge between the model synthesis and actuality.

The hallmark of the mass line concept is its balance of situational flexibility within the limits of firm operational principles. The mass line provides the aura of consistency and stability during periods of rapid policy shifts and tactical retreats. In one sense, the mass line may be viewed as the mere rationalization of opportunism as well as a system for creating and manipulating opportunities. Yet, when taken as an operational code, the mass line provides points of continuing reference for all lines of action. These reference points may not be particularly useful for the cadre in the field, but they are indispensable for maintaining the leadership's claim to infallible wisdom and revolutionary foresight. At one time (1958), for example, the party urged cadres to take a rigorous, "non-tailist" attitude toward the peasants in order to convince the peasantry of the validity of the communes. Two years later, cadres were denounced for their "commandist" errors in the former attitude. Party leaders then exhorted the cadres to journey to the villages with hat in hand to request advice from the older peasants. Both the phases of central direction and of "democracy" came within the purview of the mass line. Following the tortuous party line within the confines of the mass line, party members and cadres are also deterred from turning their sense of frustration on the elite itself. The mass line doctrine stipulates that members must adjust to sudden changes by reappraising their own knowledge in the light of the new situation. Only infrequently do individual members find the opportunity to stand aside from the flow of policy to question the mass line itself.

The next three chapters will analyze the organizational, educational, and operational forms and techniques which flow from the theoretical principles of ideology and the mass line. In the revolutionary environment of the civil war, these tactics and techniques evolved naturally in response to the demands of wartime events. Only after prolonged emersion in these events did the party's leaders abstract the general principles and rationalize ideology and the mass line into an ideal synthesis. Their first attempts at abstraction were often clumsy and haphazard—a hodgepodge of quotations from Lenin and Stalin mixed with Chinese folk wisdom and the personal experiences of war. After 1949, however, senior Communist cadres attempted to systematize their wartime generalizations and then to use the "summed up" statements as the model for future tactics and techniques. This shift in emphasis coincided with the changes in party role described in Chapter I.

The militant preservation of the revolutionary mass line progressively alienated party leaders from the postrevolutionary realities of the Chinese state. Moreover, the process of alienation continues as Communist leaders equate current struggles for economic construction with the pre-1949 revolutionary military struggle. Reasoning by analogy, they stipulate that what worked as a leadership system in Yenan must be equally effective for the same leaders a decade or so later in Peking. Believing that the mass line method must "represent the interests of the masses," Communist cadres have underestimated and misunderstood the deterioration of popular morale and support. Dissatisfied with exhortation without positive economic effects, harried peasants and workers have become listless and sullen according to many reliable but unconfirmed reports. Disheartened by ineffective leadership, even the cadres, the Communist press [81] has made clear, have departed with increasing frequency from the mass line techniques and style. The revolutionary mass line now faces its maximum trial. Should the mass line fail the test of successful applicability in the period of economic crisis, no one can predict the extent or the directions of the reaction.

[81] See, for example, the important article by Liu Ch'ung in *Jen-min jih-pao*, April 3, 1962, and *Hung-ch'i*, no. 6, March 16, 1962, pp. 1–7. At the Tenth Plenum of the Central Committee meeting September 24–27, the party specifically blamed incompetent leading cadres for failures in production teams, factories, and business establishments. (*Jen-min jih-pao*, September 29, 1962).

IV

Structure of the Communist Party

Party Membership Policies

THE Chinese Communist Party is a membership organization, which selectively recruits potential leaders who must abide by rigid standards of initiation and indoctrination. Selection of party members in the past has been flexibly oriented to attract Chinese capable of performing the priority tasks of a given period and of strengthening certain "weak" areas of the organization. Thus the typical party member before the 1949 "liberation" was the exemplary soldier whose courage and military skill were priority assets in the struggle with the Kuomintang. After the liberation, technical and intellectual youth, particularly young workers, were considered the most desirable recruits. This policy changed in 1958 with the establishment of the communes and the necessity for a vast expansion in the ranks of rural party cadres.

One of the acute problems faced by Mao Tse-tung during the "low ebb" period in the Chingkang Mountains (1927–1930) was the need for reliable party members. Faced with potential turncoats in party "careerists," Mao ordered party organizations in various *hsien* (counties) to be dissolved and a re-registration to be undertaken.[1] In the entire border area, "a drastic purge of the Party was carried out and strict restrictions were placed on membership qualifications." Mao concluded that although the party membership had been reduced, "its fighting capacity" had been substantially augmented.[2]

At the same time that Mao was devising a working balance between membership numbers and quality in the border area organizations, the Sixth National Congress of the Chinese Communist Party in Moscow, July, 1928, adopted the party's Regulations, including the following provision (Art. 2) on party membership:

Anyone who subscribes to the Constitution and regulations of the Communist International and the Chinese Communist Party, enters one of the Party organizations and works with great energy in it, obeys all the resolutions of the Communist International and the Party, and pays Party dues regularly, may become a Party member.[3]

These formal membership requirements were complicated by additional criteria applicable to the base area controlled by Mao Tse-tung. Some of these additional criteria may be inferred from *On the Rectification of Incorrect Ideas in the Party* (December,

[1] Mao Tse-tung, "The Struggle in the Chingkang Mountains" [November 25, 1928], *Selected Works* (New York: International Publishers, 1954–1956), I, 96.
[2] *Ibid.*
[3] Quoted in Ch'en Yün, *Tsen-yang tso i-ko kung-ch'an tang yüan* [How to Be a Communist Party Member] (reprinted 2d ed.; Canton: Hsin-hua shu-tien, 1950), p. 2; translated in Boyd Compton, *Mao's China: Party Reform Documents, 1942–1944* (Seattle: University of Washington Press, 1952), pp. 88–89.

1929), in which Mao added the "qualifications" of obedience and discipline, ideological activism, willingness to learn and accept criticism, and devotion to duty. The membership requirements, both explicit and inferred, were designed to foster a membership capable of carrying out the responsibilities of revolutionary leadership.

Comparing the proletariat and the party to "all social strata and political groups" of China, Mao in 1936 declared that the party (along with the proletariat) was the "most open-minded and unselfish," possessed "the most far-sighted political outlook and the highest organisational quality," and was "the readiest to learn with an open mind." [4] Two years later, Mao endeavored to strengthen this elite when he called on the party to "expand its organisation by throwing its door open to the broad masses of workers, peasants, and young and active people who are truly revolutionary, who believe in the Party's principles, support its policies and are willing to observe its discipline and to work hard." [5] Mao called for a "great party of a mass character," [6] a theme which he repeated in 1939, when he demanded a "bolshevized Chinese Communist Party of nation-wide scope and broad mass character, fully consolidated ideologically, politically, and organisationally." [7]

From 1939 to 1945, the two basic statements on conditions of party membership were Ch'en Yün's manual, *How to Be a Communist Party Member* (May 30, 1939), and Liu Shao-ch'i's *How to Be a Good Communist* (July, 1939).[8] Ch'en's book,

---

[4] Mao, "Strategic Problems of China's Revolutionary War" [December, 1936], *Selected Works*, I, 189.

[5] Mao, "The Role of the Chinese Communist Party in the National War" [October, 1938], *Selected Works*, II, 249.

[6] *Ibid.*

[7] Mao, "Introductory Remarks to *The Communist*" [October 4, 1939], *Selected Works*, III, 53.

[8] Ch'en's manual is cited above, n. 3. Liu's *How to Be a Good*

which is of major concern here, deals with formal party qualifications, while Liu discusses the "cultivation" of the best-quality
members. In addition to the formal requirements of the party
Regulations, Ch'en stressed that workers should be the "foundation" of the party, though the party should also pay attention
to poor peasants, intellectuals, and women. The prescribed
emphases in the recruitment policy were to be achieved, Ch'en
stated, by requiring applicants for membership with desired class
backgrounds to submit fewer recommendations and to undergo
a less lengthy period of probationary membership. The age
qualification for probationary party members was to be a minimum of 16 years in contrast to the post-1945 minimum of 18
years. In the fifth section of his manual, Ch'en enumerated six
primary membership conditions beyond simple participation in
a party organization and payment of dues. In brief, these were:
struggle all one's lifetime for communism; place revolutionary
interests above everything; obey party discipline and keep party
secrets; carry out decisions unflinchingly; be an example for the
masses; and study.

In the Communist Party Constitution of June 11, 1945, the
minimum age for membership was raised to 18, and a system of
differential admission requirements and probationary periods
along the lines indicated by Ch'en Yün was adopted which made
it technically easier for workers, coolies, farm hands, poor peasants, city poor, and revolutionary soldiers to become members.
In the spring of 1951, the Communist Party convened the first
National Conference on Organizational Work, and in November of the same year reportedly began the policy of "party-
reform party-construction" (*cheng-tang chien-tang*), which was
inaugurated to correct organizational and ideological weaknesses

---

Communist (Peking: Foreign Languages Press, 1951) is the official
English translation of Liu, *Lun kung-ch'an tang yüan ti hsiu-yang* [On
the Cultivation of the Communist Party Member] (reprint; Hong Kong:
Hsin min-chu ch'u-pan she, 1949).

among the members and to expand the ranks of the party by recruitment of activists, youth, and deserving nonparty cadres. From 1951, the Central Committee also gave priority to the recruitment of workers.[9] The *cheng-tang chien-tang* policy was apparently necessitated by the shake-up of the *san-fan* (three-anti) and *wu-fan* (five-anti) movements launched in 1951 and 1952. At the November, 1951, meeting, Liu Shao-ch'i, in a statement never published, reportedly recast the qualifications for party membership, and criteria established by Liu presumably became the basis for the famous "eight standards" of membership enunciated by An Tzu-wen, then deputy director of the Organization Department, on July 1, 1952.[10]

The "eight standards" substantially reaffirmed the conditions of membership given by Ch'en Yün in 1939. However, An's "standards" gave greater emphasis to motivation, discipline ("unity"), and "knowledge" (particularly ideological clarity and the use of criticism and self-criticism). On the basis of these eight standards, An attempted to establish limits so that the party would retain its elitist quality yet not become too exclusive.

We must guarantee [An stated] that new Party members admitted hereafter shall be the most elite among the workers and laboring people, those who have been educated, tested, with good character, with high consciousness, with a pure historical background, loyal to the Party, having exhibited their active zeal . . . understanding the mission of the Party and prepared to devote their whole lives . . . and capable of abiding by the discipline of the Party.[11]

[9] Hu Ch'iao-mu, *Thirty Years of the Communist Party of China*, (4th ed.; Peking: Foreign Languages Press, 1959), p. 98.

[10] An Tzu-wen, "Strengthen the Work of Party Reform and Party Expansion on the Foundations of Victory in the 3-Anti and 5-Anti Movements" (in Chinese), *Jen-min jih-pao* [People's Daily], July 1, 1952, translated in *Current Background* (Hong Kong: American Consulate General), no. 191 (1952).

[11] *Ibid.*, p. 6.

Yet An also called for "an extensive and popular party," and to balance the popular theme with the elitist quality, he announced the policy of "active and prudent" recruitment which continues to the present. This policy, reminiscent of Mao Tsetung's 1938 demand to "recruit to the Party boldly but never allow a single undesirable person to sneak in," [12] is typical of party policies in establishing an imprecise and ambiguous scale of allowed action. If successful, the party credits the all-wise leadership; if unsuccessful, the party blames the lower levels for failure to apply the policy correctly.

In the 1956 party Constitution, the 1952 "standards" of membership were more fully elaborated as ten duties (Art. 2), and former differentials in admission requirements and in probationary periods were eliminated. These differential procedures for admitting new members were removed, Teng Hsiao-p'ing reported in 1956, "because the former classification of social status has lost or is losing its original meaning." [13] To inform the leadership of the applicant's potential to fulfill the membership duties, party members who recommend an applicant for admission are now required to furnish information concerning "the applicant's ideology, character and personal history" (Art. 5). The major shift in emphasis in the 1956 membership policies is on the safeguarding of party solidarity and consolidating its unity and on Communist ethics, criticism and self-criticism, and obedience. "The most significant change about the Party," Secretary-General Teng Hsiao-p'ing said, "is that it is now in the position of leadership throughout the country." [14] This responsibility for national leadership, Teng stated, demands higher standards for party members, but, in fact, "nowadays . . . it is easy to find people who have joined the Party for the sake of

[12] Mao, "The Role of the Chinese Communist Party," p. 249.

[13] Teng Hsiao-p'ing, "Report on the Revision of the Constitution," *Eighth National Congress of the Communist Party of China* (Peking: Foreign Languages Press, 1956), I, 213.

[14] *Ibid.*, p. 208.

prestige and position." [15] To correct this discrepancy, Teng noted the importance of postrecruitment disciplinary control of members and probationary members in the 1956 party Constitution. During the probationary year, the new members are to be given "an elementary Party education" and their "political qualities" are to be closely scrutinized (Art. 7). At the end of the year, the branch general membership meeting may accept the transfer to full membership, which must then be approved by the next higher committee (Art. 8). The close supervision of members continues after full membership is conferred, and disciplinary measures including expulsion or reduction to probationary status are prescribed for violations of membership duties (Arts. 13–18).

Membership in the Chinese Communist Party continues to be selective and rigidly oriented to attract proved leaders. Many "criteria" for membership are still "understood" and not enumerated in the party's Constitution, which simply states (Art. 1): "Membership of the Party is open to any Chinese citizen who works and does not exploit the labor of others, accepts the program and Constitution of the Party, joins and works in one of the Party organizations, carries out the Party's decisions, and pays membership dues as required." The only additional formal requirements are that applicants be 18 years of age, be members of the Young Communist League if they are under 25 years,[16] have two recommendations for application, and undergo (except "under special conditions") a probationary period (one year) prior to conferment of full membership (Art. 4).

[15] *Ibid.*, p. 209.

[16] "Wei-shih-mo erh-shih-wu sui i-hsia ti ch'ing-nien ju tang shih pi-hsü shih ch'ing-nien t'uan yüan" [Why Youth under Twenty-five Years of Age When Entering the Party Must Be Members of the Youth League], in Chu Yü-chin *et al., Ho ch'ing-nien t'an ju tang wen-t'i* [Chat with the Youth about Questions of Entering the Party] (3d ed.; Hankow: Chung-nan ch'ing ch'u-pan she, 1952), pp. 32–33.

Composition and Growth of the Chinese Communist Party

These formal requirements as such would give no indication that the "working-class vanguard" is composed of a small minority of workers. According to Communist Party statistics summarized in Table 1, as of June 30, 1956, and September 27.

Table 1. Social backgrounds of Chinese Communist Party members, 1956–1957

	1956	1957
Total membership	10,734,384	12,720,000
Workers	1,502,814	1,740,000
	(14.0%)	(13.7%)
Peasants	7,417,459	8,500,000
	(69.1%)	(66.8%)
Intellectuals	1,255,923	1,880,000
	(11.7%)	(14.8%)
Other	558,188	600,000
	(5.2%)	(4.7%)

Sources: Figures for 1956 are found in Teng Hsiao-p'ing, "Report on the Revision of the Constitution," Eighth National Congress of the Communist Party of China (Peking: Foreign Languages Press, 1956), I, 209, and Shih-shih shou-ts'e [Current Events Handbook], no. 18, 1956. Figures for 1957 are given in Teng Hsiao-p'ing, Report on the Rectification Campaign (Peking: Foreign Languages Press, 1957), p. 45.

1957, 14 per cent of the 10,734,384 members in 1956 were workers; 69.1 per cent peasants; 11.7 per cent intellectuals; and 5.2 per cent of "other" class status. The only appreciable changes between 1956 and 1957 were the decline in the percentage of peasant members (69.1 to 66.8) and the increase in the percentage of intellectual members (11.7 to 14.8). In 1957, the number of intellectuals surpassed the number of workers in the party. The influx of intellectuals may be explained by Chou En-lai's January, 1956, plea for active recruitment among intellectuals and the admission by 1962 of one-third of the higher intellectuals.[17] The decline of peasant members was probably reversed in 1959 after the establishment of the communes when the party called for a rapid strenghtening of its rural organizations. By age breakdown, in 1956, 24.83 per cent were 25 or younger, 67.54 per cent were between 26 and 45, and 7.63 per cent were above the age of 46. One in ten party members in 1956 was a woman (about the same as in 1950),[18] and in 1957, about one in five members was a probationary member.

Against this brief background of membership composition, Tables 2, 3, and 4 present data on the numerical growth of the party. Table 2 graphically portrays how the growth of the membership followed the ebb and flow of party fortunes during the twenty years from 1921 to 1941. In particular, the boost in party enrollments during the preparations for the 1926 Northern Expedition and the disastrous impact of the 1927 and 1933 suppressions by the Kuomintang are strikingly evident. Then, after 1941, the expansion and contraction of the party became subject to self-imposed manipulation. No strict rule of growth may be inferred, however, from the party's "rectification" campaigns after 1942. Indeed, the 1940–1942 decline of 63,849 members occurred before the 1942–1944 campaign, and the party experienced a substantial net gain (117,269 members) during the two campaign years. During the next rectification campaign of 1947–1948, the number of party members recruited declined sharply, and in the campaign of 1950, the total number of Communist Party members dropped by more than 59,000.[19] The *cheng-tang*

---

[17] Chou En-lai, *Report on the Question of Intellectuals* (Peking: Foreign Languages Press, 1956), p. 32.

[18] *Shih-shih shou-ts'e* [Current Events Handbook], no. 16, 1951.

[19] For a discussion of the various campaigns, see the following chapter.

Table 2. Numerical growth of the Chinese Communist Party,
1921–1961

	No. of members	Years covered	Avg. annual increase
1st revolutionary civil war			
1921 (1st Congress)	57	—	—
1922 (2d Congress)	123	1	66
1923 (3d Congress)	432	1	309
1925 (4th Congress)	950	2	259
1927 (5th Congress)	57,967	2	28,508
1927 (after "April 12")	10,000	—	—
2d revolutionary civil war			
1928 (6th Congress)	40,000	1	30,000
1930	122,318	2	41,159
1933	300,000	3	59,227
1937	40,000	4	−65,000
Anti-Japanese war			
1940	800,000	3	253,333
1941	763,447	1	−36,553
1942	736,151	1	−27,296
1944	853,420	2	58,635
1945 (7th Congress)	1,211,128	1	357,708
3d revolutionary civil war			
1946	1,348,320	1	137,192
1947	2,759,456	1	1,411,136
1948	3,065,533	1	306,077
1949	4,488,080	1	1,422,547
Under People's Republic of China			
1950	5,821,604	1	1,333,524
1951	5,762,293	1	−59,311
1952	6,001,698	1	239,405
1953	6,612,254	1	610,556
1954	7,859,473	1	1,247,219
1955	9,393,394	1	1,533,921
1956 (8th Congress)	10,734,384	1	1,340,990
1957	12,720,000	1	1,985,616

Table 2 (continued)

	No. of members	Years covered	Avg. annual increase
1959	13,960,000	2	620,000
1961	17,000,000	2	1,520,000

Sources: The major sources for this table are *Shih-shih shou-ts'e*, no. 18, 1956, and *People's China*, no. 18, September 16, 1956, pp. 17–26, as well as the sources cited for Table 1. The 1959 figures are from *Ten Glorious Years* (Peking: Foreign Languages Press, 1960), p. 283; and the 1961 figures are from *Jen-min jih-pao*, July 1, 1961. Although listed in official Communist sources, these figures must be considered tentative. For example, *Jen-min jih-pao*, August 17, 1961, states that there were more than a million party members in 1942.

chien-tang campaign (1951–1954) brought a sharp increase in the annual recruitment of members, which was augmented because of the necessity for party members to supervise the post-1953 collectivization movement and the First Five-Year Plan (1953–1957). This annual increase of over 1,000,000 members (almost 2,000,000 in 1956) continued to the rectification campaign of 1957–1958, when the annual increase fell to about 620,000 members. According to the rough figure of 17,000,000 members given during the party's fortieth-anniversary celebration (July 1, 1961), the annual rate of party growth has risen once again to about 1,500,000.

The official breakdown of the 1961 membership reveals the gross dimensions of party expansion and membership attrition. According to Liu Shao-ch'i's estimates in 1961, of the more than 17,000,000 members, "80 per cent of them have joined the party since the founding of the People's Republic of China, and 70 per cent have joined since 1953." [20] Three months later, Chao Han added that "40 per cent [of the more than 17,000,000

[20] *Jen-min jih-pao*, July 1, 1961.

members] joined after the 1956 Eighth Party Congress." [21] Table 3 summarizes the figures derived from these percentages and compares the resultant breakdown of the 1961 membership to the net inputs given in Table 2. Table 3 shows that only

Table 3. Dates of admission to the party for the 1961 membership

Dates	(1) End-year membership to nearest .1 million	(2) Net input for period to nearest .1 million	(3) No. of mem- bers remain- ing in 1961 (percentage of 1961 mem- bership)	(4) Attrition (2)–(3)	(5) Annual attrition rate
Pre–1949	4.5	4.5	3.4 (20%)	1.1	2%
1950–1953	6.6	2.1	1.7 (10%)	0.4	2.9%
1954–1956	10.7	4.1	5.1 (30%)	—1.0	—
1957–1961	17.0	6.3	6.8 (40%)	—0.5	—

Sources: Jen-min jih-pao, July 1 and October 17, 1961, as well as the sources cited for Table 2. These figures are based on the rough approximations given for a general audience. For this audience the Chinese Communists have rounded percentages to the nearest 10 per cent and have said that the 1961 membership is "more than" 17,000,000. Thus the possibility of error is extremely large.

3,400,000 of the approximately 4,500,000 pre-1949 members remained in the party until 1961. Given the probable age structure of the pre-1949 group, approximately half of the 1,100,000 loss from that group may be attributed to deaths and about half to expulsion from the party. The general annual attrition rate for the pre-1949 party members equals 2 per cent. This compares

[21] *Ibid.,* October 17, 1961.

to 2.9 per cent for the 1950 to 1953 group which in the eight years from 1953 to 1961 lost 400,000 from the 2,100,000 net input. The increase in attrition rate for the 1950 to 1953 membership must be attributed both to expulsions in the various campaigns after 1950 and to deaths of group members in the Korean War. Because the party-member groups for the 1954 to 1956 and 1957 to 1961 periods exceed the numerical net input (that is, there is an apparent negative attrition for these years), it is impossible to estimate attrition rates for those groups. Scattered reports suggest a much higher attrition rate in the rectification and antibourgeois rightist campaigns of 1957 and 1958.[22] These reports indicate that rapid turnovers occurred in some units and that purges centered mainly on probationary members. On the basis of existing evidence, however, the general rate of annual attrition from all causes up to 1961 appears to be on the magnitude of less than 5 per cent. If true, the low purge rate in the party would confirm the conclusion in Chapter II that expulsions hit individuals rather than groups. Selective purging guarantees organizational continuity and, for the remaining members, simultaneously magnifies the educational lesson of "evil elements" opposed to a strong, just party.[23]

Table 4 supplements the national party figures by summarizing the available data on party memberships in certain provinces and large municipalities. Where the entire party grew from 4,488,080 members in 1949 to 13,960,000 in 1959, an increase of three times, in areas occupied by the Communist armies during the last stages of the civil war, the organizations have grown twenty or even 600 times (Canton). A similar geographical

[22] For a general discussion of the rectification campaign's effect on party members, see Teng Hsiao-p'ing, *Report on the Rectification Campaign* (Peking: Foreign Languages Press, 1957), esp. pp. 45–52.
[23] For examples of the educational use of the selective purge see *Kuei-chou jih-pao* [Kweichow Daily], April 30, 1958, in *SCMP*, no. 1813 (1958), pp. 9–13, and *Jen-min jih-pao*, July 15, 1958.

Table 4. Party statistics in selected provinces and cities

Place (1957 population)	1949	1956	1959
		PARTY MEMBERSHIP	
Anhwei (33,560,000)	70,000	—	520,000
Honan (48,670,000)	—	509,540	—
Hunan (36,220,000)	—	282,000	—
Inner Mongolia (9,200,000)	—	151,756	255,000 (1960) (39,714 local nationalities)
Kansu (12,800,000)	—	216,400	—
Kirin (12,550,000)	—	195,720	—
Kwangsi (19,390,000)	5,800	—	257,000 (97,000 local nationalities)
Kwangtung (37,960,000)	40,000	—	740,000
Kweichow (16,890,000)	—	139,000	—
Liaoning (24,090,000)	—	400,000	—
Shansi (15,960,000)	299,019	—	528,371
Shantung (54,030,000)	—	1,120,000	—
Shensi (18,130,000)	74,000	220,000	370,000
Sinkiang (5,640,000)	—	68,000	130,000 (62,000 local nationalities)
Tsinghai (2,050,000)	—	20,000	—
Yünnan (19,100,000)	—	182,000	—
Canton (1,840,000)	100	—	60,000
Peking (4,010,000)	3,300	—	257,000

Table 4 (continued)

Place (1957 population)	1949	1956	1959
Shanghai (6,900,000)	—	150,000	—
Sian (1,310,000)	1,015	—	63,724

	PARTY BRANCHES		
Anhwei	4,000	—	43,000
Kwangsi	—	—	17,700
Kwangtung	4,160	—	49,900
Shansi	13,033	—	31,913
Shensi	3,341	—	28,400
Sinkiang	—	—	8,982
Canton	—	—	3,000
Peking	395	—	14,000
Sian	—	952 (1955)	4,139

Sources: Population figures are from Chinese People's Republic, State Statistical Bureau, comp., *Ten Great Years* (Peking: Foreign Languages Press, 1960), pp. 11–12; the 1956 party membership figures are from *Current Background*, no. 411 (1956), pp. 26–27; and other party and branch figures are compiled from *Jen-min jih-pao* as found in *SCMP*, nos. 2075 (1959), 2129 (1959), 2130 (1959), 2140 (1959), 2152 (1959), and 2303 (1960).

pattern of growth is evident in the spread of party branches which were reported for all of China at 250,000 in 1950 and 1,060,000 in 1959 (see Table 5).

The impact of expanding membership is more clearly illustrated by Table 5, which presents some additional statistics on party growth since 1945. This table shows the proportion of party members to the population under Communist control. The proportion of party members to population in 1954 was

Table 5. Growth of Chinese Communist Party membership and of party branches

Year	(1) Party membership	(2) Population under CCP control	(2) ÷ (1)	(3) Branches	(1) ÷ (3)
1945	1,211,128	91,000,000 *	75.1	—	—
1950	5,821,604	553,267,000	94.8	250,000	23.3
1952	6,001,698	571,132,000	96.8	—	—
1953	6,612,254	582,600,000	88.1	—	—
1954	7,859,473	587,000,000	74.7	—	—
1955	9,393,394	596,400,000	63.5	—	—
1956	10,734,384	606,500,000	56.5	538,876	19.9
1957	12,720,000	617,400,000	47.2	—	—
1959	13,960,000	641,700,000	46.0	1,060,000	13.1
1961	17,000,000	670,000,000	39.4	—	—

* The figure 91,000,000 is used rather than 95,500,000 (Mao, *Selected Works,* IV [1956], 259) for 1945 because the base areas included in the larger figure were subject to varying forms of Communist control.

Sources: Party statistics are from the sources cited in Tables 1–3. Population figures for 1945 are from Mao Tse-tung, *Selected Works,* IV (1956), 219, 259; for 1950 and 1952 from J. E. Spencer, "Agriculture and Population in Relation to Economic Planning," *Annals of the American Academy of Political and Social Science,* CCCXXI (January, 1959), 64; and for 1953–1959 from Leo A. Orleans, *Professional Manpower and Education in Communist China* (Washington, D.C.: National Science Foundation, 1961), p. 153. The 1961 figure is an estimate based on rates given in Orleans, *loc. cit.*

roughly equivalent to that of 1945. But after 1954 this proportion rapidly increased. As an over-all 1959 average, there was one party member for each forty-six Chinese or about one member for every nine Chinese families. The number of party members relative to the general population increased to one party member for every thirty-nine Chinese (eight families) by 1961. The table further indicates that the number of party branches doubled from 1950 to 1956 and that in the three years after 1956 this number was approximately doubled again. While the dual process of increased branches and membership was under way, the net result has been to decrease the average number of members per branch from 23 to 13. Although branches may run from three members to very large numbers according to the 1956 Constitution (Art. 48), it is clear that the trend has been toward smaller units to cover the greatest possible area.

Party building from 1949 to 1959 occurred in waves following the progress of the major movements which have affected China. This wave motion is suggested by the right-hand column in Table 2, but would be more clearly portrayed in graph form. In general, the major movements affecting party development were the agrarian reform (1949–1950), the "resist-America aid-Korea" and *san-fan wu-fan* (three-anti, five-anti) campaigns (1950–1952), the rectification campaign (1957–1958), and the movement for iron and steel and the setting up of people's communes (1958–1959). As part of the continuing rectification campaign and the promotion of agricultural production, the current emphasis is on recruitment in rural areas.[24] In the various movements, Communists assert, the "political awareness of the people" was raised and the political influence of the party was enlarged.[25] Each political movement reportedly "was followed by the emergence of large numbers of activists who were of good social origin, highly awakened politically and devoted to the cause of the Party."[26] These movements "educated and

[24] See, for example, *Jen-min jih-pao*, July 7, 1959, in *SCMP*, no. 2063 (1959), pp. 1–3, and *Yün-nan jih-pao* [Yünnan Daily], July 5, 1959, in *SCMP*, no. 2084 (1959), pp. 4–6.

[25] See, for example, *Hsin-chiang jih-pao* [Sinkiang Daily], September 27, 1959, in *SCMP*, no. 2129 (1959), pp. 11–16; *Shan-hsi jih-pao* [Shensi Daily], September 26, 1959, in *SCMP*, no. 2129 (1959), pp. 16–19; *Yün-nan jih-pao*, July 5, 1959, in *SCMP*, no. 2084 (1959), pp. 1–3; and *Nan-fang jih-pao* [Southern Daily], September 28, 1959, in *SCMP*, no. 2130 (1959), pp. 11–14.

[26] *Hsin-chiang jih-pao*, p. 12.

tested each activist who wanted to join the Party." Moreover, in the course of these movements, party organizations have been drastically "overhauled"; this has meant intensive ideological rectification, technical training, and a purging of unreliable elements.[27]

An example of the use of mass movements to further party building took place in Honan in 1958 [28] and illustrates the steps by which leadership qualities are identified and tested prior to granting probationary party membership. From the meetings, competitions, mass comparisons, and checkups that comprised the Honan movement, 252,045 people in the Kaifeng district (*chuan-ch'ü*, which in this case is composed of twelve *hsien* or counties) gained the distinction of "red and expert" activists. Of this number, about 26 per cent (65,622) were declared eligible for party membership, and 15 per cent (38,261) were actually admitted as probationary party members. To ascertain levels of qualification and to improve the training of the activists, 74 per cent (186,423) of the original group were sent to schools or training classes, which numbered 1,590 for the district. Hence, three out of four activists received some immediate training as the result of the campaign. One out of three who received training was declared eligible for party membership, and one in five was admitted to the party. Of the activists admitted, 85 per cent had been "leaders of production teams or in other leadership positions" before the movement began. Thus for the vast majority of those finally admitted to the Communist Party, their leadership qualities had been recognized before the move-

[27] See, for example, *Shan-hsi jih-pao* [Shansi Daily], March 4, 1958, in *SCMP*, no. 1780 (1958), pp. 7–8; *Hei-lung-chiang jih-pao* [Heilungkiang Daily], March 16, 1958, in *SCMP*, no. 1780 (1958), pp. 9–10; *Anhui jih-pao* [Anhwei Daily], March 30, 1958, in *SCMP*, no. 1780 (1958), pp. 15–18; and *Hsin Hu-nan pao* [New Hunan], March 21, 1959, in *SCMP*, no. 2036 (1959), pp. 15–16.

[28] *Ho-nan jih-pao* [Honan Daily], December 29, 1958, in *SCMP*, no. 1959 (1959), pp. 12–13.

ment, and activation in the mass movement was a formal means of displaying these qualities in ways that would appear suitable on a recommendation form.

Recruitment has also proceeded on the basis of an assumed pattern of "coverage." Organs, communes, factories, schools, and government departments which lack party members or groups have a "need." This policy of coverage is suggested by Table 5, which indicates an average of one member for fewer than eight families in 1961. Recruitment goes on with particular fervor where "Party organizations are weak" [29] or in places which "lacked Party organizations." [30] Those who are recruited have a "sound class character" and are model "activists," but a high percentage also are nonparty cadres. For example, in Honan (1958), out of 30,606 new members recruited in two districts, 88.2 per cent were "team leaders at various people's communes, or cadres of the level of workshop leader in iron and steel works and above." [31] In a Hupei district (1959), 77.7 per cent of the new recruits were cadres; [32] and in Sinkiang (1959), a special campaign was held to recruit cadres. [33] Rigorously manipulating membership expansion, the party has rapidly gained control of all positions of leadership in the country by establishing cores of party members in all organizations and by recruiting key nonparty cadres. Even those who are not admitted during recruitment drives are bound as "activists" to the direction and supervision of the party. The hope is still held out to them that they may be admitted later if they "strengthen their

[29] *Nan-fang jih-pao*, January 14, 1960, in *SCMP*, no. 2236 (1960), pp. 45–52.

[30] *Kuei-chou jih-pao*, November 23, 1958, in *SCMP*, no. 1926 (1959), p. 11.

[31] *Ho-nan jih-pao*, December 29, 1958, in *SCMP*, no. 1959 (1959), pp. 10–11.

[32] *Hu-pei jih-pao* [Hupei Daily], April 21, 1959, in *SCMP*, no. 2042 (1959), p. 2.

[33] *Hsin-chiang jih-pao* April 6, 1959, in *SCMP*, no. 2042 (1959), pp. 3–4.

ideological advancement, rectify their motive for joining the Party, and overcome their shortcomings." [34]

The Policy Apparatus and Senior Party Leaders

In accordance with the organizational principle of democratic centralism, the apex of the party's institutional hierarchy is the National Party Congress, indirectly elected by lower party congresses for five-year terms (Arts. 21 and 31). The National Party Congress (hereafter called Congress) has formal authority to control the policies, organization, and Constitution of the party (Art. 32). Although the Constitution stipulates that the Congress should meet annually except "under extraordinary conditions," the Eighth National Congress has met only in 1956 and 1958. Each of these two sessions was concluded in less than two weeks and was a formal ritual of Central Committee proposals, member endorsements, detailed elaborations, and fraternal greetings from other Communist parties. Important decisions were approved and communicated to the membership, and both sessions of the Eighth National Congress announced significant additions to the composition of the senior party leadership. Although the term of the current Congress should have expired in September, 1961, no plans for a Ninth Congress had yet been announced in October, 1962.

The Eighth Central Committee, as shown on Chart 1, was elected by the Eighth National Congress in 1956 and expanded in 1958. Between sessions of the Congress, the Central Committee "directs the entire work of the Party, carries out the decisions of the National Party Congress, represents the Party in its relations with other parties and organizations, sets up various Party organizations and directs their activities, takes charge of

[34] *Chieh-fang chün pao* [Liberation Army News], March 30, 1957, in *SCMP*, no. 1704 (1958), p. 11.

Chart 1. Central apparatus of the Chinese Communist Party

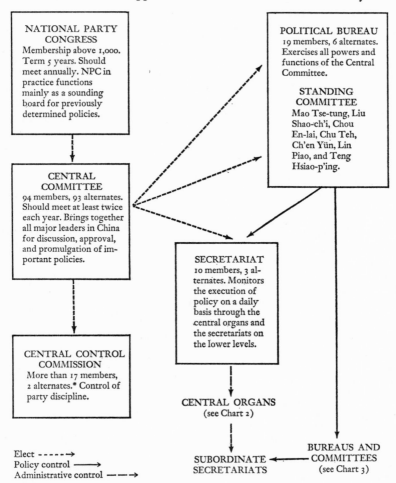

NATIONAL PARTY CONGRESS
Membership above 1,000. Term 5 years. Should meet annually. NPC in practice functions mainly as a sounding board for previously determined policies.

POLITICAL BUREAU
19 members, 6 alternates. Exercises all powers and functions of the Central Committee.

STANDING COMMITTEE
Mao Tse-tung, Liu Shao-ch'i, Chou En-lai, Chu Teh, Ch'en Yün, Lin Piao, and Teng Hsiao-p'ing.

CENTRAL COMMITTEE
94 members, 93 alternates. Should meet at least twice each year. Brings together all major leaders in China for discussion, approval, and promulgation of important policies.

SECRETARIAT
10 members, 3 alternates. Monitors the execution of policy on a daily basis through the central organs and the secretariats on the lower levels.

CENTRAL CONTROL COMMISSION
More than 17 members, 2 alternates.* Control of party discipline.

CENTRAL ORGANS
(see Chart 2)

Elect ----->
Policy control ⟶
Administrative control — — →

BUREAUS AND COMMITTEES
(see Chart 3)

SUBORDINATE SECRETARIATS

* The communiqué of the Tenth Plenum stated that the Central Control Commission membership was increased, but no details were given.

Sources: Biographic Information, no. 2, May 9, 1962; U.S. Department of State, Bureau of Intelligence and Research, *Directory of Party and Government Officials of Communist China* (B.D. no. 271, unclassified; Washington, D.C.: U.S. Government Printing Office, 1960), vol. I; and *Jen-min jih-pao*, September 29, 1962. The general information is based on the 1956 party Constitution. The chart reflects personnel shifts made at the Tenth Plenum in September, 1962.

and allocates Party cadres" (Art. 34). The Central Committee elects the members of the Political Bureau, the Standing Committee of the Political Bureau, the Secretariat, and the Central Control Commission, as well as the chairman, the vice-chairmen, and the secretary-general. It is also charged with guiding the work of the government, the army, and the various people's organizations through the party organizations in them (Arts. 34–35). The Eighth Central Committee, which is directed to meet in plenary session at least twice a year, has met ten times from 1956 to September, 1962. Twenty months elapsed between the January, 1961, Ninth Plenum and the September, 1962, Tenth Plenum. With the deaths of the regular Central Committeemen Lin Po-ch'ü in 1960, Ch'en Keng in 1961, and Li K'o-nung in 1962 and of 3 alternate Central Committeemen (Chang Hsi, Ts'ai Shu-fan, and P'eng T'ao), the Eighth Central Committee is comprised of 94 regular members and 93 alternates as of October, 1962. The numbers of regular members attending the Eighth (August, 1959), Ninth, and Tenth plenums were 75, 83, and 82, respectively, and the comparable figures for alternate members were 74, 87, and 88. (The alternate membership was increased from 73 members in May, 1958.)

The wide dispersal of Central Committee members to superintend key party, state, and mass organizations and army commands is suggested by the fact that 24 of the 28 first secretaries at the provincial level (or the equivalent) are (as of July 1, 1962) Central Committee regular and alternate members, as are 28 members of the Standing Committee of the Second National People's Congress (Chu Teh, chairman), the premier (Chou En-lai) and all 16 vice-premiers of the State Council, the chairman (Liu Shao-ch'i) and 10 of the 14 vice-chairmen of the National Defense Council, and all but one member of the general staff of the People's Liberation Army.[35] This diverse coverage does not indicate "representation" of independent organiza-

[35] Biographic Information, no. 2, May 9, 1962.

tions but the extension of the party's policy apparatus to all significant areas of Chinese society.

The composition of the Central Committee provides an important insight into the central leadership of Communist China. According to figures compiled by Chao Kuo-chün in 1959,[36] of the then 97 regular members of the Central Committee, 80 per cent would in 1962 be between the ages of 49 and 63, while probably less than 8 per cent of the total party membership would be between those ages. Moreover, as far as is known, all regular members of the Central Committee except possibly Yang Hsiu-feng probably joined the Communist Party before 1938. What is significant in the backgrounds of the regular members is that 10 have attended middle school, 22 have attended military academies, and 51 have had some college, normal school, or professional training. Thus at least 83 out of the 97 regular members would qualify as intellectuals, according to the Communist Party definition. Ch'en Yi also admitted in August, 1961, that "many leaders in our party Central Committee came from the upper or middle classes. Those who came from the worker-peasant classes are very few." [37] The Central Committeemen are not only old comrades-in-arms but also highly trained comrades. Their education was, in the main, undertaken in China; only 40 out of the 97 are known to have received some training abroad (25 in the Soviet Union, 9 in France, 5 in Japan, and 1 in Germany), while 56 (1 unknown) received no training outside China. The party is led by men and women (4 are women) who bring to their posts long service, common sacrifice, and extensive education and training in China. They know how to read, and most have written frequently and knowledgeably on a variety of political and technical subjects.

[36] Chao Kuo-chün, "Leadership in the Chinese Communist Party," *Annals of the American Academy of Political and Social Science*, CCCXXI (January, 1959), 40–50.

[37] Speech of August 10, 1961, quoted in *Jen-min shou-ts'e 1961* [People's Handbook 1961] (Peking: Ta-kung pao she, 1961), p. 321.

Speculation has run high since 1958 concerning the presence of factions within the central party leadership. Frequently, for example, both journalists and scholars have concluded that the different emphases given in the statements made by various specialists within the party elite—such as Chou En-lai for state administration, Ch'en Yün for the economy, or Teng Hsiao-p'ing for the party apparatus—indicate the lack of support for, or even outright opposition to, general policies or statements by other specialists. They assume, therefore, that the "dominant" group permits dissident elements to deliver official speeches in "opposition" and to undermine collective solidarity with impunity. Without additional evidence, however, groups of specialists cannot be equated with party factions. Official statements do not necessarily represent the views of the individual leaders making the statements. Indeed, according to the doctrine of democratic centralism, the fact that an individual makes a policy statement might indicate that he opposed the particular policy prior to the decision and is symbolizing continued leadership unity by his announcement of the new policy.

That senior members of the elite have been criticized in the past for failure to abide by the rules of solidarity is beyond dispute, however. In addition to the struggle for power in 1953 and 1954 between a group loyal to Mao Tse-tung and an "anti-party group" led by Kao Kang and Jao Shu-shih,[38] many provincial party secretaries, including secretaries concurrently regular or alternate Central Committee members, have been criticized and replaced. The latter include the secretaries of such provincial committees as those in Honan, Hunan, Kansu, Liaoning, Shantung, and Tsinghai provinces and the Kwangsi Chuang and Ningsia Hui autonomous regions. In addition, such

[38] The documents of the dispute are found in *Daily News Release*, February, 1954, pp. 111–116, and *Documents of the National Conference of the Communist Party of China (March 1955)* (Peking: Foreign Languages Press, 1955).

key Central Committeemen as P'eng Te-huai (formerly Minister of National Defense until 1959) and Huang K'o-ch'eng (formerly Chief of Staff of the People's Liberation Army and Vice-Minister of National Defense until 1959) have been dropped from leading posts in the government. At the Central Committee's Tenth Plenum in September, 1962, Huang K'och'eng and T'an Cheng were dismissed from the Secretariat. What generalizations may be drawn from these apparent high-level purges have not yet been shown in the Chinese case. The necessity for caution particularly applies to inferences from who is "in the news" or who attends which conference in this or that order. Widespread guessing concerning the "fate" of Chang Wen-t'ien and Ch'en Yün, among a host of others "out of the news," has somehow bypassed the consideration of simple explanations such as illness, an active work schedule, or travel. These explanations may not excite the imagination, but they may be closer to reality in many cases. Doctrine makes the appearance of leaders before the people an important, but not a decisive, consideration. On balance, existing sources do not tell the extent or even the clear-cut presence of factionalism within the current central leadership apparatus, and hasty judgments following mercurial press reports are probably ill-advised. The basic fact is that the real world of the Political Bureau and the Central Committee of the Chinese Communist Party remains closed to outsiders save for blurred glimpses, and contradictory judgments concerning the cohesion of the central elite can be supported on the basis of our present evidence.

In Chart 1 the central party apparatus is depicted. As already indicated, the Central Committee elects the Political Bureau (now 19 members, 6 alternates); the Standing Committee of the Political Bureau (7 members: Mao Tse-tung, Liu Shao-ch'i, Chou En-lai, Chu Teh, Ch'en Yün, Lin Piao, and Teng Hsiao-p'ing); the chairman (Mao Tse-tung) and 5 vice-chairmen of the Central Committee (who are concurrently chairman and vice-chairmen of the Political Bureau); the Secretariat (10 members, 3 alternates); and the Central Control Commission (more than 17 members, 2 alternates; enlarged at the Central Committee's tenth plenary session in September, 1962, but no details were given). The central work of the party is organized under the Political Bureau with supreme authority in its 7-member Standing Committee. According to Article 37 of the Constitution, when the Central Committee is not in session, the Political Bureau and its Standing Committee exercise the powers and functions of the Central Committee. These powers and functions under the principle of democratic centralism gravitate to the Standing Committee under Chairman Mao Tse-tung and include the decision making for and the supervision of all the central apparatus of power in China.

In 1956, Liu Shao-ch'i argued that the concept of collective leadership did not "in any way negate the need for personal responsibility or the important role of [the] leader." [39] At the zenith of the command structure is the party leader and the Standing Committee of the Political Bureau. Mao, as party leader, must be the epitome of unity and the essence of correctness and purpose within the entire apparatus. When speaking of the leader, the Chinese usually quote Lenin that leaders are those who are "the most authoritative, influential and experienced." [40] Leaders stand within the masses as a matter of definition of the mass line, and to popularize this theme in 1958, a three-volume work called *Chairman Mao among the Masses* and a volume called *Comrades Liu Shao-ch'i, Chou En-lai, and Chu Teh among the Masses* were sold throughout China.[41] Because party leaders stand within the masses, Secretary-General Teng Hsiao-

[39] Liu Shao-ch'i, "The Political Report of the Central Committee," *Eighth National Congress of the Communist Party of China*, p. 104.

[40] Quoted in Teng Hsiao-p'ing, "Report on the Revision," p. 200.

[41] *Mao chu-hsi tsai jen-min ch'ün-chung chung* (Peking: Wen-wu ch'u-pan she, 1958); *Liu Shao-ch'i Chou En-lai Chu Te t'ung-chih tsai ch'ün-chung chung* (Peking: Jen-min ch'u-pan she, 1958).

p'ing told the party in 1956 that "they must set an example in maintaining close contact with the masses, in obeying the Party organizations and observing Party discipline." [42] All the people love the leader because they love the party and the class, Teng continued, but this is not deification of the individual. As "proof," he cited the party decision to prohibit both birthday celebrations of party leaders and use of party leaders' names to designate places, streets, and enterprises.[43]

Mao as the supreme party leader, moreover, plays an important charismatic function. His revolutionary background is made to symbolize the rise of the Chinese nation and its revolutionary future.[44] Communist policies are made personal in such slogans as "Be a good student of Chairman Mao." [45] In Mao, ideological leadership is real and visibly unified. Moreover, communism is no longer an imported ideology; communism is Chinese because Mao is Chinese. The works of Mao are placed on a par with the classics of Marx, Engels, Lenin, and Stalin, and it is Mao, the leader, who has made communism a vital fact in China's national life.

The Political Bureau and its Standing Committee under Chairman Mao Tse-tung normally direct the routine daily work of the apparatus through the Secretariat (Art. 37). Chart 2 details the subordinate apparatus superintended by the Secretariat, and Chart 3 outlines the basic structure of bureaus and committees which maintain policy direction over the subordinate secretariats. Below the central level, six regional bureaus direct the work of

[42] Teng Hsiao-p'ing, "Report on the Revision," p. 200.
[43] *Ibid.* But see "Record Run by 'Mao Tse-tung' Locomotive," Hsinhua News Agency release, September 27, 1960, in *SCMP*, no. 2350 (1960), pp. 17–18.
[44] Li Jui, *Mao Tse-tung t'ung-chih ti ch'u-ch'i ko-ming huo-tung* [The Early Revolutionary Activities of Comrade Mao Tse-tung] (Peking: Chung-kuo ch'ing-nien ch'u-pan she, 1957), pp. 239–244.
[45] *Tso Mao chu-hsi ti hao hsüeh-sheng* (Peking: Chung-kuo ch'ing-nien ch'u-pan she, 1960).

Chart 2. Principal divisions of the Secretariat

POLITICAL BUREAU

SECRETARIAT
Teng Hsiao-p'ing, secretary-general

GENERAL OFFICE
Yang Shang-k'un, director

PROPAGANDA DEPART-
MENT
Lu Ting-yi, director

ORGANIZATION DEPART-
MENT
An Tzu-wen, director

SOCIAL AFFAIRS DEPART-
MENT (?)
(Unknown)

UNITED FRONT WORK
DEPARTMENT
Li Wei-han, director

RURAL WORK DEPART-
MENT
Teng Tzu-hui, director

INDUSTRIAL WORK DE-
PARTMENT
Li Hsüeh-feng, director

FINANCE AND TRADE
WORK DEPARTMENT
Ma Ming-fang, director

COMMUNICATIONS WORK
DEPARTMENT
Tseng Shan, director

INTERNATIONAL LIAISON
DEPARTMENT (?)
Wu Hsiu-ch'üan, director

MILITARY AFFAIRS COM-
MITTEE
(Unknown)

WOMEN'S WORK COM-
MITTEE
Ts'ai Ch'ang, 1st secretary

SENIOR PARTY SCHOOL
Wang Ts'ung-wu, director

COMMITTEE FOR CEN-
TRAL STATE ORGANS
Kung Tzu-jung, director

COMMITEE FOR PARTY
ORGANS DIRECTLY
UNDER THE CEN-
TRAL COMMITTEE
Yang Shang-k'un, director

POLITICAL RESEARCH
OFFICE
(Unknown)

BUREAU FOR TRANSLAT-
ING THE WORKS OF
MARX, ENGELS, LENIN,
AND STALIN
(Unknown)

Sources: Biographic Information, no. 2, May 9, 1962; "Chinese Communist Party Organization," unclassified chart no. 27092.1 9–58 (Washington, D.C.: U.S. Government Printing Office, 1958); and U.S. Department of State, Bureau of Intelligence and Research, *Directory of Party and Government Officials of Communist China* (B.D. no. 271, unclassified; Washington, D.C.: U.S. Government Printing Office, 1960), vols. I–II.

Chart 3. Probable groupings of bureaus and provincial committees

POLITICAL BUREAU

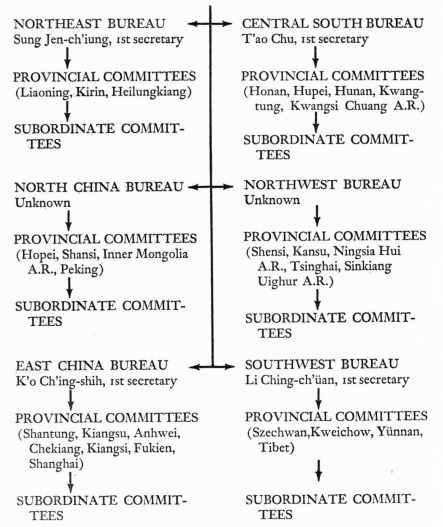

NORTHEAST BUREAU
Sung Jen-ch'iung, 1st secretary

PROVINCIAL COMMITTEES
(Liaoning, Kirin, Heilungkiang)

SUBORDINATE COMMIT-
TEES

CENTRAL SOUTH BUREAU
T'ao Chu, 1st secretary

PROVINCIAL COMMITTEES
(Honan, Hupei, Hunan, Kwangtung, Kwangsi Chuang A.R.)

SUBORDINATE COMMIT-
TEES

NORTH CHINA BUREAU
Unknown

PROVINCIAL COMMITTEES
(Hopei, Shansi, Inner Mongolia
A.R., Peking)

SUBORDINATE COMMIT-
TEES

NORTHWEST BUREAU
Unknown

PROVINCIAL COMMITTEES
(Shensi, Kansu, Ningsia Hui
A.R., Tsinghai, Sinkiang
Uighur A.R.)

SUBORDINATE COMMIT-
TEES

EAST CHINA BUREAU
K'o Ch'ing-shih, 1st secretary

PROVINCIAL COMMITTEES
(Shantung, Kiangsu, Anhwei,
Chekiang, Kiangsi, Fukien,
Shanghai)

SUBORDINATE COMMIT-
TEES

SOUTHWEST BUREAU
Li Ching-ch'üan, 1st secretary

PROVINCIAL COMMITTEES
(Szechwan, Kweichow, Yünnan,
Tibet)

SUBORDINATE COMMIT-
TEES

Sources: Biographic Information, no. 2, May 9, 1962, and *Peking Review,*
no. 4, 1961, p. 7. The "A.R." in this chart stands for "Autonomous Region."
The standing of the Peking and Shanghai committees is equivalent to that of
a provincial committee.

provincial-level (or the equivalent) committees, which in turn supervise the descending hierarchy to the district committees, *hsien* committees, and basic-level committees. At each of these levels, the committee organizations recapitulate the central apparatus with party committees executing policy through counterpart secretariats (or the primary committee secretaries at the basic levels). Only at the national, provincial, *hsien*, and basic levels (or the equivalent) is there a general membership meeting or congress to which the given-level committees are responsible. Committees and secretariats at the intermediate levels are set up by the next higher level for administrative convenience.

The work load of the Secretariat is functionally distributed to departments and committees (Chart 2), many of which remain secret as to operation and personnel. Moreover, it is not altogether clear what the differences are between departments and working committees, though the latter may be convened irregularly for specific purposes rather than in continuous operation and may be directly responsible to the Central Committee rather than to the Secretariat. A General Office under the secretary-general (Teng Hsiao-p'ing) and a director (Yang Shang-k'un) serves as the central body for clearing and coordination. Known current departments are the Propaganda Department (Lu Ting-yi, director), Organization Department (An Tzu-wen, director), Social Affairs Department, United Front Work Department (Li Wei-han, director), Rural Work Department (Teng Tzu-hui, director), Industrial Work Department (Li Hsüeh-feng, director), Finance and Trade Work Department (Ma Ming-fang, director), Communications Work Department (Tseng Shan, director), and probably International Liaison Department (Wu Hsiu-ch'üan, director). All known directors and many deputy directors are members of the Central Committee. Known committees and other bodies under the Secretariat include a Military Affairs Committee, Women's Work Committee (Ts'ai Ch'ang, first secretary), Senior Party School (Wang Ts'ung-wu, director), Committee for Central State Organs

(Kung Tzu-jung, director), Committee for Party Organs Directly under the Central Committee (Yang Shang-k'un, director),[46] Political Research Office, Bureau for Translating the Works of Marx, Engels, Lenin, and Stalin, and several other probable committees (cultural affairs, minorities, overseas Chinese, youth, education, etc.).[47] The most nebulous administrative division is the Social Affairs Department, supposedly headed by Li K'o-nung until his death in February, 1962,[48] and reportedly charged with inner-party secret policing. With the exception of this department, as far as is known all other departments have responsibilities covered by their descriptive titles, and all departments and committees presumably have both intra-party and national policy functions. Only two departments have been authoritatively described in recent published reports: the Finance and Trade Work Department under Ma Ming-fang and the Organization Department, the latter being discussed in the next section. According to Ma, the Finance and Trade Work Department is

entrusted with the task of control, circulation and distribution. It is the bridge between the different sections of production, between production and consumption and between the cities and rural areas. It has a close connection with the broad masses . . . [and] is also in control of quite a number of processing enterprises.[49]

[46] The existence of nonparty and party functionaries within the party apparatus possibly explains the establishment of this committee, which acts as a special kind of branch to bring together the party members who work at the central level.

[47] For a list of probable committees, see Fei-wei-shih tzu-liao tiao-ch'a yen-chiu hui [(Communist) Bandit Materials Investigation and Research Committee], ed., Fei-wei jen-shih tzu-liao hui-pien: tsu-chih piao [Collection on (Communist) Bandit Personnel and Activities: Organization Tables] (Taipei: Szu-fa yüan, 1958), vol. III.

[48] New China News Agency, February 13, 1962, and Jen-min jih-pao, February 27, 1962, report some of the biographical details of Li's life. The first citation states that Li was head of the Social Affairs Department from 1945 to 1949.

[49] Jen-min jih-pao, May 25, 1960.

The work of several other departments may be inferred from the reports of their directors or deputy directors, particularly from their speeches delivered at the Eighth National Congress in 1956.[50]

Administration of Personnel

The Organization Department under the supervision of the Secretariat directs the central administration of party personnel. The work of the department was authoritatively discussed in a party handbook published in 1959.[51] Stressing the interaction of the party's organizational line and its political and mass lines,[52] this handbook also noted that the organizational tasks of the party required the support and devotion of all party members. Within the scope of over-all organizational work—including recruitment, assignment, training, struggle, inspection, and policy—the Organization Department handles routine work consisting "largely of cadres' work, administration of party members, review of policy concerning organizational work of the party, and review of the performance of resolutions, etc."[53] In addition to these routine organizational and personnel tasks, the

---

[50] See *Eighth National Congress*, vol. II. A more complete selection of speeches at this congress may be found in *Hsin-hua pan-yüeh k'an* [New China Semimonthly], nos. 20–21, October 26 and November 6, 1956.

[51] Chinese Communist Party, Central Committee, Research Office of the Organization Department, ed., *Tang ti tsu-chih kung-tso wen-ta* [Questions and Answers on Party Organization Work] (Peking: Jen-min ch'u-pan she, 1959), translated in *U.S. Joint Publications Research Service*, no. 7273 (1961), pp. 14–27.

[52] *Ibid.*, pp. 8–14. This part of the handbook draws heavily on Liu Shao-ch'i, *On the Party* (2d ed.; Peking: Foreign Languages Press, 1950), pp. 1–5, and Mao Tse-tung, "Appendix: Resolution on Some Questions in the History of Our Party" [April 20, 1945], *Selected Works*, IV, esp. 189–211.

[53] Chinese Communist Party, *op. cit.*, p. 15.

Organization Department determines optimum timing for party congresses and other meetings in order to strengthen the prevailing political line. Its role in coordinating political and organizational lines also concerns the growth and ideological solidarity of the party organizations commensurate with current political tasks. For this reason the organization departments must work closely with the propaganda departments at all levels.[54] Repeating a 1941 resolution on propaganda and agitation, the 1959 handbook compared propaganda and organization to "two wings of a bird or two wheels of a cart." [55] Thus in the administrative work of the various departments of the party, the propaganda and organization departments play an equal and "organic" role.

These structural considerations give focus to the administration of personnel. With respect to the utilization of personnel, for example, Teng Hsiao-p'ing reported in 1956 that the administrative work of the party had been divided up "so that each division covers groupings of certain ranks and departments and is thus co-ordinated with the work of political and professional inspection and supervision." [56] Since cadre ranking is usually given by seniority within a unit and by the rank of the geographic unit (commune, hsien, district, province, etc.), it is not clear whether cadres and members within the party carry ratings which assign priority and administrative identity to achieve the "groupings of certain ranks" as suggested by Teng. Presumably the requirement of obeying superiors in accordance with the principle of democratic centralism would require clear-cut, military-type rankings, though ranking is not brought into discussions on qualifications, on transfers, or on reorganization.

The key principle in personnel administration within the party is apparently organizational solidarity. In 1945, Liu Shao-ch'i stated that reorganization of the party should not "take its own course or be handled with carelessness. . . . Random transfers

[54] Ibid., pp. 22–24.   [55] Ibid., p. 23.
[56] Teng Hsiao-p'ing, "Report on the Revision," pp. 221–222.

should not be made even in elections as provided by the Party Constitution. The reorganisation and reconstruction of any leading body of the Party is advisable only when it is assured of a turn for the better, and will be more beneficial to the people." [57] Nominations, meetings, and assignments (including conferment of full membership) are all controlled by committees above the level at which the given action occurs, and above the basic-level organizations all elections are indirect. Personnel exist in the apparatus to effect policy, and personnel organization and scheduled elections must support, not deter, the basic policy objectives. Tours of duty for convenience are objectionable if disruptive and are prohibited. Party solidarity was the theme, for example, of the 1958 "overhauling" of party organizations as a matter of purification and ideological remolding.[58] The preoccupation with solidarity may also explain in part the erratic scheduling of party meetings, particularly congresses which have not met at the prescribed intervals. Even in the *hsia-fang* (lit.: to go to the lower levels) movement transferring cadres to the production levels, attention was paid to minimizing the effects of transfers so that the unity and integration of the party would not be disrupted.[59]

Party solidarity is ensured by a disciplinary and performance control system. This system is headed by the Central Control Commission, whose secretary is Tung Pi-wu. Within the Central Control Commission, Tung directs the work through a standing committee of 9 members and 2 alternates and a secretariat with 5 deputy secretaries. The hierarchy of semiautonomous control commissions was established in 1955, replacing the central and local discipline inspection committees.[60] The new control com-

[57] Liu Shao-ch'i, *On the Party*, p. 127.
[58] Cited in no. 27 above.   [59] See below, Chapter VII.
[60] *Documents of the National Conference of the Communist Party of China (March 1955)*, pp. 21-25. This document, which reports the 1955 organizational changes, primarily describes the authorized version of the famous 1949-1954 inner-party power struggle precipitated by Kao

missions were given additional powers to investigate independently and to mete out punishments. Moreover, higher-level control commissions were authorized to overlap the investigations
of lower bodies and to maintain a direct chain of command with
lower control commissions. Party members were directed to
report on one another. At all levels the control commissions were
integrated with the mass organizations and with the procuratorial
and control organs of the state. According to the 1956 Chinese
Communist Party Constitution (Art. 53), the tasks of the central
and local control commissions are to (1) examine regularly and
deal with cases of violation of the Constitution, discipline, ethics,
state law, and decrees; (2) decide on or cancel disciplinary
measures; and (3) deal with appeals and complaints.

Articles 13 through 18 of the 1956 party Constitution establish
the requirements for membership discipline. The Constitution
permits party organizations at the various levels to "take disciplinary measures against any Party member who violates Party
discipline, such as warning, serious warning, removal from posts
held in the Party, placing on probation within the Party, or
expulsion from the Party" (Art. 13). Decisions regarding discipline are usually taken by the general membership meeting of the
party branch of the offending member, and these decisions are
subject to the approval of higher party committees or control
commissions (Art. 14). Special regulations apply to higher-
ranking members (Arts. 15–16) and to the rights of the person
considered for disciplinary action (Art. 18). According to Mao's
dictum, penalties are part of an educational process "to treat the
illness in order to save the man," [61] and discipline thus pertains
to "comrades" who must be distinguished from the "enemy." [62]

Kang, who committed suicide in 1954, and Jao Shu-shih. This anti-Mao
faction was also the major topic discussed at the 1954 Fourth Plenum
of the Central Committee, which passed the well-known resolution on
party unity.

[61] Mao, "Appendix," p. 216.
[62] Chinese Communist Party, *op. cit.*, pp. 132–133.

The party has also spelled out the fate of party members who receive administrative punishments in their state posts and has defined by a series of regulations in 1957 both the levels of approval for various punishments and the detailed process of arriving at a punishment.[63]

As a sign of the stresses of the past four years, patterns of control and discipline have steadily grown within the party.[64] In the past, imposed discipline was viewed as necessary for uniformity when there existed wide inner-party discrepancies in experience and training and because of military emergencies. Discipline was an adjunct of ideological education and ensured unity of action despite different levels of ideological consciousness.[65] But, irrespective of the recent trends toward increased organizational discipline to bolster party solidarity, recent inner-party disciplinary campaigns such as the 1959 campaign against "right opportunism" should not be viewed as an elimination of the objectives of ideological unity and self-discipline. Inner-party dissension and the use of imposed discipline are more than the function of simple inner-party disunity. As the model vanguard party, the promotion of internal unity must be weighed against the greater tasks of party expansion and of rapid progress in the socialist revolution beyond the current limits of solidarity. Furthermore, the Communists hold that the disciplined control of inner-party struggle can be exploited to motivate the organization and to ferret out undesirables.

The division of functions and the integration of personnel and policy are achieved at the basic level of the party administration

[63] *Ibid.*, pp. 137–142.

[64] See *Tung-feng* [East Wind], no. 5, 1960, in *ECMM*, no. 211 (1960), pp. 1–6; *Shang-yu* [Upstream], no. 4, 1960, in *ECMM*, no. 210 (1960), pp. 33–36; *Hung-ch'i*, no. 24, December 16, 1959, pp. 9–15; and *Jen-min jih-pao*, November 15, 1961. For an official discussion of discipline, see Chinese Communist Party, *op. cit.*, pp. 130–146.

[65] Teng Hsiao-p'ing, "Report on the Revision," p. 212.

by the leadership of the branch first secretary.[66] At the crucial branch (*chih-pu*) level which is the fundamental unit within the so-called "basic-level organization" (see Table 6, below), the administration of personnel is personal and complete, for in theory every member of the Chinese Communist Party must belong to a branch organization regardless of his rank or position. As of 1959, there were 1,060,000 branches established in the various cities, villages, factories, mines, communes, offices, schools, and army commands. Established on the basis of "production, work or residence" (Art. 48), branches are conceived of as "the basic links between the Party and the broad masses" [67] as well as the core of the organizational life of the members. According to Article 50 of the party Constitution, eight general tasks befall the basic-level organizations and are thus the special responsibility of the branches: (1) propaganda and organizational work among the masses; (2) mass line relationship with the masses; (3) recruitment and discipline of members; (4) political education of the members; (5) political leadership of the masses; (6) leadership of the masses in production; (7) innerparty struggle; and (8) revolutionary education of the members and the masses.

The position of the branch first secretary is probably the most critical in the entire party organization. The first secretary guarantees the leading role of the party in China and promotes the intensive, united relationship of party members and the solidarity of party and masses. On him depends the success of balanced external and internal operation of the party and the supervision of the elite standards of the vanguard. The first secretary assumes over-all responsibility at the lower level and is the key administrative link to the rank and file and through them to

[66] An authoritative discussion of the branch level is found in Chinese Communist Party, *op. cit.*, pp. 115–130.

[67] Teng Hsiao-p'ing, "Report on the Revision," p. 224.

the Chinese people. According to a *People's Daily* description of the branch first secretary: "Here, democracy and centralism, the party leadership and the mass line, and the collective leadership of the party committees and the command of the first secretary are interdependent, interrelated, and supplementary." [68] Under the command of the first secretary, the branch deputy secretaries have been delegated the responsibility to guide the work of the rank and file—to recruit and train and to coordinate the assigned tasks of personnel. At this pivot level, the party first secretary strives to expand the influence and control of the party by personnel assignments and by recruitment of new members who have demonstrated leadership capabilities.

The party press gives an endless stream of advice and homilies to party cadres on how to run branches, how to be model branch secretaries or committee members, and how to make the branch a vital force among the Chinese people. A typical *People's Daily* article in November, 1961, lauded the intraparty democracy exemplified by an urban commune party branch in Kirin, the excellent mass line working style of a Tsinghai branch, the progress in educating women party members in Hopei branches, and the training in party discipline of a rural commune branch in Heilungkiang.[69] The following month the same newspaper discussed the individual members of a model branch committee and their fine collective leadership.[70] Other articles show the role of the branch secretary in "patiently assisting and seriously rectifying" the "commandist" errors of a subordinate.[71] Many articles are written in the first person to "tell my story of success after great difficulty." [72] Virtually every aspect of branch life receives some daily comment in the central and local party press.[73] These include warnings on personal conduct, directives

[68] *Jen-min jih-pao*, December 5, 1959.
[69] *Ibid.*, November 23, 1961.   [70] *Ibid.*, December 14, 1961.
[71] *Ibid.*, January 22, 1962.   [72] *Ibid.*, December 21, 1961.
[73] *Ibid.*, January 24, 26, and 30, 1962.

on "too many meetings and documents," and statements on holding brief regular meetings.[74]

The administration of personnel and the performance of party responsibilities at the basic level are carried out through a variable organizational structure which depends on the size of the basic-level membership (Constitution, chap. VI). The minimum size comprises three full party members. The variations in the structures are summarized below in Table 6. The committees

Table 6. Basic-level organization of the Chinese Communist Party

	Over 100 members	50–99 members	Less than 50 members
Primary party committee (1st sec.; 1–4 deputies; term 1 year)	Usual	Permitted	Unusual
General branch committee (sec.; 1–3 deputies; term 1 year)	Several *	One	Unusual
Branch committee (sec.; 1–3 deputies; term 1 year)	Several	Several *	One *
Group (leader, deputy)	Permitted	Permitted	Permitted

* Formed on the basis of production, work, or residence.

shown in this table are elected by counterpart general membership meetings with the approval of the next higher party committee (usually the *hsien* committee). For a basic-level organization with a primary party committee, the general membership meeting (or delegate meeting) is held at least once each year. The general membership meeting (or delegate meeting) for the general party branch is held at least twice each year, and the party branch general meeting convenes at least once in three months. As a consequence of the command functions of the primary party committee, it may elect a standing committee in addition to the first secretary and deputies given in Table 6.

[74] *Ibid.*, February 23 and 25 and March 15, 1962.

Interaction of Party Apparatus and Nonparty Organizations

Although the leading role of the party has steadily expanded with respect to state and nonparty organizations (see the discussion of "directness" in Chapter I), the manipulation of state and mass organizations is conceived in consistent leadership terms. As in internal organization, the principle of overt command is muted by the policy of self-motivation and the ideological agreement that binds party members irrespective of their current assignment. Party members in nonparty organizations must follow the central leadership responsively and with an excellent style of work. Mao Tse-tung in 1938, describing the nature of the party's model role, said:

Communists engaged in government work should be exemplary in being absolutely incorruptible, free from favouritism in making appointments, and doing much but taking little reward. Communists engaged in mass movements should act as the friends of the masses and not as their bosses; they should be indefatigable teachers and not bureaucratic politicians.[75]

Party groups form the nucleus of leadership organization in nonparty organizations.[76] These groups, which are conceived as vital links in the policy chain, have the following duties stipulated by the 1956 party Constitution: "to assume the responsibility of carrying out Party policy and decisions, to fortify unity with non-Party cadres, to cement the ties with the masses, to strengthen Party and state discipline and to combat bureaucracy" (Art. 59). Party groups must form when "three or more Party members holding responsible posts" work within "the leading

[75] Mao Tse-tung, "The Role of the Chinese Communist Party in the National War," Selected Works, II, 247.

[76] For an official discussion of the role of party groups in extraparty organizations, see Chinese Communist Party, op. cit., pp. 146–156.

body of a state organ or people's organization." They provide the leadership core in all organizations outside the party except for the army where "there is no party group, since the system of separate responsibility by heads under the collective leadership of the party is practiced." [77] According to a 1959 handbook of the Organization Department, the single chain of command system throughout the Communist hierarchy determines the guidance of the party group.[78] Thus leadership comes from a specific party committee and not from departments of that committee even though the department may be concerned with the work of a group's organization. Although the party committee entrusts the group to lead and supervise the work in an organization, the group "is not a level of party committee." [79] Moreover, the group as a body created under the authority of the committee for a special leadership purpose has no leadership relationship to other party groups in organizations or departments, superior or inferior. Should the same organization have a party group and a basic-level organization, the group directs the basic-level organization in matters of work guidance and assistance but the latter guides in matters of administration and personnel.[80] Both the group and the basic-level organization are led by the pertinent party committee.

Administratively assisted by the functional divisions within the Secretariat (United Front Work Department, Committee for Central State Organs, Rural Work Department, etc.), the Central Committee or Political Bureau "must regularly discuss and decide on questions with regard to the guiding principles, policies and important organizational matters" concerning their special area of responsibility.[81] In the past, party members have

[77] Chinese Communist Party, op. cit., pp. 147–148. For an official discussion of leadership principles in the army, see "Speech by Comrade Peng Teh-huai," Eighth National Congress of the Communist Party of China, II, 17–44.

[78] Chinese Communist Party, op. cit., pp. 153–156.

[79] Ibid., p. 154.   [80] Ibid., pp. 154–156.

[81] Teng Hsiao-p'ing, "Report on the Revision," p. 202. In this discus-

looked to the party not only for policy decisions but for training in techniques and adaptable forms of organization as well. The substance of Political Bureau decisions, discussions, and recommendations for techniques and organizational forms is transmitted via the apparatus of the Secretariat to the leading party groups in the state and mass organizations. These groups "must see to it that these decisions are put into effect with the harmonious co-operation of non-Party personalities." [82] The relevant divisions of the Secretariat are also required to "conscientiously and systematically look into the problems and work" of the nonparty organs, and thus the Political Bureau is enabled "to put forward correct, practical and specific proposals or revise them in time in light of actual practice." [83] The departments and committees of the Secretariat and the control commissions must exercise constant administrative and disciplinary supervision over party groups in state organs, and nonparty organizations are warned not to become "independent kingdoms." [84]

In a recent discussion on the question of "cooperation and collaboration" between party members and "democrats" in the government, *People's Daily* stated that "during the past eleven years . . . the party organizations in the government seriously enforced the party's basic policy of placing, exploiting, educating, and transforming nonparty-member democrats [in the government]." [85] The article in examining "cooperation and con-

---

sion, Teng uses only vague references to "the Party." I have made the terms more specific, according to other party documents.

[82] *Ibid.*

[83] *Ibid.* As in such matters, the Chinese Communist press emphasizes that proposals and advice must be specific, realistic, and concrete, but party writers also dictate the line on such mundane topics as whether the Communists in official organs should call one another "comrade" or by their organizational title. For an amusing set of articles on the importance of being a "comrade," see *Jen-min jih-pao,* February 23 and March 23, 1962.

[84] Teng Hsiao-p'ing, "Report on the Revision," p. 203.

[85] *Jen-min jih-pao,* March 16, 1961.

sultation" in 1961 fundamentally restated an important 1954 article on the leading role of party organizations in the state apparatus. "The leading role of the party," *People's Daily* wrote on November 18, 1954,

finds expression in such ways as these: (1) the party gives exact directives to the organs of state power on the nature and direction of their work; (2) the party enforces party policies through the organs of state power and other work departments and exercises supervision over their activities; and (3) the party selects and promotes loyal and capable cadres (party and nonparty) for work in the organs of state power.

The central organs of the party reserve the formulation and supervision of policy and the control of personnel to themselves and delegate routine and technical implementation—and thus the immediate blame for failure—to nonparty bodies.

In 1956, Liu Shao-ch'i singled out the trade union organizations, the Young Communist League (YCL), and the Democratic Women's Federation as the most important of the people's organizations linking the party with the Chinese people. Of these three, the Young Communist League (formerly called the New Democratic Youth League) is central in the over-all Communist structure of leadership. Directly controlled by the Communist Party, the YCL maintains an organizational apparatus parallel to that of the party and is assigned major responsibility in socialist construction and in implementing the party's policies and decisions. As examples of the projects undertaken by the 25,000,000 YCL members (1959), it organized 90,000,000 youth to collect manure (1958), 60,000,000 young people to participate in water conservation projects (1958), and 30,000,000 youth to work in 1,780,000 youth shock brigades.[86] The league, which is open to youth between the ages of 14 and 25, also

[86] These figures are based on *Chung-kuo ch'ing-nien pao* [China Youth News], September 25, 1959, in *Current Background*, no. 600 (1959), pp. 8–13.

supervises the Young Pioneers, an organization for youngsters between the ages of 9 and 15 and numbering 50,000,000 in 1962.[87] The YCL is probably the most important source of new party members because of the requirement that applicants for Communist Party membership under 25 years of age be league members. As a general average between 1949 and 1959, approximately 4 out of 10 new members came from the league.[88]

In general, both outside the party and internally, the central leadership manipulates the party and nonparty cadres to provide the greatest access to the various parts of Chinese society for policy control and mass motivation. Functional division of labor and mass movements under party leadership are handled as administrative routine in order to get the most qualified cadres on the spot to supervise and lead nonparty organizations and the masses. The organizational structure provides the effective framework for internal operation and effective leadership of China. Through that organizational instrument, the Communist elite maintains command of China's fate.

[87] Hsinhua News Agency release, May 25, 1962, in *SCMP*, no. 2750 (1962), p. 19.
[88] *Chung-kuo ch'ing-nien pao*, p. 13.

V

The Organization of Cadre and Party Training

The Development of Study Programs

ALTHOUGH the Chinese Communists place extraordinary priority on organization as a political weapon, their first priority is always on the preparation of the cadres and party leaders who will perform in organizations. In Chapter II, ideology was analyzed in terms applicable to the state of mind of the party leadership. With that background, the next two chapters discussed basic elements of leadership or mass line doctrine and the apparatus of party leadership. The principal technique by which these ideological, conceptual, and organizational precepts have been given real content for party members is the organized use of "study." After the consideration of education and study in this chapter, the remaining chapters will turn to the practical operation of Communist leadership in China particularly in the forms by which leadership is projected outside the party and within the Chinese population.

The most conspicuous form of party education, the rectification campaign, is a maximal concentration of the techniques of ideological education which are regularly applied within the party. This consistency and regularity are most clearly seen in the uninterrupted stress on study. *Hsüeh-hsi*, the term which the Communists invariably use for "study," is the systematic acquisition of knowledge in the Communist sense of the word "knowledge" (Chapter II). In 1938, Mao Tse-tung wrote: "It is impossible for a party to lead a great revolutionary movement to victory if it has no knowledge of revolutionary theory, no knowledge of history and no profound understanding of the actual movement." [1] Mao urged that study be systematic and practical.[2] Three years later as a prelude to the 1942–1944 rectification campaign, Mao declared that correction of existing defects in study methods required attention to "the study of the contemporary situation," "the study of history," and "the study of international revolutionary experiences and of the universal truth of Marxism-Leninism." [3] He emphasized that "bad style in work" in these respects resulted in a ruining and corrupting "subjectivism." In contrast, the correct Marxist-Leninist attitude on study would "combine revolutionary sweep with practical spirit," and Marxism-Leninism would be the "arrow" in this study needed "to hit the 'target' of the Chinese revolution and the revolution of the East." [4]

A Central Committee resolution on the in-service education of cadres (passed by the Political Bureau on February 28, 1942) established basic study priorities.[5] Generally, "cadre education"

---

[1] Mao Tse-tung, "The Role of the Chinese Communist Party in the National War," *Selected Works* (New York: International Publishers, 1954–1956), II, 259.

[2] *Ibid.*

[3] Mao, "Reform Our Study" [May, 1941], *Selected Works*, IV (1956), 13–14.

[4] *Ibid.*, pp. 17–18.

[5] Text in *Cheng-feng wen-hsien* [Rectification Documents] (rev. ed.;

was to "occupy first place in the general educational program," with primacy given to cadres in actual service. In addition to the education of the "more than 90 per cent" of the cadres in service, a small group of cadres were to be detached for systematic education in party schools. "The sphere of in-service cadre education," the resolution stated, "should include professional, political, cultural, and theoretical education." As the first of these, professional education for on-the-job proficiency became "the primary task in education and study." Professional party education comprised five fields of study: (1) "investigation and research" (*tiao-ch'a yen-chiu*) on the total conditions intimately connected with assigned duties; (2) research on applicable party policies, regulations, directives, and resolutions; (3) research on concrete experiences related to the work of each department; (4) research on the historical background of the particular department's work; and (5) research on the scientific principles required for a specialized knowledge of each department.[6]

Diligent study in these five fields was designed to bring success to the Communist Party cadre on the job. To cope with the variety of cadre jobs, the party supervised the preparation of hundreds of training manuals and handbooks. For a cadre in propaganda work, for example, a post-1949 manual presented as models for his own conduct the brief accounts of fifty other propaganda cadres who had successfully met special propaganda problems of general interest.[7] In mass campaigns and for other unique displays such as the nationwide signing of "patriotic declarations" in 1951, supplementary manuals based on actual

---

Shanghai: Chieh-fang she, 1950), pp. 66–71, translated in Boyd Compton, *Mao's China: Party Reform Documents, 1942–1944* (Seattle: University of Washington Press, 1952), pp. 80–87.

[6] *Cheng-feng wen-hsien*, pp. 67–68.

[7] Jen-min ch'u-pan she pien-chi pu [People's Press, Editorial Office], ed., *Tsen-yang tso hsüan-ch'uan yüan* [How to Be a Propagandist] (Peking: Jen-min ch'u-pan she, 1951).

trial experiences were issued and gave specific examples of problems expected and standard methods of solution.[8] In addition to manuals for assigned duties and special problems, complete, general study guides for "investigation and research" have been issued. In the manual widely used after 1949, for example, the first chapter deals with the ideological significance and Marxist-Leninist foundation of "investigation and research." [9] The second chapter gives instructions on investigation preparation, methods, organizational leadership, how to collect and handle materials, and a practical introduction to common types of investigation. The field of "investigation and research" distills and standardizes Mao's survey technique developed first in the famous 1927 *Report of an Investigation into the Peasant Movement in Hunan* (see above, Chapter I) and adheres to Mao's thesis on "the quantitative aspect of a situation or problem." [10] Thus the final chapter of the 1949 manual presents elementary statistics with an emphasis on simple, accurate statistical decisions necessary to fill in standard forms on production, census-type data, and planning estimates.

"Investigation and research" must also be considered against the background of the major Central Committee resolution on

[8] *Tsen-yang ting-li ho chih-hsing ai-kuo kung-yüeh* [How to Draw Up and Carry Out Patriotic Declarations] (Hankow: Chung-nan jen-min ch'u-pan she, 1951). For a different type of manual, cf. *T'u-ti kai-ko shou-ts'e* [Land Reform Handbook] (Hankow: Hsin-hua shu-tien, 1950).

[9] Yü Kuang-yüan, *Tsen-yang tso tiao-ch'a yen-chiu ho t'ung-chi* [How to Do Investigation, Research, and Statistical (Work)] (rev. 4th ed.; Peking: Jen-min ch'u-pan she, 1951). A recent authoritative collection on "investigation and research" is *Mao Tse-tung lun tiao-ch'a yen-chiu* [Mao Tse-tung on Investigation and Research] (Hong Kong: San-lien shu-tien, 1961).

[10] Mao, "Methods of Work of Party Committees" [March 13, 1949], *Selected Works* (Peking: Foreign Languages Press, 1961), IV, 379–380. For recent articles, see *Hung-ch'i* [Red Flag], no. 13, July 1, 1961, pp. 25–29, and *Jen-min jih-pao* [People's Daily], March 7, 1961.

that subject of August 1, 1941.[11] This resolution was written to combat "subjectivistic and formalistic tendencies" and to correct "immature lack of knowledge" and "our understanding [which] is still roughly finished, a caricature, lacking system and thoroughness." [12] For the purpose of collecting materials and performing research, the resolution directed the establishment of investigation and research organizations, the holding of investigation meetings of three to five "men of experience," the "detailed investigation" of villages, the writing of biographical sketches, and the interrogation of a wide range of individuals. Full use was to be made of enemy, allied, and Communist materials. In addition, this resolution was explicitly related to an earlier resolution on "strengthening the party spirit" (passed by the Political Bureau on July 1, 1941). This July, 1941, resolution attacked independent political actions and improvisations, personal systems of organization, and the "failure to gain an understanding of concrete conditions through observation of fact." [13]

"Investigation and research" are the practical means by which theory and practice are combined. Recent Chinese Communist writings have linked Communist standpoint, class analysis, and the mass line style of work to "investigation and research." Standpoint provides the ability to discriminate between classes, while revolutionary practice through the mass line heightens standpoint. Discrimination and practice are assisted by "investigation and research" which provide a ready formula to teach and apply theory in daily mass line practice.[14] Properly conducted research, therefore, advances knowledge, and when incorporated in the

[11] Text in *Cheng-feng wen-hsien*, pp. 57–60, translated in Compton, *op. cit.*, pp. 69–73.

[12] *Cheng-feng wen-hsien*, p. 57; Compton, *op. cit.*, p. 69.

[13] Text in *Cheng-feng wen-hsien*, pp. 131–134, translated in Compton, *op. cit.*, pp. 156–160; quotation from *Cheng-feng wen-hsien*, pp. 132–133.

[14] *Kuang-ming jih-pao* [Bright Daily], August 4, 1961, translated in *U.S. Joint Publications Research Service*, no. 10896 (1961), pp. 33–35.

mass line process this research bears fruit in successful party policies. As was seen in conjunction with the party line, the rewards of mass line successes are personal as well as evident in completed programs (see above, pp. 95–97). Thus typical party commentaries on "investigation and research" state that the "right to speak" can be earned only through diligent research. This "right to speak" presumably derives from an inner confidence associated with this kind of habitual, painstaking study.[15] *Red Flag* in May, 1961, reasserted the role of "investigation and research" as a fundamental Marxist-Leninist method and implied that short cuts from this method had cost the party dearly.[16]

In addition to study for professional on-the-job effectiveness, a second essential part of in-service cadre study in the 1942 resolution was "political education," including "education on current affairs and general policy." [17] As it developed in the following years, political education—which had the purpose of "the mastery of specialized work" as well as the "understanding of general conditions and policy, the broadening of vision, and the avoidance of prejudice and the error of narrow specialization"— became divided into two types. The first type was the study of current events, particularly newspapers. By 1949, this study requirement had made increasing demands on cadre time. Mandatory reading included not only *Jen-min jih-pao* (People's Daily) and local newspapers but also *Shih-shih shou-ts'e* (Current Events Handbook), *Hsin-hua yüeh-pao* (New China Monthly; from 1956, a semimonthly), *Hsüeh-hsi* (after 1958, replaced by *Hung-ch'i* [Red Flag]), and from 1955 *Cheng-chih hsüeh-hsi* (Political Study). If read carefully, this reading alone would average approximately two hours daily for the Chinese reader. In addition,

[15] *Chung-kuo ch'ing-nien* [China Youth] no. 3, 1961, in *SCMM*, no. 254 (1961), pp. 10–15; *Chung-kuo ch'ing-nien*, no. 10, 1961, in *SCMM*, no. 266 (1961), pp. 60–65.

[16] *Hung-ch'i*, no. 9–10, May 5, 1961, pp. 1–10.

[17] *Cheng-feng wen-hsien*, pp. 68–69; Compton, *op. cit.*, pp. 83–84.

study guides multiply the load and detail the "right way" to study newspapers, current events, and documents. For example, one typical pamphlet tells how to study current events and presses the theme of the correct standpoint and ideological background necessary for a cadre to study, analyze, and utilize current events.[18] Another manual outlines the standpoint, outlook, and method required to study all documents and defines ideologically what a document is.[19]

The second type of political education complements reading and theory and focuses on the writing of political reports and articles. The conclusions derived from investigations and political study must be written out by cadres and submitted to their superiors for review and possible publication. The study manual for cadres dealing with this type of writing lists autobiographies, news articles, summation of experiences, letters, and book notes as the most common types of writing for political education.[20] Traditionally, the party has stressed the use of individual diaries and the inspection of the diaries at regular intervals. In the Communist judgment, training remains incomplete unless its results are committed to paper so that they can be checked, inadequacies and errors can be revised, and specific judgments can be reached concerning their utilization.

That the results of study and experience can be brought to full form only in concrete writing illustrates the significance attached to the unity of theory and practice as described by Mao Tse-tung in *On Practice*. The critical stages of knowledge, which coincide with similar stages in the mass line method, are summing up and generalization and then putting into practice (mass line

[18] Ch'en Chung-ta, *Tsen-yang hsüeh-hsi shih-shih* [How to Study Current Events] (Canton: Kwangtung jen-min ch'u-pan she, 1957).

[19] Liao Yüan, *Tsen-yang hsüeh-hsi wen-chien* [How to Study Documents] (Hong Kong: Nan-fang shu-tien, 1950).

[20] Chang Chu-shih, *Tsen-yang hsieh* . . . [How to Write . . .] (3d ed.; Peking: Hsüeh-hsi shu-tien, 1951).

implementation) for verification. Improper study in this regard is labeled "empiricism," [21] which is "knowledge for its own sake" and, in the Communist definition of "knowledge," is not knowledge at all. Through practice, the purpose and process of knowledge become welded together. The Communist undergoes revolutionary cultivation, Liu Shao-ch'i wrote in 1939, "for the purpose of revolutionary practice and effectively to lead the actual revolutionary movement of the masses." [22]

The third essential part of the 1942 study program, in addition to "investigation and research" and political education, is "cultural education"—which means primarily literacy and general educational level. Subjects included in the study of "culture" are the national language, history, geography, arithmetic, nature, society, and politics. The party has prescribed classes, small groups, self-study aids, and teacher training as effective methods to develop the cadre's cultural level. In addition, cultural study supplements political education. "New-democratic culture," Mao wrote in 1940, "is national." [23]

It opposes imperialist oppression and upholds the dignity and independence of the Chinese nation. It belongs to our own nation, and bears our national characteristics. It unites with the socialist and new-democratic cultures of all other nations . . . to develop, and form together the new culture of the world.[24]

Mao also characterized the new culture as scientific and as belonging to the masses. In cultural training, Mao added, "the

[21] Ai Szu-ch'i, "Fan-tui ching-yen-chu-i" [Oppose Empiricism], in Chung-kuo kung-ch'an tang chung-yang Hua-nan fen-chü hsüan-ch'uan pu [Communist Party of China, Central Committee, South China Regional Propaganda Department], ed., Kan-pu hsüeh-hsi tzu-liao [Cadre Study Materials] (Canton: Hua-nan hsin-hua shu-tien, 1951), V, 29–31.

[22] Liu Shao-ch'i, Lun kung-ch'an tang yüan ti hsiu-yang [On the Cultivation of the Communist Party Member] (Reprint; Hong Kong: Hsin min-chu ch'u-pan she, 1949), p. 8.

[23] Mao Tse-tung, "On New Democracy," Selected Works, III, 153.

[24] Ibid., pp. 153–154.

knowledge to be imparted to the revolutionary cadres and the knowledge to be imparted to the broad revolutionary masses must be qualitatively distinguished" [25] in order for the cadres in cultural work to assume command of the various ranks on the cultural front. At the same time, however, Mao advocated linking culture to the people and proposed a reform of the written and spoken language to bring it "close to the people."

The fourth (and final) part of in-service cadre education, theory, is organized around three aspects of Marxism-Leninism: the philosophy of dialectical and historical materialism; political economy; and "scientific communism." In essence, the first aspect shows how mankind got to its present state; the second, how and why mankind should advance to a new, Communist society; and the third, what that Communist society will be. The substance of theory as imparted to party cadres was examined above in Chapter II. In general, Communist authors emphasize the direct relationship between theoretical study and ideological training. "We Communist Party members cannot divorce theoretical study from ideological cultivation," Liu Shao-ch'i said in the 1962 revised edition of *On the Cultivation of the Communist Party Member*. "We must reform ourselves and steel our proletarian ideology not only in revolutionary practice but also in the study of Marxist-Leninist theory." [26] In the 1942 resolution on in-service cadre education, assigned readings in theory were based on differences in cultural (literacy) level and the need for selective and progressive development of the readings. Because of the limited supplies of study materials in Yenan, moreover, the Central Committee devised special schemes for the distribution of materials, for self-study, and for collective discussions.

[25] *Ibid.*, pp. 155–156.
[26] Liu, "On the Cultivation of the Communist Party Member" (in Chinese), *Hung-ch'i*, no. 15–16, August 1, 1962, p. 9. These sentences do not appear in the comparable earlier edition, Liu, *Lun kung-ch'an tang yüan ti hsiu-yang*, p. 27.

After 1949, the study of theory was brought up to date with the new conditions in translation, printing, and distribution. A complete, standard training series for the study of Marxist-Leninist theory was organized around twelve "cadres must read" (*kan-pu pi tu*) volumes. These twelve were (1) Marx and Engels, *Communist Manifesto;* (2) Lenin, *State and Revolution;* (3) Lenin, *Imperialism: The Highest Stage of Capitalism;* (4) Engels, *Socialism, Utopian and Scientific;* (5) Lenin, *Left-Wing Communism, an Infantile Disorder;* (6) Marx, Engels, Lenin, and Stalin, *On Ideological Methods;* (7) Lenin and Stalin, *On China;* (8) Stalin, *Foundations of Leninism;* (9) Lenin and Stalin, *On Socialist Economic Construction* (two volumes); (10) *The History of the Communist Party of the Soviet Union (Bolshevik);* (11) *Political Economy* (replaced in 1955 with a Chinese translation from the Russian of *Political Economy Textbook* [Peking: Jen-min ch'u-pan she]); and (12) *The Short History of Social Development.* According to various 1950 regional committee directives, these twelve volumes published by Liberation Press were to serve as the "basis" for a continuing course of theoretical study.[27] For example, in addition to the twelve "cadres must read" volumes, the party leaders directed cadres to study Mao Tse-tung's newly published *Selected Works* and other current materials. As volumes of Mao's works appeared in the early 1950's, they were accompanied by study guides.[28] In addition, books of specialized, compiled readings such as *On Cadre Theoretical Study* and the 1957 *Collected Readings and Documents for the Curriculum in Socialist Education* [29] augmented the general study load. After 1949, new journals for

[27] Text of Kwangtung directive in Chung-kuo kung-ch'an tang, *Kan-pu hsüeh-hsi tzu-liao,* II, 1–8.

[28] For example, Cheng Ch'ang, Shen Chih-yüan, Li Ta, *et al., Hsüeh-hsi "Mao Tse-tung hsüan-chi" ti-i chüan* [Study the First Volume of the "Selected Works of Mao Tse-tung"] (Peking: Hsin chien-she tsa-chih she, 1952).

[29] *Lun kan-pu li-lun hsüeh-hsi* (3d ed.; Shenyang: Tung-pei jen-min ch'u-pan she, 1951); *She-hui-chu-i chiao-yü k'o-ch'eng ti yüeh-tu wen-chien hui-pien* (Peking: Jen-min ch'u-pan she, 1957, 1958).

national, provincial, and local area distribution were published that dealt with aspects of theoretical study, the most important of which were *Hsüeh-hsi* until 1958, and after 1958 *Hung-ch'i* (Red Flag). The various collected works of Marx, Engels, Lenin, and Stalin and the reprinted writings of the best-known Chinese Communists have contributed to the flow of required reading.

The coordination of study and cadre work assignments has become a mounting problem within the party because of the rising number of publications for required reading. The 1950 provincial directives cited in the previous paragraph, for example, placed a two-hour daily minimum on reading and also required note taking, reports, examinations, specified reading quotas, and methods of rewarding with the stipulation that levels of achievement be weighed in judging and promoting cadres. Since the unity of theory and practice discourages Marxist-Leninists from becoming mere bookworms, moreover, party leaders have considered it essential to balance study with practical work. Put differently, study without adequate participation in and supervision of production and mass-level work is a form of cadre failure. Study which does not lead to action is wasted and frustrates the process of knowledge.

Since 1950, party leaders have experimented with hundreds of *ad hoc* systems to integrate study into the heavy work loads. At Tsinghua University, for example, administrative cadres use the "3-2-1-1" system whereby they "spend three days a week at the basic level, two days for holding meetings to study work, one day for study, and one day for rest." [30] This system was in response to complaints that meetings were too many and too long and that there were too many documents. Other systems arrange the time for study in a way that is similar to military "plans of the day."

No administrative problem seems to have been quite so perplexing to the Communists as the integration of study time, ad-

[30] *Kuang-ming jih-pao* [Bright Daily], July 17, 1960, in *SCMP*, no. 2339 (1960), p. 8.

ministrative work, and production supervision.[31] Although these may appear to involve different orders of cadre problems, in the Communist mind they all relate directly to the effective means to unite theory and practice for over-all cadre training. Training, operation, and administration are interchangeable aspects of the same totalitarian system which in this case concerns cadre remolding. The most important system which bears explicitly on study is the "2-5 system," or its variants, the "3-7 system" and the "3-3 system."[32] The "2-5 system" unites study, administration, and production supervision and provides for two days in the office for study and administration and five days participating in and superintending production at the work levels.

By burdening cadres with a study load almost beyond their capacity and by arranging cadre schedules to integrate that load with other supervising and administrative duties, the Commuists believe that the cycle of knowledge will bound "forward" in great leaps. In the Communist judgment, the cycle will be accelerated within the controlled framework of study programs and small study groups. The old teach the new, the more advanced guide the less advanced, and all engage in criticism and self-criticism. Study is always fundamental in cadre training. At times—such as the pre-rectification period in 1941–1942—the study of Marxist-Leninist literature, the retreat to the library of "truth," outweighs in importance all other forms of activity to refurbish the mind and prepare for even greater tasks ahead.

Formal Organizations for Study

In the past, heavy reliance has been placed on the use of two types of organization for controlled and systematic study: party

[31] See *Nan-fang jih-pao*, October 7, 1960, in *SCMP*, no. 2380 (1960), pp. 12–15. For a more complete discussion of this problem and the various systems, see below, Chapter VII.

[32] These three systems are examined in detail below, Chapter VII.

or cadre schools and small groups. A resolution of the Central Committee (December 17, 1941) established a hierarchy of cadre schools for the regulated study and indoctrination of a select core of party members and cadres.[33] The function of these schools compares to that of military academies and of officer and staff training colleges. In 1958, the party leaders modified party and cadre schools to rely more heavily on the mass line method of leadership in response to the new general line of socialist construction.[34] Short-term training classes were inaugurated and combined with the sending of cadres and Communist Party members to participate in production. New methods such as debates and the use of large-character posters for "struggle" training supplanted formal instruction, and in one school "more than 3,000 large-character posters were posted, thinking was laid bare, and all kinds of individualistic and rightist conservative thought of the bourgeoisie were criticized." [35] The party supplemented lectures with visits to factories and communes, summer "vacations" were planned for work experience, and "free" time was regimented. The party leaders emphasized speed, correctness of thinking, and "shock training." [36] Politics and ideology were "placed in command." [37] By 1961, however, the party was seeking to reestablish the classroom focus of party schools, and typical articles stressed the need for improved quality in teaching, in content and methods of courses, and in the cadre students.[38] In addition, greater emphasis was placed on the routine rotation of a portion of the cadre force into party schools.[39]

The small study group as a second type of cadre training organization does not constitute an alternative to the cadre or party school. All classes of these schools—all factories, government

[33] *Cheng-feng wen-hsien*, pp. 61–65, translated in Compton, *op. cit.*, pp. 74–79. In the Compton translation, the date of this resolution is erroneously given as 1944 rather than the correct 1941.
[34] *Jen-min jih-pao*, August 13, 1958.   [35] *Ibid.*   [36] *Ibid.*
[37] *Ibid.*   [38] *Ibid.*, October 24, 1961.
[39] *Ibid.*, November 18, 1961.

organizations, street committees, mass organizations, communes, and army units—have been organized into small groups. The small group (*hsiao-tsu*) has the intimacy of the traditional family, which it resembles in size and in the rules of direct and frank relationship. This group form is the one which the Communists in Yenan found effective for retraining Kuomintang prisoners and for indoctrinating party and cadre personnel. In this small group, which ranges from three to fifteen members, all the inter-personal pressures can be brought to bear including criticism, self-criticism, "frank speaking" (*t'an-pai*), ostracism, and "mutual help." In the past, daily meetings of the small groups were the rule, though the times have varied greatly, and during the post-1958 agricultural crises meetings have become increasingly sporadic. In 1949, a daily, two- or three-hour session was considered optimum.

At the small-group meeting, all must speak and take an active interest. Usually the chairman begins the discussion, and the activists follow in turns. Chinese interviewed in Hong Kong have said that by the time it was their turn to speak they knew what to say from listening to the chairman and the activists. For the participants in the meeting, the essential requirements are to prepare in advance, to hold to the key theme without repeating, to participate actively with equal use of time, to respect the speaking order, and to take notes.[40] These requirements are self-explanatory except that the key theme should be related to concrete production tasks and to what the members already know well. "Equal time," moreover, means a minimum contribution as well as a limitation on talkative members who might monopolize the discussion. All are directed to listen to and learn from others. Study is arranged to coincide with the discussions, and a concrete lesson plan is written with the least-educated member in mind so that he will "receive a clear impression easily

[40] *Hsüeh-hsi* [Study], I, no. 1 (September, 1949), 40–41.

when he hears the lesson." [41] For competitive spirit, students are exchanged between groups, periodical checkups are held, and the results are published.

The leader of the small group may be any person in the group, and his selection is rotated over a period of time. The leader, who becomes a cadre by virtue of his position, appoints meeting chairmen, draws up the general study plan, and assists and supervises the meeting chairmen.[42] Frequently, the most "backward" person is chosen as chairman in order to place him in full view of the group and to force him to "elevate" himself. Study directives admonish the group chairman to control the discussion time and to ensure that all abide by the basic requirements of membership given in the previous paragraph. The chairman must keep tempers down, prepare before the meeting, and, after careful note taking, sum up the collective results of the meeting.[43]

Although the small-group routine is the basis for cadre study, the form of the group itself has varied. Under some conditions, attending classes has been prescribed, while in others the main form has been self-study. Classes have been divided according to literacy and ideological levels with different reading assignments made accordingly. In usual reading lists, the divisions are "minimum list," "maximum list," and "abridged list." Self-study has been as fully planned as classwork and has placed the burden for remolding and improvement on the individual. After the completion of scheduled phases of self-study, it is mandatory that at least three to five cadres get together for collective discussions.[44] In all cases, these and other small-group collective discussions must make the general concrete; make a clear explanation; reduce the results of the discussion to a few, simple principles; be made applicable to the errors of the participants; and be connected to what the participants have already learned.[45]

[41] *Ibid.*, I, no. 4 (January, 1950), 50.
[42] *Ibid.*, I, no. 1 (September, 1949), 40.   [43] *Ibid.*
[44] *Ibid.*, IV, no. 3 (May, 1951), 4.   [45] *Ibid.*, no. 4, 1954, p. 3.

To achieve these explicit goals, all small-group discussions, even those to sum up self-study, have a meeting chairman. This responsible chairman begins the meeting with a report and ends with "summing up" so that study intimately relates to practical production experiences and special problems in production are anticipated.

Criticism and Summing Up

This brief section will comment on one critical technique by which the training of the cadre is brought to the point of total and automatic reconciliation with the collective spirit and the leadership of the Chinese Communist Party. This technique, summing up, begins with a general orientation to criticism and self-criticism, which were introduced in Chapter III in discussing the rectification of deviations.[46]

"No political party or person," states the Constitution of the Communist Party, "can be free from shortcomings and mistakes in work. The Communist Party of China and its members must constantly practice criticism and self-criticism to expose and eliminate their shortcomings and mistakes so as to educate themselves and the people." Criticism and self-criticism are the operative techniques and the most concrete forms of intraparty struggle. In the unity-criticism-unity rectification method, criticism and self-criticism play the central role.

These things are essential about criticism and self-criticism: (1) each must take place within organization;[47] (2) it must be open and frank and focus on what in principle is wrong; (3) it must be normal routine; and (4) it must not be confused with disciplinary action. A central adjective in the moral character

[46] For a recent, practical discussion of criticism and self-criticism, see *Jen-min jih-pao*, January 11, 1962.

[47] Mao Tse-tung, "On the Rectification of Incorrect Ideas in the Party" [December, 1929], *Selected Works*, I, 110.

of the party member is "honesty," [48] and the moral cadre must be honest to the point of self-exposure or the exposure of mistakes of friends. Concealment or distortion of facts is an infraction of membership duties, and criticism and self-criticism are expressions of the dutiful, honest member and are essential to his training. As a tool of education, criticism and self-criticism call forth an endless stream of analysis and self-analysis, confession, apology, and public resolution. Opinions, errors, and shortcomings are all in the open, are written down for future use, and are known quantities for evaluation and decision.

The most sophisticated form of solving the group "contradictions" raised in study meetings and in criticism and self-criticism is summing up.[49] The summing up of experiences, ideas, opinions, and agreements ranges from a small meeting to the entire nation and from local problems to the whole of history. "Marxism-Leninism," Mao Tse-tung said in 1937, "has in no way summed up all knowledge of truth, but is ceaselessly opening up, through practice, the road to the knowledge of truth." [50] Summing up, which takes place during the second and third stages of the mass line method to become the party's line and policy, assumes that Chinese having the same clear standpoint and directed by the policies and principles previously summed up and verified in revolutionary practice will arrive at the same conclusions. However, because unity of conclusions is so essential in the acquisition and promotion of collective knowledge, the Communists hold that practice has proved the necessity of leadership direction in

[48] Teng Hsiao-p'ing, "Report on the Revision of the Constitution," *Eighth National Congress of the Communist Party of China* (Peking: Foreign Languages Press, 1956), I, 211–212.

[49] This discussion is based on Hung Yen-lin, *Tsen-yang tso kung-tso tsung-chieh* [How to Sum Up Work] (Hong Kong: Hsin min-chu ch'u-pan she, 1949), and *Ta-kung pao* [Impartial], ed., *Szu-hsiang tsung-chieh* [Ideological Summing Up] (Shanghai: T'ang-ti ch'u-pan she, 1950). See also *Jen-min jih-pao*, September 10, 1959.

[50] Mao Tse-tung, *On Practice* (rev. trans.; Peking: Foreign Languages Press, 1958), p. 20.

summing up. Various reasons such as bourgeois contamination, mass inexperience, and the variety of levels of consciousness are given. The party does not merely deserve to lead; proved reality "demands" that it lead. Evidence of disunity in summing up is taken not only as a sign of faulty standpoint or insufficient experience but also as a denial of the absolute requirement of party leadership, a denial which would destroy the mass line and betray history.

Summing up is the means by which the individual brings together his entire conscious activity. As a technique learned in the "investigation and research" phase of training, summing up extends to all forms of theory and practice. The member or cadre lays himself on the line for analysis, discussion, and criticism and self-criticism. He and his comrades scrutinize his own and the group's cognition, practice, struggle attitude, and standpoint. One party resolution states: "Every comrade may have shortcomings and commit mistakes, every comrade needs other people's help, and the purpose of Party unity is precisely to develop this kind of comradely mutual help." [51] To refuse to be unified in the collective summing up is to deny the party and to reveal an individualistic motive and a bourgeois standpoint. Willingness to participate in and accede to the party's summing up separates the "real" Communist from the nominal party member. Disagreement after summing up of the lines and policies is unthinkable for the "real" Communist, because his will has been collectivized. He "understands" the party's policies for they are his policies perfected and heightened in the summing up process. If at no other time, the remolding of thought and action takes place in summing up. Constant writing, reporting, and talking in addition to a system for comparison of past efforts provide safeguards against superficial unity. Given time, the inconsistencies will be revealed, and the struggle for "true" unity will be renewed.

[51] Quoted in Teng Hsiao-p'ing, "Report on the Revision," p. 205.

Recent Developments
in Party and Cadre Training

Cadre and party member training continues to undergo changes in response to the demands of new policies and tasks of the socialist revolution and socialist construction. The following recent developments are critical.[52]

(1) *Increased cadre work load.* Because "the basic-level cadres of today have much more work to do than those of . . . any previous period," [53] the Communists have intensified the planned arrangement of study under such divisions of time as the "2-5 system," the "3-7 system," and the "3-3 system" (see below, Chapter VII). Common programs for regular study days also have included training periods every week on the 5th, 15th, and 25th of each month.[54] Given the "proper" use of such systems, "busy work is no excuse for having no time for one's study." [55] The organized leadership and planned arrangement of study time come within the purview of party committees (particularly at the *hsien* level), and these party committees are directed to "take as keen an interest in the studies of basic-level cadres as they do in the food and clothing of the popular masses." [56] Under the increased work load, cadres must abide by a regimen that calculates every minute of activity. For convenience and simplicity the student is urged to study "advanced models" from which he purportedly gains advanced, general knowledge applicable to other situations.[57]

[52] For a typical recent article, see *Jen-min jih-pao*, May 6, 1961.
[53] *Nan-fang jih-pao*, October 7, 1960, in *SCMP*, no. 2380 (1960), p. 13.
[54] *Jen-min jih-pao*, December 2, 1961; *Chung-kuo ch'ing-nien pao* [China Youth News], January 27, 1962, in *SCMP*, no. 2681 (1962), pp. 3–6.
[55] *Nan-fang jih-pao, loc. cit.*
[56] *Ibid.* See also *Jen-min jih-pao*, April 5, 1962.
[57] *Jen-min jih-pao*, April 29, 1961.

By 1962, the Communist Party had settled on a regular training system of party lessons,[58] often provided for through "study stations" scattered throughout the area of party committee responsibility. Although lost in the hectic period from 1958 to 1960, party lessons had been a basic training technique since the Yenan period. Earlier "on-the-spot schools" used for rapidly training large numbers of basic-level cadres overloaded by practical work were held less frequently and apparently were in large measure superseded by routine lesson periods. The dilemma of the cadre student faced with party lessons is revealed in the reported testimony of a brigade leader in Kiangsi Province:

To tell the truth, I found study quite a headache. . . . First, because of my low cultural standard, I was unable to understand clearly some common terms, much less the spirit and substance of the books. Second, I was very busy and always afraid that my work might be delayed because of study. It struck me that rather than spend time on study, it would be better to have more work done.[59]

This cadre, as one would expect from the prominence of the story in the Communist press, overcame his resistance to study and gradually "understood" the importance of study for his daily work. To assist similar cadres in overcoming the problem of coordinating party lessons with the increased work load, the various party committee departments have compiled simplified readers and textbooks, and great emphasis is placed on intensified learning during slack farming seasons.

(2) *Greater sense of urgency in training.* The subject matter of study is also organized for maximum effectiveness in the shortest possible time. For cadres in service (rather than detached for special training in party schools) the current emphases in training are the study of Marxism-Leninism and "Comrade Mao Tse-

[58] On party lessons, see, for example, *ibid.*, September 13 and October 21, 1961, and June 12, 1962.
[59] *Ibid.*, September 13, 1961.

tung's great works," [60] the study of party documents (directives, lines, and policies), the study of newspapers, and the "study" of current central production tasks through participation and supervision.[61] For cadres at the basic level, the reading of newspapers and the study of party documents are considered "the best ways of studying Marxism-Leninism" since these are "typical examples of the application of the universal truth of Marxism-Leninism to the actual conditions of China" and are "the most practical and most useful parts of Marxism-Leninism." [62] Condensed, rapid courses especially in the slack farming season teach the "red and technical" fundamentals and depend on practical experience for continued advancement and greater depth of knowledge.

(3) *More deliberate planning and wider scope.* Cadre and party-member training comprises more than study and production training. Organized life itself provides an environment for indoctrination and the educational development of the Communist. Mao Tse-tung has consistently stressed the importance of an organizational life which brings cadres and masses together on a basis of mutual benefit, but this form of training received little practical notice until the rectification campaign of 1957–1958. At that time the Central Committee took deliberate steps to give actual content to cadre training within the masses by instituting the *hsia-fang* movement (see below, Chapter VII). This program vastly accentuated the scope of training and regularized cadre work at the production levels. The redistribution and rotation of more than 1,300,000 cadres in the 1958–1961

[60] In late 1961, *China Youth News* reported on a compilation of twenty-two of Mao Tse-tung's writings by the General Political Department of the People's Liberation Army and suggested its use by youth. See *Chung-kuo ch'ing-nien pao*, December 8, 1961, in *SCMP*, no. 2645 (1961), pp. 1–5.

[61] *Nan-fang jih-pao*, p. 14. The details of what to read in the course of this study are spelled out in *Chung-kuo ch'ing-nien pao*, November 25, 1961, in *SCMP*, no. 2646 (1961), pp. 4–5.

[62] *Nan-fang jih-pao*, *loc. cit.*

phase of the *hsia-fang* movement made the systematized visits to the production levels an integral part of the over-all organizational life. This movement placed first priority in the minds of party cadres on the basic-level organizational life, particularly on the party branch. In the main, the bulk of the training activities described in this chapter occur within the branch apparatus, which includes small groups. One party committee, for example, in 1961 "held a three-week training for 243 members of the rural Party general branches, secretaries of Party branches, and leaders of production brigades who are Party cadres." [63] The committee cadres lectured, held small-group discussions, and participated in open debates with branch members. In late 1961 and early 1962, party branches reportedly paid increasing attention to the use of party lessons and to training within mass campaigns.[64]

Moreover, as most cadres have belonged to the Young Communist League,[65] which is open to youth from 14 to 25 years, this organizational training usually has begun at middle school age, and for an increasing number who joined the Young Pioneers,[66] life in Communist organizations reaches back to primary school. The entire educational apparatus [67] is geared to the Communist indoctrination of Chinese youth, and as an idea of the numbers processed in this educational system, over 96,000,000 youth attended schools in 1959.[68] Everyone under the age of

[63] *Pei-ching jih-pao* [Peking Daily], March 22, 1961, in *SCMP*, no. 2478, pp. 2–3.

[64] *Jen-min jih-pao*, September 13, 1961.

[65] The membership of the Young Communist League was 25,000,000 in September, 1959. On YCL cadre training, see *Chung-kuo ch'ing-nien pao*, February 22, 1960, in *SCMP*, no. 2267 (1960), pp. 2–4.

[66] The membership of the Young Pioneers in 1962 was 50,000,000.

[67] For a recent comprehensive study on the educational system, see Leo A. Orleans, *Professional Manpower and Education in Communist China* (Washington, D.C.: National Science Foundation, 1961).

[68] For two official commentaries on Communist education, see Lu Ting-yi, *Education Must Be Combined with Productive Labour* [Septem-

27 or 28 who has studied in China has had some Communist education, and every graduate of middle school since 1960 has had a complete Communist education from kindergarten.

(4) *Increased proliferation of forms and emphasis on beginning with probationary members.* The organized training of party members and cadres has assumed a wide variety of forms in recent years: party schools for a minority detached from service, "red and expert" training classes and schools, organized lectures, and special integrated systems for new members of the party. The party lessons described under the first point above largely applied to probationary party members. According to *China Youth News,* moreover, "There are multifarious forms in which the lessons were given: general lecturing, class meetings to hear reports, discussions on proper topics and the educating method by way of making investigations." [69] Of these forms, the training systems for probationary members of the party demonstrate most clearly the recent complexities in Communist training.[70] In general, each new member becomes the specific responsibility of a full member of the party under the system of "one help" ("helping probationary members overcome difficulties and improve themselves incessantly") and "two responsibilities" ("responsibility to the party organization and responsibility to the new member").[71] "Instruction" is given probationary members in the difference between materialism and idealism and the

---

ber 16, 1958] (Peking: Foreign Languages Press, 1958), and an article by Yang Hsiu-feng, Minister of Education, in *Jen-min jih-pao,* October 8, 1959.

[69] *Chung-kuo ch'ing-nien pao,* January 27, 1962, in *SCMP,* no. 2681 (1962), p. 5.

[70] This section is based on a selection of typical articles on new-member training. See *Ho-nan jih-pao* [Honan Daily], December 29, 1958, in *SCMP,* no. 1959 (1959), pp. 13–16; Hsinhua News Agency release, June 30, 1959, in *SCMP,* no. 2057 (1959), pp. 3–4; *Jen-min jih-pao,* July 28, 1959; and *Kuei-chou jih-pao* [Kweichow Daily], November 14, 1959, in *SCMP,* no. 2158 (1959), pp. 38–40.

[71] *Kuei-chou jih-pao,* p. 38.

"proletarian road" and the "bourgeois road" (Chapter II, above), in the party lines, programs, and Constitution, and in "socialist construction and [the] prospects for Communism, the mass line, class struggle, materialistic dialectics, all kinds of erroneous thought and practice" with the use of production practice, mass movements, lectures, debates, wall posters, and criticism.[72] Members are indoctrinated to "establish six ideas" (the ideas of state, labor, collectivism, class, mass, and party organization), to "play five roles" ("fighter for production, director of work, professional technician, political agitator, and servant of the people"), and to "lead in five things" (participation in labor, learning of techniques and skills, enduring of hardships, observance of labor discipline, and execution of policies and resolutions).

The formal education of probationary members may take place in party schools, "red and expert" schools, party night schools, "on-the-spot" party schools, or "spare time" schools. Some of these party schools have been "moved to the front lines" for education at basic production levels. In these schools probationary members receive instruction during "spare moments immediately before and after meals and in rest periods." [73] The typical story disseminated by the party concerning cadres attending these schools pertains to the rapid development of personal motivation and skill and a revolution in the working style of the member, who is thus enabled to work more effectively within the masses. In addition to the "front line" schools, there are periods of short-term education by rotation when a few are detached from production and sent to regular party schools.

(5) *Intensified stress on practical performance.* To initiate new members into party duties, special "tasks and demands" are imposed on them. Competitions are arranged, public declarations of intent to reform are made, and comparisons are used to assess the results. Shock brigades of probationary members and "leap

[72] *Ho-nan jih-pao*, p. 14.   [73] *Ibid.*

forward" classes "request" assignment to the most difficult production sites and eagerly accept the challenge to invent new systems, tools, and labor-saving techniques and to engage in public experiments particularly experimental or "model" farms. All these activities to demonstrate performance ability are centered in the organizational life of the party. At the party meetings, probationary members "tell one another their achievements since their joining the Party, how they have overcome their own personal shortcomings, and how they are trying to win full membership." [74] When the probationary members "voice their views" of the party and their own lives, the leading cadres "will be able to promptly understand the thoughts of the probationary members and the condition of their work."

After each meeting, the probationary Party members are required to voluntarily draw up plans for spurring themselves onward. . . . These personal plans for advancement are first of all turned over to the Party group of the unit to which the makers of the plans belong for examination and amendment, and then turned over to the head of the Party group or to the sponsors of the probationary Party members concerned, so that execution of these plans may be constantly checked and supervised.[75]

Once committed to an approved plan of self-reform, no thought or action is exempt from a rigid comparison. In making the new Communist man, nothing is left to chance.

Study and Mass Movements

At those times when problems become acute or when critical new stages in the revolutionary movement occur, study is expanded into a campaign. All the techniques of study are opera-

[74] *Kuei-chou jih-pao*, p. 39. Minor changes have been made in this translation to bring it into conformity with the original.
[75] *Ibid.*

169

tive during these campaigns though at a greatly increased tempo. A high emotional intensity pervades these periods, during which the party affords its members and cadres a special opportunity for general political education, for testing in criticism and self-criticism, and for purging unreliable elements. In one article in *People's Daily*, the rectification campaign was called a "powerful magic weapon" [76] and "the principal method for correctly handling contradictions inside our party." By means of self-education and criticism, its purpose is "to clear up ideological matters, to improve our understanding, and to distinguish between what is Marxist and what is not." [77]

Prior to 1957, there were four major periods of rectification for party members in Communist China.[78] The explicit purpose of the 1942–1944 movement was to correct the party's style of work and to reform the study habits of its members.[79] In 1947–1948, an inner-party rectification movement was linked to the land reform in Communist-controlled areas and emphasized education and the correction of style in basic-level party organizations. A 1950 rectification movement directed primarily against the deviation of "commandism" (see above, Chapter III) was coordinated with a mass campaign for fiscal economy. The 1950 movement also stressed the basic techniques of the mass line and the correct use of class analysis, study, summing up of work, and criticism and self-criticism. A 1951–1954 campaign was associated with several other national movements such as the "resist-America aid-Korea" campaign and the *san-fan* campaign

[76] *Jen-min jih-pao*, January 5, 1961. See also *ibid.*, September 1, 1959.
[77] *Ibid.*, January 5, 1961.
[78] For a typical survey of these campaigns, see Chao Han, ed., *T'an-t'an Chung-kuo kung-ch'an tang ti cheng-feng yün-tung* [Talk about the Rectification Campaigns of the Chinese Communist Party] (Peking: Chung-kuo ch'ing-nien ch'u-pan she, 1957), esp. chap. ii.
[79] For a recent discussion of this campaign, see *Jen-min jih-pao*, August 17, 1961. The major documents of this campaign are found in Compton, *op. cit.*

(against corruption, waste, and bureaucracy) in 1952. Its fundamental purpose was to "purify" basic-level party organizations and to promote party education.

When these periods of intense education are related to the events which followed, it is clear that the purposes of unity and of high-level preparation in the campaigns were to promote the greatest possible mastery of proved organizational and leadership techniques. Maximum-intensity training within strict time limits characterized these earlier campaigns. Since the 1957 campaign to rectify the party's style in work, however, the Communist Party and Chinese in general have taken part in scores of overlapping and continuous campaigns, which feature massed rallies in city and village squares, displays of banners with red and gold characters, the rhythmic chant of slogans, and the orations of party leaders. In one dramatic moment of raised fists and shouts of action, the mass will is collectivized, and all are committed. By prolonging this emotional experience from 1957 through 1962, therefore, the party has transformed the nature of campaigns from a special, reserve weapon into a regular tool of leadership.

In addition, the 1957 rectification campaign was extended to all parties and nonparty democrats, and a further, extraparty dimension was added to the intensive study and education which had previously characterized inner-party rectification. Moreover, in May, 1957, all cadres in the government, mass organizations, the military, and the various enterprises were brought within the scope of the campaign by the directive on physical labor.[80] By this extension, all party and nonparty cadres and intellectuals who were responsible for the operation of every aspect of Chinese society not directly supervised by the party leaders were brought within the intensive training system of the party and made to abide by the party's guidance and discipline

[80] *Hsinhua News Agency Release*, May, 1957, item 051421, pp. 120–121.

as if they were party members. Study not only serves to indoctrinate adherents but also has become in the form of mass movements a primary technique of mass line leadership in Communist China.

Most of the post-1957 campaigns have involved specific parts of the five-year plan such as steel production or water conservancy. In point of emphasis rather than mere numbers of campaigns, however, the party has clearly given priority to ideological reform. It has been the extension of the inner-party rectification techniques to nonparty circles that has received such worldwide publicity since 1957. Academicians and intellectuals became a principal target for ideological reform at the time of the Central Committee meeting in January, 1956, to discuss the question of intellectuals,[81] when Mao inaugurated the long-term campaign for the controlled "self-reform" of intellectuals under the slogan "let a hundred flowers blossom, a hundred schools of thought contend!" [82] The "hundred flowers" directive was revitalized in 1961,[83] after a year of experimenting with the "hundred flowers" method of debate and struggle ("blooming and contending") among industrialists, businessmen, and all democratic party members. This experimentation in the method of "uniting, educating, and remolding bourgeois elements" was popularized during 1961 as "meetings of immortals," a method that

observes the spirit of mild rain and gentle breeze under the correct leadership of the party, by which they [the bourgeois elements] are enabled to analyze and solve problems themselves and, on the

[81] Chou En-lai, *Report on the Question of Intellectuals* (Peking: Foreign Languages Press, 1956).

[82] Lu Ting-yi, *"Let Flowers of Many Kinds Blossom, Diverse Schools of Thought Contend!"* [May 26, 1956] (Peking: Foreign Languages Press, 1957); Mao Tse-tung, *On the Correct Handling of Contradictions among the People* [February 27, 1957] (Peking: Foreign Languages Press, 1957), pp. 48–59.

[83] See *Hung-ch'i*, no. 5, March 1, 1961, pp. 1–5, and *ibid.*, no. 11, June 1, 1961, pp. 23–26.

foundation of heightening their self-consciousness continuously, carry out criticism and self-criticism and self-remolding.[84]

In accordance with Central Committee directives, the party provincial committees have ruled that a "large-scale rectification campaign be organized in the province every year." [85] In addition, local echelons are authorized to conduct small-scale campaigns several times each year. At the ninth plenary session of the Central Committee (January 14–18, 1961), the party leadership determined to continue the campaign for functionaries and cadres

throughout the country stage by stage and area by area to help the cadres enhance their ideological and political level, improve their method and style of work and purify the organizations by cleaning out the extremely few bad elements who have been verified by careful check-up as having sneaked into the Party and Government organizations.[86]

This call for an intensive rectification campaign was expanded to all party members and particularly party cadres by Liu Shao-ch'i on July 1, 1961. "The primary purpose of this campaign," Liu said, "is to help all Party cadres further to understand and grasp the objective laws of China's socialist construction." [87]

At the same time that the party extends the rectification movements in scope and coverage, however, greater emphasis is placed on self-study and self-analysis. It is almost axiomatic in Communist China that the more extensive the scope of the Chinese covered by remolding the more intensive the probing of the human mind becomes. In the Communist view, not only are superficial leadership techniques ineffective, but they can also become a self-defeating trap. The ideological cultivation of the

[84] *Jen-min jih-pao,* May 16, 1961.
[85] *Chung-kuo ch'ing-nien* [China Youth], no. 10, 1960, in *SCMM,* no. 220 (1960), p. 31.
[86] *Peking Review,* no. 4, 1961, p. 6.
[87] *Ibid.,* no. 26–27, 1961, p. 10.

party member, Liu Shao-ch'i said, "is the struggle of the proletarian ideology in each and every party member against all
nonproletarian ideologies within him." [88] The Chinese Communists have staked their future on the practical efficacy of a
dialectically united extensive-intensive remolding technique. By
struggling within a mass rectification movement, the individual
theoretically becomes integrated with the party-led "collective."
Concerning the struggling individual, *China Youth* in 1960 wrote
that the most important aspect of a comrade's lifelong struggle
was that "he should use well the weapon of self-criticism, should
examine his brain for the presence of bad thoughts, and, if bad
thoughts are found there, should struggle against them fiercely
till the end and struggle against them if they arise again." [89]
China Youth continued that a comrade should treat mistakes and
shortcomings as an enemy with whom the comrade can never
be at peace. Carried along in the tide of the campaign, each comrade carries his own sentinel against the internal enemy. To ex-
tend the Communist analogy, when the sentinel is on full-time
alert, the operation of the Communist-trained responses of the
individual will become completely automatic.

The remolding of all cadres establishes the basis for the total
ordering of all Chinese within the "direct," unified totality of the
people led by the party according to the rules of democratic
centralism and the mass line. All leadership personnel, thinking
alike, will operate within the masses who have been prepared in
study groups and mass movements to respond affirmatively to
party guidance. If successful, the resolution of so high an order
of contradictions would solve in theory all the major problems
between leaders and led, in agriculture and in business, for intellectuals, and with respect to national minorities as listed in
Mao's *On the Correct Handling of Contradictions among the
People*. In Marxist-Leninist theory, this would release a tide of

[88] *Hung-ch'i*, no. 15–16, August 1, 1962, p. 14.
[89] *Chung-kuo ch'ing-nien*, no. 10, 1960, in *SCMM*, no. 220 (1960), p. 31.

human creativeness and energy undreamed of in history and would create a great leap forward in production. This is the theory of the most-unified collective in the world, the theory of the "single spark" which would enflame the Chinese people. These are the stakes in the great social gamble that put rectified relationships before economic plenty and rational industry. That gamble is not yet won or lost.

VI

Communist Party Operation and Cadres

The Totality of Operation

MAO TSE-TUNG'S essays *On Contradiction* and *On Practice*, reportedly delivered first as lectures in the summer of 1937, deal with complementary, theoretical aspects of cadre operation. These two essays fit the operational concepts of the mass line to the precepts of dialectical and historical materialism. This integration of effective methods of operation in China with the theory of Marxism-Leninism marks an essential step in the total systematization of Chinese communism. In particular, *On Practice* set the foundation for active, creative, directed participation as summed up in one-half of the principle of democratic centralism—democracy under centralized guidance. *On Contradiction*, on the other hand, as the basis for authoritative leadership and decisive direction to resolve principal contradictions supported the other half of the principle—centralism based on democracy.

An organization whose membership professedly adheres to the

principle of democratic centralism is a manifestation of the epistemological process detailed in *On Practice* and of the total historical movement from relative to absolute outlined in *On Contradiction*. Cadres trained in Marxism-Leninism and the revolutionary practice of the mass line method must progressively comprehend the totality of objective knowledge (*On Practice*) at the same time they are solving the primary contradictions of each relative stage (*On Contradiction*). In this integrated and organized context of knowing and doing, revolutionary cadres guide the resolution of contradictions of the total system. Cadre knowledge constitutes the subjective reality required to lead this total resolution. Cadres, cadre organization, the Chinese people, and the modes of production, to name a few examples, however, are parts of the objective reality of base and superstructure. Thus cadres consciously guide the integration of the system into a democratically centralized whole and are at the same time themselves integrated in that system.

The directed resolution or "synthesis" of contradictions within human relationships simultaneously creates democratically centralized organization. In fact, this synthesis of relationships may be said to define in Marxist-Leninist terms the nature of an organization founded on the principle of democratic centralism. In 1957, Mao listed the critical contradictions in human relationships which were then pertinent for China's socialist society as those contradictions occurring within the "people" and between the working class and peasantry, between these two classes and the intelligentsia, between the working class and the national bourgeoisie, within the national bourgeoisie, and between the government and the masses.[1] The synthesis of these contradictions theoretically should "release" the unified social energy to create more-advanced forms of social cohesion and "great leaps" in socialist construction. Social progress occurs when these ad-

[1] Mao Tse-tung, *On the Correct Handling of Contradictions among the People* (Peking: Foreign Languages Press, 1957), pp. 8-16.

vanced forms and great leaps upset the previous balanced unity. New perception, new summaries, and new lines and policies are then required to reconstitute the synthesis of democratic centralism at a "higher level." Theoretically, a more creative form of "democratic" participation evolves to promote a more-unified, centralized social system. At each high point of integration, leadership operation proceeds according to the complete unity of democracy and centralism. At these points, flexibility and rigidity, opposed in logic, engulf the mind and body in creative, eager activity that upholds and develops the rigidly integrated system. When the mind of the Chinese comes automatically to respond to this complex of point-counterpoint, the revolutionary process itself will have been completed. The various elements—collective and individual, objective and subjective—will have been brought into total unity; and the superstructure and economic base will have been so completely attuned that party and state theoretically will cease to function.

Operational Phases and Cadre Action

The mass line method of leadership was defined above (Chapter III) as "from the masses, to the masses" and "linking the general to the specific." The process of coming from and going to the masses was seen to involve four stages: perception, summarization, authorization, and implementation. These four stages, however, are cyclically completed during the process of absolute movement of history. This historical process has its own cycle of operation which is compatible with the progressive mass line method. Each cycle basically incorporates the period from the emergence to the resolution of a given principal contradiction (see above, p. 50). Indeed, the existence of cycles in the historical process justifies the stages in the mass line method. Yet, as "proved" in the experience of the Communist Party of China, historical process has implications for leadership action beyond (though inclusive of) the mass line. Mao Tse-tung discussed these implications in "On Methods of Leadership" (June 1, 1943), which detailed the positive aspects of leadership operation that had been verified in the course of the 1942–1943 rectification campaign.

Briefly, as stated by Mao and other party leaders, three points for leadership operation stand out: (1) action must be based on the unity of internal party relations and on trained, proved cadres;[2] (2) success in action depends on over-all, daily performance of cadres at the working level;[3] and (3) each stage of the mass line method (perception, summarization, authorization, and implementation) must be well defined, concrete, and pretested and must utilize all available devices (meetings, propaganda, etc.) to arouse and involve the people.[4] Success is particularly important at the stage of implementation, for it causes deeper commitment and involvement, especially if the participants believe that their "conquest" has been over notable hardships and demanded extraordinary effort.[5] Failure when it occurs

[2] Mao Tse-tung, "On Methods of Leadership," *Selected Works* (New York: International Publishers, 1954–1956), IV, 111–117; Mao, "Rectify the Party's Style in Work," *Selected Works*, IV, 37–43; Liu Shao-ch'i, *Lun kung-ch'an tang yüan ti hsiu-yang* [On the Cultivation of the Communist Party Member] (reprint; Hong Kong: Hsin min-chu ch'u-pan she, 1949); Ch'en Yün, *Tsen-yang tso i-ko kung-ch'an tang yüan* [How to Be a Communist Party Member] (reprint; Canton: Hsinhua shu-tien, 1950).

[3] Mao Tse-tung, "On Methods of Leadership"; "Economic and Financial Problems during the Anti-Japanese War," *Selected Works*, IV, 109–110.

[4] Mao Tse-tung, "On Methods of Leadership"; "Spread in the Base Areas the Campaign for Rent Reduction, for Production, and for the Army's Support of the Government and Protection of the People," *Selected Works*, IV, 126–130. For a recent example of this point, see documents which introduced the communes in *Hsin-hua pan-yüeh k'an* [New China Semimonthly], nos. 17–20, 1958.

[5] Mao Tse-tung, "On Methods of Leadership." On the hardship

179

results essentially from an incorrect relationship between the cadres and the general population and between the individual and collective operation.[6] Establishment of a correct balance between individual and collective operation requires (1) the gathering of information, which may be collective or individual; (2) decision, which is the responsibility of the individual cadre; (3) implementation, which is collective; and (4) control, which utilizes collective supervision and individual responsibility.[7] Where the process is collective, it emphasizes participation and "democratic" creativeness; where it is individual, it stresses responsibility and organizational centralization.

As the most comprehensive statement of the Communist code of operation, Mao's "On Methods of Leadership" begins with the mass line leadership method. "The two methods which we Communists should employ in carrying out any task," he began, "are, first, the linking of the general with the specific and, second, the linking of the leadership with the masses." Mao then covered most of the points above on leadership operation with special emphases to correct particular leadership deficiencies. Moreover, he wrote the leadership resolution against the background of other party resolutions in force and to summarize the specific lessons drawn from experience during the 1942–1943 rectification campaign.

---

aspect, see Mao, "Economic and Financial Problems," pp. 109–110; Mao, "On the Chungking Negotiations," Selected Works (Peking: Foreign Languages Press, 1961), IV, 58; and Ai Szu-ch'i, "Nan" [Difficulty], in I-wang wu-ch'ien [Go Forward Regardless of What Is Ahead] (Hong Kong: Hung-mien ch'u-pan she, [1948?]), pp. 33–35.

[6] Mao, "Appendix: Resolution on Some Questions in the History of Our Party," Selected Works, IV, 171–218; Jen-min jih-pao [People's Daily], August 6, 1958.

[7] Mao, "On Methods of Leadership"; Teng Hsiao-p'ing, "Report on the Revision of the Constitution," Eighth National Congress of the Communist Party of China (Peking: Foreign Languages Press, 1956), I, 171–228; "Speech of Comrade Sung Jen-chiung," Eighth National Congress, II, 147–156.

After the general introduction of "On Methods of Leadership," Mao stated the necessity for careful pretesting of general directives in a few selected areas and units in order to make a thorough study of a "typical" sample and to gain practical experience. He then turned to the problem of the "leading group" which operates within the ranks of the people, a problem which bears on policy implementation and the requirement for maintaining a tight relationship with the people at the working level. "The fundamental reason for failure to advance our work in various places and organisations," Mao wrote, "is precisely the absence of such a permanently healthy leading group firmly united and linked with the masses." The "leading group" (*ling-tao ku-kan*) in this resolution refers to the official functionaries ("cadres") who are the leadership nucleus of all levels of the party leadership organs and official nonparty organs (see below, next section). At the production or working levels within the general population, these leading groups are composed of party and nonparty cadres who superintend the work and education of the people—that is, the production group and team leaders, the police officers who head street committees, the army squad leaders, the class leaders in schools, and the leaders of the small study groups. The working-level leading groups stand at the administrative base of the official party, commune, government, industrial, education, or other apparatus and direct the work of the broad masses.

In overseeing the implementation of policy, the cadres at the working level give general policy its specific form and are responsible for all daily implementing decisions. Thus, by thoroughly indoctrinating its cadres, the party creates the means for delegating authority for daily decisions to the working level. It was this purpose which was noted above (pp. 65 ff.) as being the significance of the proletarian type of individualism. In 1935, Stalin proposed the slogan "Cadres decide everything," [8] and in

[8] Joseph Stalin, "Address Delivered in the Kremlin Palace to the

1939, he added that "after a correct political line has been worked out and tested in practice, the Party cadres become the decisive force in the leadership exercised by the Party and the state." [9] These are the considerations Mao had in mind concerning assignments to working-level cadres who implement party lines as specific work tasks, build mass line relationships, and report on performance.

To avoid cadre confusion concerning the order in which general policies are to be implemented, Mao specified that in the assignment of tasks higher departments should limit their contacts to counterpart lower departments, that leading cadres at each level be kept fully informed, and that higher organs assign only one priority task with clear rankings for secondary tasks. [10]

In assigning a task . . . to a subordinate unit [Mao wrote in "On Methods of Leadership"], the higher (party) leading group and its various departments should act through the main responsible person in the lower organization concerned, so that he can take on the responsibility of achieving a division of work with a unified purpose (a common denominator). [11]

Mao focuses here on the question of staff and line relationships within the cadre apparatus. Administrative and policy-command functions amalgamate in the apparatus, but Mao cautions cadres to maintain the central leadership priority of the policy function. A recent (1959) authoritative handbook written by the Central Committee's Organization Department has further clarified the role of policy control at each level in the apparatus through the

Graduates from the Red Army Academies," *Problems of Leninism* (Moscow: Foreign Languages Publishing House, 1954), pp. 660–661.

[9] Stalin, "Report to the Eighteenth Congress of the C.P.S.U. (B.) on the Work of the Central Committee," *Problems of Leninism*, p. 784.

[10] Mao, "On Methods of Leadership," pp. 115–116.

[11] "Kuan-yü ling-tao fang-fa ti jo-kan wen-t'i," *Mao Tse-tung hsüan-chi* [Selected Works of Mao Tse-tung] (Peking: Jen-min ch'u-pan she, 1951–1960), III, 922–923.

party committee at each respective level.[12] The manual reminds the reader that the party committee sets up departments to conduct its business. Departments such as the Organization Department, Rural Work Department, or Finance and Trade Work Department thus receive their policy direction from their committee for which they are the executive staff, not from their counterpart department at the higher levels. For example, one organization department does not *lead* or *direct* the work of lower-level organization departments. In Communist terms policy demands that there be only one "leadership relationship" for any particular body, even though for administrative convenience a higher organization department (or any other department) "may inspect the status of performance of party policies and resolutions by a similar department of [a] lower level party committee." The higher department, however, "has no right to make decisions or issue directives concerning problems involving policy or other vital problems concerning the work of a similar department of a lower level party committee." Leadership and policy flow through the "line" hierarchy of the party committees at the higher levels. "Staff" departments "watch the work of a similar department of a lower level party committee and . . . give concrete assistance and guidance to it" as well as study conditions, offer suggestions, sum up and exchange work experiences, and explain practical problems.

The party leading group maintains a mass line process with the working-level cadres, and the working cadres maintain a mass line process with the masses. To repeat the point made above in Chapter III, the first mass line becomes the model for the second.

[12] Chinese Communist Party, Central Committee, Research Office of the Organization Department, ed., *Tang ti tsu-chih kung-tso wen-ta* [Questions and Answers on Party Organization Work] (Peking: Jen-min ch'u-pan she, 1959), translated in *U.S. Joint Publications Research Service*, no. 7273 (1961), pp. 25–27. This discussion supplements the statements on the single chain of command of party groups in nonparty organs in Chapter IV, above.

For clarity, Mao labeled the first mass line as the party's line of organization or democratic centralism.

To make sure that it [the party's political line] does come "from the masses" and particularly that it does go "to the masses" [Mao wrote in 1945], close contact must be established not only between the Party and the masses outside the Party (the class and the people), but first of all between the leading bodies of the Party and the masses within the Party (the cadres and the membership).[13]

According to Secretary-General Teng Hsiao-p'ing, "Democratic centralism . . . is the fundamental organizational principle of the Party, the mass line in Party work applied to the life of the Party itself." [14]

Within the party, operational delegation of responsibility is governed by Article 25 of the 1956 Constitution, which stipulates how the functions and powers of the central and local party organs are to be divided:

All questions of a national character or questions that require a uniform decision for the whole country shall be handled by the central Party organizations so as to contribute to the centralism and unity of the Party. All questions of a local character or questions that need to be decided locally shall be handled by the local Party organizations so as to find solutions appropriate to the local conditions. . . .

Decisions taken by lower Party organizations must not run counter to those made by higher Party organizations.

The explicit purpose of this article is to allow appropriate administrative decisions to be made as low in the bureaucracy as possible in order to promote "the activity and creative ability of the lower organizations." [15] By analogy, functional delegation of authority is extended to the nonparty organizations and, as in the

13 Mao, "Appendix," p. 205.
14 Teng Hsiao-p'ing, "Report on the Revision," p. 187.
15 Ibid., p. 190.

party, has been identified as a key operational problem.[16] Because all cadres must operate within the rigid limits defined by the party's lines, leading cadres are enabled to delegate implementing, administrative, and technical responsibility, but no party level can delegate policy responsibility to nonparty cadres.

Policy authority is the single, clear standard which distinguishes the party cadres from the nonparty cadres at the working levels of government, the communes, the factories, and mass organizations. The mass line within the party is differentiated from the mass line between the party and the masses, therefore, not only by its locus of application but also by its substantive content. It is the distinction based on policy authority that requires the organizational precision provided by the principle of democratic centralism. Party leaders claim the right to limit policy making to those who share the intensive, intraparty relationship which provides special training, discipline, and advanced techniques of mass line operation. However, the line between policy and nonpolicy is continuously blurred by the pervasive character of politics in socialist construction. All decisions have a political character, and no position occupied by a nonparty cadre is logically exempted from the policy control of the party. All operational decisions inevitably gravitate to Communist Party cadres.

Communist Cadres and Party Policy

In 1956, the ratio of party members to party cadres [17] of and above the rank of *hsien* (county) party committee members

[16] Liu Shao-ch'i, "Report on the Work of the Central Committee," *Second Session of the Eighth National Congress of the Communist Party of China* (Peking: Foreign Languages Press, 1958), pp. 57–58.

[17] For an early account of cadre policy, see W. E. Gourlay, *Chinese Communist Cadre: Key to Political Power* (Cambridge, Mass.: Russian Research Center, Harvard University, 1952). A typical recent summary

was approximately 36 to 1 (10,734,384 to 300,000).[18] As the number of committees at the *hsien* level and above has changed because of the reduction in the number of *hsien* and the addition in 1961 of six regional bureaus, the figure of 300,000 cadres is undoubtedly inaccurate, though the possible error cannot be estimated. Added to these cadres are the cadres for the primary party committees, general branch committees, and branch committees. There were 1,060,000 branches in 1959, but no figures were published on the numbers or sizes of the branch committees, and party regulations do not require cadres at the branch level to be full-time committee members. Thus the party cadres may number between two and three million. These cadres are contrasted to the party rank and file, who do not hold leading positions in the party apparatus. The rank and file may be assigned to cadre posts outside the party in the government, mass organizations, communes, or factories, or they may be ordinary workers or peasants without official rank.

The definition of cadres, even party cadres, has been the subject of debate.[19] The precise definition of "cadres" (*kan-pu*) is difficult because the word, which can also be applied outside party circles, can mean "leader," "functionary," "responsible person," or "supervisor." But, even with respect to the party cadres, Communist usage of the term has been inconsistent. For example, in May, 1937, when Mao Tse-tung first examined the question of cadres at length, he distinguished cadres from "leaders" (*ling-hsiu*).[20] By 1938, however, apparently after reading Stalin's works on cadres, Mao began to talk about "leading

article on cadres is in *Hung-ch'i* [Red Flag], no. 12, June 16, 1962, pp. 1–13.

[18] Teng Hsiao-p'ing, "Report on the Revision," pp. 209, 220.

[19] The issue of the debate is whether or not the term "cadre" includes "leaders" of the party or is applicable only to the group between "leaders" and "rank and file."

[20] *Mao Tse-tung hsüan-chi*, I, 275–276.

cadres" (*ling-tao kan-pu*) and leading nuclei in organizations.[21] In general Mao's views on party cadres after 1938 came to coincide with Stalin's views, which were clearly expressed by Stalin's *Defects in Party Work and Measures for Liquidating Trotskyite and Other Double-Dealers* (March 3–5, 1937).[22] In this important report, Stalin divided the Soviet cadres into 3,000 to 4,000 "generals," 30,000 to 40,000 "commissioned officers," and 100,-000 to 150,000 "non-commissioned officers." [23]

As currently defined, a cadre is an official in a responsible or leading position within any organization, including the party, state, communes, army, factories, and schools. "A cadre," states an official handbook, "is someone who can be high or low, who can be an 'official' or a citizen, who can come from production, and return to production, who can lead the mass, or accept leadership from the mass." [24] Party cadres function through committees, departments, and offices and are ordered within a hierarchical system governed by a precise chain of command. Specific areas of activity are assigned to groups of cadres who also are individually charged with less comprehensive spheres of responsibility. Cadres at the production or "basic" levels stand on the lowest rung of the hierarchical ladder and have the critical task of transforming general policies into specific assignments for the general masses. Individuals become cadres by virtue of the position they hold, not because of their party membership or other personal qualifications. "A cadre is not a permanent profession; nor is he a special class." [25] Cadres perform all the leadership functions theoretically assumed by the proletarian vanguard. An idea of this central leadership role played by cadres was conveyed in a rather effusive way by *People's Daily* in 1960:

[21] *Ibid.*, II, 488–489; in the notes to this 1938 report, Mao cites Stalin, *Problems of Leninism*, pp. 644, 661, 784.

[22] Stalin, *Defects in Party Work* . . . (Moscow: Cooperative Publishing Society of Foreign Workers in the U.S.S.R., 1937), p. 27.

[23] *Ibid.*   [24] Chinese Communist Party, *op. cit.*, p. 29.   [25] *Ibid.*

For the sake of our splendid cause, they [the cadres] have even strained their eyes through sleepless nights. Their footprints can be found during violent rain or snow storms. . . . When the party says that tools must be improved, they will, together with the masses, improve tools. . . . When the party says that we must have a bumper harvest, they will put up tents in the fields. . . . If any person opposes socialism, they will immediately mobilize the masses to launch a clear-cut struggle against him. The party is the truth, and they are the personification of all truths.[26]

Thus party cadres are the responsible elements within the party apparatus who "get things done." "The cadres of the party," Liu Shao-ch'i said in 1945, "are the nucleus of the party leadership and of the Chinese revolution." [27] This cadre nucleus is substructured within the apparatus into leading cadres and working cadres (usually called "basic-level cadres" or simply "cadres" in the party press) along the lines suggested by Stalin in 1937. Common references to the cadre apparatus also divide cadres into "high, middle, and low levels." Commenting on the absolute requirement for leadership, an article in *Red Flag* stated that within the Chinese Communist Party "we have the party center and the leading organs at the different levels; the party Central Committee headed by Comrade Mao Tse-tung is the head of our party; the party committees at the different levels led by the first secretaries are the heads of the party organs at those levels." [28] The cadre nucleus forms the party leadership hierarchy which runs from the party branch committee at the lowest level through the levels of committees and standing committees and which culminates in the Central Committee and the Political Bureau. The cadre apparatus existed prior to the establishment of the party congress system. It determines the timing of all congresses and the bases of representation.

[26] *Jen-min jih-pao*, March 26, 1960.

[27] Liu Shao-ch'i, *Lun tang* [On the Party] (Peking: Chieh-fang she, 1950), p. 104.

[28] *Hung-ch'i*, no. 24, December 16, 1959, p. 14.

Some examples should help to clarify the cadre's position. The elected members of the committees from the basic level to the Central Committee are the leaders of the bodies which elected them and of all lower bodies. At the basic level, the branch membership elects a first secretary and his deputy secretaries who thus become cadres. Other branch cadres may be elected by the rank and file or appointed by the first secretary. The first secretary and deputy secretaries are the leading cadres for the rest of the committee, and the full committee is the leading body (*ling-tao chi-kuan*) for the general members of the branch. To handle clerical and administrative work of the party, several party or even nonparty personnel may be hired by the committee to work full time in the committee's departments or offices. Most of these are simply "functionaries" (*kung-tso jen-yüan*), and only the functionaries who head departments or offices qualify as cadres. If the branch first secretary is elected to the *hsien* (or municipal) committee, he then becomes also a "working" cadre of that committee, while remaining a "leading" cadre of the branch committee. In the unlikely event that a branch rank-and-file or working cadre member is elected to the *hsien* committee, he then becomes a leading cadre for the branch committee for interlevel matters and resumes his former status for intrabranch matters. The hierarchical ordering of cadres under the control of the organization department at each level presumably prevents such organizational entanglements of cadres, and these departments reportedly strive to utilize cadres efficiently and with the least impediment to operation.

The primary function of the cadre apparatus within the party is to make and supervise the implementation of policy. Democratic centralism requires that central directives promote and be integrated with "democratic" participation. This is "centralism on the basis of democracy." Policy is the broad decision made by leading cadres after, or at least theoretically after, consultation with working-level cadres and the rank and file. The constitutional definition of democratic centralism poses limits on the scope of predecision debate and on the kinds of alternatives which the rank-and-file party members and working cadres can propose and discuss (Art. 19). After decision, the effect must not be to terminate the participation begun in consultation but to encourage maximum participation within the policy guidelines and according to mass line leadership methods. In other words, policy is a general expression, but the manner of determining it makes it also a form of advanced approval for a wide latitude of implementing action. Where specific, detailed decisions at the top would tend to stifle initiative and would greatly tax the central leaders, general directives leave an important area of working cadre discretion which can provide a motivating challenge, a flexibility to meet local conditions, and a reduction of the burden on leading cadres. Equally significant, policies expressed in vague generalities preserve the aura of leadership infallibility by shifting the blame for the possible failures of (but not the credit for the success of) specific implementing decisions to the working levels.

"The leading body of the Party," Mao said in 1929, "must give a correct line of guidance and find solutions when problems arise, in order to establish itself as a leading centre." [29] To achieve this, "all resolutions and all regulations to be decided must be fully prepared and carefully examined by the leading cadres." [30]

[29] Mao Tse-tung, "On the Rectification of Incorrect Ideas in the Party," *Selected Works*, I, 109.

[30] Chung-kung chung-yang Hua-pei chü tang hsiao chiao-wu ch'u [Communist Party of China, Central Committee, North China Regional Party School, Education Office], ed., *Chung-kuo kung-ch'an tang tang-chang chiao-ts'ai* [Teaching Materials on the Constitution of the Communist Party of China] (rev. 3d ed.; Peking: Jen-min ch'u-pan she, 1951), p. 90. For an identical discussion on the 1956 Constitution, see Chung-kung Hu-nan sheng wei hsüan-ch'uan pu [Communist Party of China, Hunan Provincial Committee, Propaganda Department], ed., *Chung-kuo kung-ch'an tang chang-ch'eng chiao-ts'ai* [Teaching Materials on the Constitution of the CCP] (Changsha: Hunan jen-min ch'u-pan she, 1957), p. 45.

All party meetings are convened by leading cadres and led by those cadres.[31] Leading cadres absolutely determine the formulation of general policy directives. Without this determination, the party leaders assert, centralization would fall victim to "extreme democratization." As early as 1929, Mao denounced as extreme democracy the proposal of " 'democratic centralism from the bottom to the top' or 'ask the lower levels to discuss first, then let the higher levels decide.' " [32] Participant democracy must support centralized policy in a unified and disciplined way. "Democracy sometimes seems to be an end, but it is in fact only a means," Mao said in 1957. "Our democratic centralism means the unity of democracy and centralism and the unity of freedom and discipline." [33]

As the responsible echelon between the masses and the leading cadres, the "working" cadres seek out the information basic to policy and make the decisions to implement policy. They must make all the "democratic" decisions for effecting the general policy and for breaking policy into specific tasks.[34] If problems or conflicts arise, working cadres are, however, directed to request instructions from the higher party levels.[35] Working cadres have the continuous responsibility to conduct investigations, to surpervise implementation, and to submit reports on the results of their investigations and the implementation of assigned tasks. The basic directive for reporting was written by Mao in 1948.[36] This directive, which may have been superseded or modified since 1948, places the actual writing task on the first secretary of organs subordinate to the Central Committee for bimonthly reports covering definite military, political, land reform, party,

[31] Ibid.   [32] Mao, "On the Rectification," p. 108.
[33] Mao, On the Correct Handling, p. 15.
[34] Mao Tse-tung, "On Methods of Leadership," pp. 111–114.
[35] 1956 Constitution, Art. 19 (4); Teng Hsiao-p'ing, "Report on the Revision," pp. 191–192.
[36] Mao, "On Setting Up a System of Reports" [January 7, 1948], Selected Works, IV (Peking), 177–179.

economic, propaganda, and cultural headings; these are probably periodically revised and standardized throughout the party. The first secretary reports conditions, problems, and trends in a concise form limited to about one thousand characters. If reports are longer, separate regulations apply including regulations for special reports.

The key link in this information process is the working cadre (including the branch committee first secretary from the upper levels' point of view), who must act as a channel of the most sensitive kind. For cadres to fail in this respect would not only destroy the mass line but would stifle organizational leadership, which brings ideology and policy within the scope of administrative routine. By this routine, the trained Communist responses continuously pick out and resolve problems ("contradictions," errors, etc.). One of the serious cadre errors, therefore, is to fail to function effectively as a two-way communicator between the upper echelons and the broad masses. "It often happened that there were Party cadres who liked to make their particular department a little world of their own," Teng Hsiao-p'ing said with respect to the bureaucratic deviation of "departmentalism." [37] These cadres acted "according to their own ideas on political questions, disliked the Party's direction and supervision, and did not respect the decisions of higher organizations and the Central Committee." [38]

By the centralization of the movement and review of information, policies are kept up to date and over-all direction is maintained.[39] Yet in the total division of functions between leading cadres and working cadres, it would be a mistake to overemphasize the control aspect and to obscure the real strength of the operation of the principle of democratic centralism. The great strength and flexibility of Communist organization rests on the

[37] Teng Hsiao-p'ing, "Report on the Revision," p. 189.   [38] *Ibid.*
[39] Chung-kung chung-yang, *op. cit.,* pp. 87–88; Chung-kung Hu-nan sheng wei, *op. cit.,* pp. 43–45.

emphasis which the definition of democratic centralism places on the working cadres. This echelon has wide discretionary powers in transforming general policies into specific actions and in building the necessary tight relationship with the rank and file and, through them, with the Chinese people.[40]

Special directives set out in detail policies concerning cadre evaluation, selection, and promotion. The critical standard for judging cadres is their performance on the job.[41] In 1938, Mao propounded the line on cadre evaluation as follows: "The criterion should be whether a cadre is resolute in carrying out the Party line, observant of Party discipline, closely connected with the masses, capable of working independently, active and hardworking and self-denying; this is the line of 'employing only the worthy.' " [42] He argued this line in opposition to an "erroneous" line of "employing only the near and dear." [43] He added that the ability of cadres to conform to these standards depended in part on the adeptness of the leading cadres. "This means, on the one hand," Mao wrote, "to allow them [the working cadres] a free hand in their work so that they will have the courage to assume responsibilities themselves.[44] On the other hand, the leading cadres must give the lower-level cadres "timely directions so that they can put forth their creative power on the basis of the Party's political line." [45] Mao also emphasized cadre training to "raise their theoretical understanding and working ability to a higher level" and the checking up, assistance in summing up, and correction by leading cadres. When mistakes were found, Mao concluded, the method of persuasion was preferable to struggle,

[40] Mao, "On Methods of Leadership," pp. 111–113.
[41] By the twin techniques of "experimental farming" and "on-the-spot conferences" developed in the 1957–1958 rectification campaign, practical results of cadre performance can be directly ascertained and compared by leading cadres and the masses. See below, Chapter VII.
[42] Mao, "The Role of the Chinese Communist Party in the National War," *Selected Works*, II, 252–253.
[43] *Ibid.*, p. 253.   [44] *Ibid.*   [45] *Ibid.*

though later, as already brought out, persuasion was fused in the concept of inner-party struggle (see above, pp. 56 ff.). The essential point for the working cadre was unity in thought, action, and comradely relationship.

Although varied Communist reports emphasize the necessity for "promoting and fostering" cadres, the actual numbers of cadres selected and promoted and the sequence of promotion are not known.[46] In the party, most cadres are selected by election according to the principle of democratic centralism. "Anyone who is elected becomes a cadre; the one who fails to get elected should return to his productive post to participate in productive labor, and be a common laborer." [47] Several criteria for the promotion of cadres are given in the following Canton report, which is typical of many:

The outstanding cadres of proven ability with Communist consciousness and zeal for work who had been tested in the rectification campaign and trained in the great leap forward should be promoted to leadership posts. . . . We must persist in the criteria that all cadres must be Red and vocationally proficient.[48]

To gain a full picture of an individual cadre's merit for promotion, the leadership purportedly weighs its own judgment with the views and complaints of nonparty Chinese. According to Liu Shao-ch'i in 1945, the cadre is to be examined both by the leading cadres and by the rank and file.[49] The effective techniques for this rank-and-file examination, Liu stated, were criticism in

[46] In a 1959 article from Kansu, the following statistics were given: 10,000 cadres promoted in 1958 to be "leadership hard cores" (i.e., cadres at the senior levels), 30,000 transferred to lower levels (hsia-fang), and a "few" demoted "who did not prove equal to the situation of big leaps forward" (Kan-su jih-pao [Kansu Daily], March 10, 1959, in SCMP, no. 2036 [1959], p. 10).

[47] Chinese Communist Party, op. cit., p. 32.

[48] Nan-fang jih-pao [Southern Daily], May 28, 1959, in SCMP, no. 2075 (1959), p. 33.

[49] Liu Shao-ch'i, Lun tang, p. 118.

meetings, listening to periodic reports, and the machinery of election and nomination.[50] With respect to cadre "demotion," the more abundant information on the redistribution of cadres to lower levels (*hsia-fang*) will be examined in connection with rural leadership techniques (Chapter VII).

Democratic Centralism and the Chain of Command

The operation of the Communist Party in China has been analyzed in its theoretical complexities, as a code of action, and as a process of cadre decision making. One other important way of examining Communist Party leadership operation is as a chain of command. It is the chain of command function of democratic centralism which Secretary-General Teng Hsiao-p'ing had in mind in 1956, when he said that "what is of special significance is to correctly regulate relations between the Party organization and its members, between higher and lower Party organizations, and between central and local Party organizations."[51] In essence, the correct regulation of these relationships in party operation is a balance between the active participation of party members and central leadership command.

Stripped of the details, the party chain of command emanates from the Standing Committee of the Political Bureau under Mao Tse-tung and proceeds through the party committees at each major geographical division down to the branch first secretary who is in charge of his working cadres (see above, Chapter IV). Through the working cadres, the command system reaches out to the rank and file and the Chinese people. Command "levels" conform to geographical divisions from the national level to 6

[50] *Ibid.*, pp. 118–119.
[51] Teng Hsiao-p'ing, "Report on the Revision," pp. 187–188.

regional bureaus (since January, 1961),[52] 28 provincial (or the equivalent) committees, more than 2,000 *hsien* (or the equivalent) committees, and an estimated 1,000,000 branch committees. The basic interlevel system of command was discussed in Chapter IV with respect to party apparatus. The party Constitution summarizes the interlevel command as follows:

Party decisions must be carried out unconditionally. Individual Party members shall obey the Party organization, the minority shall obey the majority, the lower Party organizations shall obey the higher Party organizations, and all constituent Party organizations throughout the country shall obey the National Party Congress and the Central Committee [Art. 19 (6)].

Within each level, the Communists base chain of command on the principle of combining collective leadership with individual responsibility. Where democratic centralism primarily (though not exclusively) concerns command relationships of and between organizational units, collective leadership pertains to relationships among cadres within a unit. The practical ramifications of this principle were summarized by Mao Tse-tung in two party directives published in 1948 and 1949.[53] Mao in the 1948 directive, for example, stipulated the rules for systematically holding meetings and the necessity of advanced preparation of these meetings through "personal consultations." He explicitly warned that "neither collective leadership nor personal responsibility is [to be] overemphasized to the neglect of the other." Teng Hsiao-p'ing in citing this 1948 directive at the Eighth Party Congress (1956) condemned certain failings that violated the directive and were made more serious by the events surrounding the Twentieth Congress of the Communist Party of the Soviet Union and

[52] This restored a situation which existed prior to 1954.

[53] Mao, "On Strengthening the Party Committee System" [September 20, 1948], *Selected Works*, IV (Peking), 267–268; "Methods of Work of Party Committees" [March 13, 1949], *Selected Works*, IV (Peking), 377–381.

Stalin's "cult of the individual." [54] Teng denounced the practice of irregular and infrequent meetings and those meetings which were "mere formality." The latter, Teng reported, "neither give the participants a chance to prepare themselves beforehand . . . nor create an atmosphere conducive to free discussion at the meetings; hence decisions are virtually imposed on the members." [55]

An Tzu-wen, head of the Central Committee Organization Department, wrote in 1960 that proper utilization of the committee under the principles of democratic centralism and collective leadership required notice in advance of meetings so that later decisions not only would be made more feasible but could be promulgated on the supposition that meetings, consultations, and "mental preparation" of a democratic nature had been thoroughgoing.[56] Moreover, An singled out what is probably the most important function of the ideology in training members to respond to mass line leadership and to democratic centralism—the function of giving members of committees a common way of looking at problems or what Mao called a "common language" [57] for discussion and decision. "Collective leadership of the party committee presupposes a common language," An wrote, "and in order to seek the common language, much work has to be done." [58] In addition to exchange of information and regular meetings, An stressed the key importance of study "to raise the Marxist-Leninist level." [59]

Within committees, therefore, the party seeks to promote a special commonalty based on ideological training. The assumed counterpart of this ideological common denominator is constant

[54] Teng Hsiao-p'ing, "Report on the Revision," pp. 192–196.
[55] *Ibid.*, p. 195.
[56] *Hung-ch'i*, no. 24, December 16, 1960, pp. 12–13.
[57] Mao, "Methods of Work," p. 378.   [58] *Hung-ch'i*, p. 12.
[59] *Ibid.* Several Chinese interviewed in Hong Kong stated that the purpose of the Chinese Communist emphasis on collective leadership was to frustrate the growth of Soviet-style favoritism (*blat*).

commitment to party actions, a commitment which is reinforced by predecision discussion and consultation. Given this commitment and knowledge by committee members and theoretically by party rank and file, not only is responsibility delegated, but it is in theory also willingly and even eagerly accepted. In contrast to a system of command based on fear and rigid obedience, the Communists argue for command based on mutual respect born from knowing what to expect and from common involvement.

This responsibility is delegated, assumed, and centralized at each successive level. The individual working cadres have responsibility in specific areas of implementation and follow-up, while total-area responsibility is centralized in the first secretary of every branch and higher committee. It was in this sense that Mao Tse-tung in his 1949 directive compared the committee to the army squad (*pan*).[60] The squad leader manages his unit so that its work may be coordinated with that of all other squads. He is to his squad as his senior commanders are to him. His relationship to his commanders, moreover, by inference depends on the effectiveness of his relationship with his juniors. As in military planning, the squad (committee) must be regarded as uniform, with equal capabilities when compared to other squads. This is the critical importance of style of work and of systematic cadre training for "if the 'squad members' are not uniform in action, it is out of the question to lead millions of people to fight and construct." [61]

In the 1949 directive, Mao elaborated the basic committee "rules" which were compatible with the uniform command relationship within the "squad." Mao directed cadres "to place problems on the table" for discussion and itemized decision, to "exchange information" freely and reciprocally, and to ask the lower levels when things were not understood. They should be adept at using all resources to the best of their individual pur-

[60] Mao, "Methods of Work," p. 377.
[61] *Ibid.*; translation is made from the original Chinese.

poses and capabilities as when using ten fingers to play the piano, Mao cautioned.[62] "Grasp firmly" the essential, but do not forget the entire work. These were the hard-core principles on which party command would succeed, but Mao also reiterated some of his favorite themes regarding ideological and work method: "have a head for figures"; give advanced notice of meetings "to reassure the public"; "talks, speeches, articles and resolutions should all be concise and to the point"; unite with "comrades who differ with you"; "guard against arrogance"; and make analyses clearly distinguish between what is revolutionary and what is counterrevolutionary and then what is good or bad, first or second, within the revolutionary.[63]

These "rules" provide the context in which Mao's 1938 principles of command and discipline conform to democratic centralism. The 1938 principles, adopted from the Soviet Communist Party, are "(1) that individuals must subordinate themselves to the organisation; (2) that the minority must subordinate itself to the majority; (3) that the lower level must subordinate itself to the higher level; and (4) that the entire membership must subordinate itself to the Central Committee." [64] As restated in the present party Constitution (and quoted above, p. 196), these principles of obedience and subordination are tempered within each level in order to foster democratic participation and organizational solidarity.

The proper functioning of this system of command thus rests on a fine balance of participation and obedience, a balance maintained by "squad" unity in thought and action. It is evident that serious disagreement could strike far more quickly at an organization maintaining discussion, criticism, and delegated responsibility than at one in which central direction is complete and

[62] For a recent discussion of the "play the piano" work method, see *Hung-ch'i*, no. 20, October 16, 1961, pp. 15–20.

[63] Mao, "Methods of Work," pp. 377–381.

[64] Mao, "The Role of the Chinese Communist Party," p. 254.

one in which the leader's immunity is guaranteed by instruments of fear. As an organization for action, however, the delegation of responsibility within a "democratically active" organization has far greater potential for flexible, responsive creativity and, because of genuine commitment, a higher probability of survival in a crisis. It is action potential and survival probability which make the great effort to achieve actual ideological and behavioral unity within the Chinese Communist Party worth the gamble of disintegration before such unity is achieved. If it is to be genuine and permanent, moreover, this unity must be instilled and practiced under the most positive conditions rather than in an atmosphere of purge and fear. Fear would run counter to every principle of "command" given above and would inevitably lead to a basic distrust of the mass line system. This is not to say that the Communists in China within the party as in the society in general have not used secret police and terror, but their usage must be discreet, extremely selective, and progressively eliminated. It is in this light that the brilliance of ideological rectification in a spirit of self-reform becomes sharply focused, for it not only unites the loyal without overt constraint but also disastrously discredits any who become disloyal and subject to purge.

In 1945, Liu Shao-ch'i commented on the extreme importance of genuine internal unity if the particular command relationships within the party were to operate properly. He noted that class origin, party seniority, and kinds of assignments had created differences detrimental to this inner-party solidarity.[65] To correct this, Liu reiterated that the party was not "a family body or a trade guild." Its basis of unity must be common ideology and the party's political program. Steeled in this ideology and having faith in the line and program, cadres, Liu predicted, could overcome all lack of solidarity.[66] "The unity of our cadres is inseparable from their progress," Liu reminded the party. "They are two

[65] Liu Shao-ch'i, *Lun tang*, pp. 106–109.　　[66] *Ibid.*, pp. 108–109.

sides of the same thing." [67] In 1956, Teng Hsiao-p'ing stressed the continuing importance of this unity and urged members to "build a comradely relationship." [68] A united relationship was to be the foundation for democratically centralized command.

Some Conclusions on Party Operation

Unified Communist leadership combining flexibility, devotion, and centralized direction follows a conscious, staged scheme for the complex restructuring of Chinese society and every Chinese in it. The Communists believe that complex social goals require an equally complex method of operation. This operation comprises a code of action which is linked to the mass line, a process of decision making based on a cadre apparatus, and a chain of command closely integrated with the principle of democratic centralism. In practice, however, these abstracted elements of operation complement or supplement one another and form a dialectical synthesis of leadership technique and Marxist-Leninist ideology.

Amazingly successful in operation, Chinese Communist leadership incisively analyzes its own failings and strengths so as to prepare in the most comprehensive and realistic way for its vanguard mission. Current crises in agriculture only serve to reinforce the judgment that the Communist social experiment in China remains subject to unique internal controls in the hands of party leaders. Mass hunger and unfulfilled material objectives have apparently not yet weakened the ideological core of leadership in operation or provoked the masses to threaten or even to consider threatening seriously the all-encompassing paternalism of Communist cadres.

[67] *Ibid.*, p. 115.
[68] Teng Hsiao-p'ing, "Report on the Revision," p. 221.

A substantial portion of this discussion of Communist leadership has attempted to establish a clear picture of the Communist state of mind and the spiritual-conceptual charisma that surrounds party leadership. The unity of theory and practice pervades the emotional structure of Communist society to the extent that Communist cadres willingly devote unusual effort to the materialization of Communist principles. In theory, cadres have been indoctrinated to the point that the real world of China has for them become a dialectical cosmos.

Chinese Communist Party leadership subsumes all human activity within the legitimate scope of its operation and depends for its success on the cadre. The ideal of the unified party weapon reaches fruition in the party cadre who theoretically epitomizes the best in ideological insight and technical competence. None the less, obvious Communist successes in China should not blind us to the fact that party cadres have at times shown a marked proclivity toward bureaucratic lethargy and venality. In his story "A New Young Man Arrives at the Organization Department" (September, 1956), Wang Meng describes a factory manager of questionable morality who "never did anything but run around in circles, hide in his office and approve papers and play chess." [69] He further tells of the lives of young cadres enmeshed by Marxist-Leninist sophistry which conceals corruption and mismanagement and causes them to exclaim bitterly: "We party workers have created a new life but this new life is incapable of arousing us." [70] Similar stories of pompous, ill-trained cadres are repeated endlessly by refugees in Hong Kong. In the documents on rectification campaigns (see above, pp. 169–175) and in subsequent statements on the purging of certain cadres the Communists confirm the fact that many cadres have failed to match the vanguard ideal. Furthermore, by mid-1962 there could be

[69] *Jen-min wen-i* [People's Literature], September, 1956, in *Current Background*, no. 459 (1957), p. 7.
[70] *Ibid.*, p. 26.

no doubt that the party leaders were deeply troubled by the disillusionment spreading among the cadres and general population alike.[71]

Nevertheless, the party has demonstrated a remarkable capacity for self-criticism and internal reform. In fact, as noted earlier, the techniques of reform have served the leadership in a positive way by heightening training and commitment and "purifying" the ranks. To a remarkable degree, the highest echelons of the party have reacted to deepening crisis by even further reliance on proved operational techniques and their working cadres. Inner-party struggle reinforces operation by adding to organizational techniques a personal dimension which provides conscious motivation and self-correction to achieve the moral "character" of communism. Since 1956, when Wang Meng's story of party organization appeared, the party has come a long way in integrating ideological and operational techniques to account for weaknesses and crises and to exploit areas of potential support such as that among intellectuals, the youth, and the women. On the whole, the party has undoubtedly consolidated and strengthened its ranks by this integrating process.

[71] See above pp. 99–100. For typical recent Communist comment see *Jen-min jih-pao*, April 3, 1962, and *Hung-ch'i*, no. 6, March 16, 1962, pp. 1–7. At the Central Committee's Tenth Plenum in September, 1962, the party leaders paid unusual attention to the strengthening of the party control commissions, to the reliability of the army and security organs, and to erroneous thinking within the party (*Jen-min jih-pao*, September 29, 1962).

VII

Rural Leadership in Action

One Model Commune

IN order to get a clearer picture of rural leadership in practical operation, an examination will be made of the problems of a specific Chinese commune. The lessons derived from this commune's experience typify the lessons drawn by the party leaders from successful rural communes throughout China. Moreover, the lessons learned by rural leadership have in the past been directly applied to urban and industrial situations, and, in the main, urban cadres continue to take their cue from lessons and techniques developed in rural areas.

The village of Hsip'u, Hopei, is a cluster of 154 houses on the northern slope of Mount Changyu.[1] Located in Tsunhua *hsien*

---

[1] This section is based on *Chung-kuo nung-ts'un ti she-hui-chu-i kao-ch'ao* [Socialist Upsurge in China's Countryside] (Peking: Jen-min ch'u-pan she, 1956), I, 3–26; Hsinhua News Agency releases of December, 1960, and May, 1962, reprinted in *SCMP*, no. 2410 (1961), pp. 1–12, and in *SCMP*, no. 2741 (1962), pp. 15–16; *Kung-jen jih-pao* [Daily Worker], August 29, 1961, in *SCMP*, no. 2586 (1961), pp. 17–21; and Mao Tse-tung, *On the Correct Handling of Contradictions among the People*

(county) about eighty miles northeast of Tientsin and approximately ninety miles east of Peking, Hsip'u lies across a narrow valley from China's Great Wall. The farm land is hilly and rocky, and the climate is subject to extreme drought. In 1939, one out of three Hsip'u households was reduced to begging for food and clothing during a dry spell that lasted over 200 days, and all but eight or nine families lived on wild vegetables and the bark of trees. In good years, on the other hand, the Hsip'u peasants have grown maize, sweet potatoes, wheat, cotton, and some minor crops such as groundnuts, but even in years of relative abundance one out of ten persons in Hsip'u formerly begged for food each spring before the summer crops were harvested.

In sharp contrast, 1960 was reported to be a good year for Hsip'u despite a far more severe drought (more than 300 days) in North China than that of 1939. There were no beggars. All major crop yields in 1960 were higher than previous years, waste land had been reclaimed, and "from the interplanting practiced on 300 hectares, the results all round, in this terrible farming year, are outstanding." [2] This remarkable transformation of Hsip'u, the Communists assert, has directly resulted from the correct leadership of Communist cadres, particularly one leading cadre, Wang Kuo-fan.

In 1934, Wang, then 16 years old, ran away from poverty-stricken Hsip'u and joined the Communist revolution. Six years later, he was admitted to the Chinese Communist Party. After the Communist victory in 1949, Wang was offered the leading post in a *hsien*, but instead "he requested to be allowed to return home as a rank and file Party member and help in the transforma-

---

[February 27, 1957] (Peking: Foreign Languages Press, 1957), pp. 33–34. On the theoretical importance of "models," see *Jen-min jih-pao* [People's Daily], April 8, 1961.

[2] *SCMP*, no. 2410 (1961), p. 4. *Kung-jen jih-pao*, p. 17, reported that "production in 1959 was up 17 per cent, compared with 1958. Output of 1960 rose again 8.6 per cent over that in 1959. A higher production this year [1961] than last is predicted by the veteran peasants."

tion of his homestead." [3] In Hsip'u, Wang led the land reform confiscation and redistribution of "landlord" holdings and then organized mutual aid teams.[4] On December 15, 1951, the Central Committee of the Chinese Communist Party circulated the "draft decisions" on mutual aid and cooperation in agricultural production,[5] and after the autumn harvest in 1952, when Wang was informed by a higher party committee of these decisions, he led the formation of twenty-three households into a "lower-level" agricultural producers' cooperative.[6]

[3] *SCMP*, no. 2410 (1961), p. 11.

[4] In accordance with the Common Program of the Chinese People's Political Consultative Conference (September 29, 1949), the Central People's Government on June 30, 1950, promulgated the "Agrarian Reform Law of the People's Republic of China." This law basically conformed to the CCP Central Committee's "Basic Program for the Chinese Agrarian Law," passed on October 10, 1947. The text of the 1947 "Basic Program" is found in *Mu-ch'ien hsing-shih ho wo-men ti jen-wu* [The Present Situation and Our Tasks] (Hong Kong: Hsin min-chu ch'u-pan she, 1949), pp. 12–16. The text of the 1950 "Agrarian Reform Law" and "Decisions concerning the Differentiation of Class Status in the Countryside" are found in *The Agrarian Reform Law of the People's Republic of China* (Peking: Foreign Languages Press, 1950).

[5] From the description, Wang appears to have organized a permanent mutual aid team in contrast to a seasonal mutual aid team. For these distinctions and the text of the "Decisions on Mutual Aid and Co-operation in Agricultural Production" (officially adopted on February 15, 1953), see *Mutual Aid and Co-operation in China's Agricultural Production* (Peking: Foreign Languages Press, 1953), pp. 1–23.

[6] Generally, the lower-level agricultural producers' cooperative prepared the way for the advanced agricultural producers' cooperative. The lower-level form differed from the advanced form in that only the lower-level form allowed the peasant member to derive compensation proportionate to his share of land in the cooperative and for a limited time to retain title to land which he had pooled in the cooperative. The land reform eliminated the landlords, the transformation to the lower-level cooperatives (1951–1955) struck at the rich peasants, and the advanced cooperative movement in 1955–1956 was aimed at the middle peasants. In addition to the documents cited above, see *Co-operative Farming in China* [Central Committee decisions adopted on December 16, 1953] (Peking: Foreign Languages Press, 1954); Teng Tze [Tzu]-

The more than 100 members of this cooperative were the poorest peasants in the village, owning in total 230 *mou* (about 37.7 acres) of land but lacking carts, draft animals (except for a three-quarter share in the ownership of a donkey), and even farm tools. Before 1952, the government annually distributed grain and clothing for the relief of the Hsip'u peasants. The landless farm laborers were hired as coolies, and plowing was frequently accomplished by hitching three of these coolies to a primitive wooden plow. Thus, when the poorest of this destitute village banded into a cooperative, it was natural for it to be ridiculed as the "paupers' co-op."

The wretched conditions of the new cooperative reportedly began to show improvement after the five party members of the village met to discuss the future of Hsip'u. Under Wang Kuo-fan's instruction and the leadership of the other four party members, the peasants in the cooperative then assembled to plan a "diligent and frugal" operation that later so impressed Mao Tse-tung that he called for a similar tactic in all enterprises as part of a policy to make China prosperous.[7] To initiate this operation, the co-op needed money, and Wang organized the male members of the co-op under the vice-chairman to go into the next *hsien* to forage for wood which might be sold for cash. Wang and a woman party member, on the other hand, stayed

hui, *The Outstanding Success of the Agrarian Reform Movement in China* [April, 1954] (Peking: Foreign Languages Press, 1954); Mao Tse-tung, *The Question of Agricultural Co-operation* [July 31, 1955] (Peking: Foreign Languages Press, 1956); *Decisions on Agricultural Co-operation* [Central Committee decisions of October 11, 1955] (Peking: Foreign Languages Press, 1956); *The Draft Programme for Agricultural Development in the People's Republic of China 1956–1967* [January 23, 1956] (Peking: Foreign Languages Press, 1956); *Model Regulations for an Agricultural Producers' Co-operative* [March 17, 1956] (Peking: Foreign Languages Press, 1956); and *Model Regulations for Advanced Agricultural Producers' Co-operatives* [June 30, 1956] (Peking: Foreign Languages Press, 1956).

[7] *Chung-kuo nung-ts'un ti*, p. 16.

in Hsip'u and directed the co-op women in the collection of manure, the clearing of stones, and the mending of irrigation ditches. Three weeks later, the men returned with sufficient wood to purchase a cart, an ox, a mule, nineteen sheep, and some tools. Despite these auspicious beginnings, however, a series of calamities including near starvation harassed the co-op in its first year, but because of Wang's insistence the co-op members kept to the policies of economy and self-sufficiency. In spite of the poor first-year showing of the "paupers' co-op," sixty additional households were induced to join that year, and in its second year the cooperative reported abundant crops, a reserve fund, and a new spirit of collective morale. All households which were qualified to join (148 out of 154 households) [8] became members by the cooperative's third anniversary.

Wang's cooperative, officially called the Chienming Agricultural, Forestry, and Livestock-breeding Cooperative, became a model for Tsunhua *hsien*. The district (*ch'ü*) party committee organized educational tours during the slack season so that cadres could see the successful "paupers' cooperative." The visiting cadres were reportedly so impressed by Wang's efforts to raise money that after one tour thirty-eight cooperatives cut 2,300,000 catties (1 catty equals about 1.1 pounds) of brushwood which they bartered for implements and animals. Wang, moreover, was elected to the National People's Congress and was called upon to describe his experiences in articles which appeared in *People's Daily* and *Red Flag*.[9] After the Central Committee's Resolution on the Establishment of People's Communes in the Rural Areas (August 29, 1958), thirty-three cooperatives in Tsunhua *hsien* merged into one commune, and the members of

[8] Former landlords, rich peasants, and certain other categories of peasants were forbidden to join the cooperatives during the initial period of their establishment. See *Model Regulations for an Agricultural Producer's Co-operative*, Art. 11 (3) and (4).

[9] See, for example, his article praising the communes in *Hung-ch'i*, no. 17, September 1, 1959, pp. 26–30.

the commune adopted the name of the paupers' co-op, "Chien-ming," and elected Wang the commune director.

According to Communist reports, the Chienming commune has continued to prosper under Wang's guidance, and the pace-setter for the commune has remained the "paupers' co-op," now called the Hsip'u Production Brigade. Four out of five of its 3,000 hectares of farm land can be irrigated. Seventeen tractors and other farm machinery (including 7 trucks) are used on 70 per cent of the land. The commune has radio facilities and a telephone system which links all 125 villages in the commune. One out of four of the commune's 4,700 families now owns a bicycle. The commune has six new factories employing 800 workers, a winery, a synthetic ammonia plant, two or more work-shops for each of the forty-three production brigades of the commune, a vast irrigation and reservoir system, and over 200,-000 *yüan* (approximate 1962 exchange rate for non-Communist countries is 2.45 *yüan* for one U.S. dollar) in bank deposits. The commune has both a grain reserve for emergencies and a surplus to sell to the government. For the 25,000 people in the commune (who are organized into 100 production teams), libraries, schools, and various service and entertainment facilities have been estab-lished. Although the success of the Chienming commune hardly typifies China's crisis-ridden communes,[10] the progress of this model commune is impressive and provides the kind of example which the Communist Party is attempting to duplicate in all of the more than 25,000 communes in the rural and urban areas.[11]

[10] An example of an official statement on the agricultural crisis is the communiqué issued at the Central Committee's Ninth Plenum, the text of which is in *Peking Review*, no. 4, 1961, pp. 5–7.

[11] There is now some question as to the actual number of communes in China. In 1958, the 740,000 agricultural producers' cooperatives averaging 160 households were combined into 26,425 communes averag-ing 4,614 households. After the 1959 "amalgamation and reorganization" the number was reduced to "over 24,000" communes averaging about 5,000 households. In early 1960, the movement for urban people's com-

In commenting on the Wang Kuo-fan cooperative in 1957, Mao Tse-tung told the Supreme State Conference: "What this co-operative could do, other co-operatives should also be able to do under normal conditions, even if it may take a bit longer. It is clear then that there are no grounds for the view that something has gone wrong with the co-operative movement." [12]

Five direct leadership lessons may be drawn from the experience of the paupers' co-op and commune. The most obvious, but none the less critical, lesson is that party leadership in its model form is specific, concrete, and practical. It capitalizes on common sense and collective effort. A second leadership lesson, "get organized," may also be abstracted from the collective action and Wang Kuo-fan's coordinating direction. Collectivity and direction, though essential ingredients of organization, do not, however, fully convey the picture of organized interaction between cadres and common Chinese, which, as will be seen in the next section, has also been a vital lesson to be derived from the party's rural experience. The third lesson is that during adversity Communists should stick to what they believe is correct. Those who sing the praises of Wang Kuo-fan stress that his tactics for maintaining the correct line were based on his persuasiveness. No hint concerning the use of pressure is given, though Wang's policy of self-sufficiency may have justified force had the starvation level been reached during the first crucial year of the Hsip'u co-op. Fourth, the Communists evidently assume that lessons similar to those which are drawn here may be taken from situations of success and failure. They believe that ideal, universal principles of leadership exist and that these principles can be discovered by alert leadership personnel in the "summing up" of experiences. Those leadership lessons which "truly" reflect the universal principles can be independently transferred to other

_____

munes became active, and by July, 1960, there were reportedly 1,027 urban people's communes.

[12] Mao, *On the Correct Handling*, p. 34.

situations and must therefore receive the widest possible publicity. Finally, the fifth lesson, which by now should require little elaboration, is that leadership depends completely on the cadre who is willing to take responsibility and *consciously* abide by the correct leadership principles.

Rural Party Organization

The Communists assert that the key to the success of the Chienming commune was political leadership, the dedicated leadership of Wang Kuo-fan and a few subordinate cadres.[13] The transformation of the "paupers' co-op," the Communists point out, was marked by opposition and discontent, but in the end "correct" leadership of the party was vindicated. In view of the poverty existing in Hsip'u, what other than party leadership, they seem to say, could account for this remarkable development of the co-op, and what other than a new system of Communist leadership could create a sufficient number of successful communes to revolutionize China's agriculture, which since late 1959 has been termed the "foundation of the national economy." For the agricultural revolution, the Communist Party of China has staked its hopes on the leadership of its rural cadres and has given priority to their political organization.

The cadre organization for rural work in China is an administrative and control chain that emanates from the Standing Com-

[13] The general "tone" of this section regarding the vital role of rural party organization is based on An Tzu-wen, "Further Strengthen the Leadership Function of the Party's Organization in Communes" (in Chinese), *Hung-ch'i*, no. 24, December 16, 1959, pp. 1–8; Hsü Pi-hsin, "On the Basic System of Rural People's Communes at the Present Stage" (in Chinese), *Hung-ch'i*, no. 15–16, August 10, 1961, pp. 27–38; and Hsü Pang-i, "Bring into Fuller Play the Role of Rural Basic-Level Party Organizations as Cores of Leadership" (in Chinese), *Hung-ch'i*, no. 20, October 16, 1961, pp. 21–25.

mittee of the Political Bureau under Mao Tse-tung to small party groups working among the masses. The organizational core is the party group which directs and controls counterpart government and technical administration. At the commune levels, the functional departments of the party and government have in many cases been merged under party leadership as shown by Chart 4, which presents the basic leadership hierarchy for rural policy making and administration.

Chart 4 omits many of the more complex (though less essential) aspects of the organizational hierarchy, particularly the representative and supervisory bodies at each of the commune levels. Newly restored regional bureaus (on which detailed information is lacking),[14] various intermediate administrative levels,[15] and variant titles for levels and names of organizations have not been included.[16] On the other hand, Chart 4 does include information on the hierarchy which does not necessarily apply uniformly to all parts of China; for example, party branches may be established at the team or brigade levels in accordance with the size of the party membership in the commune.

With these qualifications in mind, Chart 4 shows the general organizational structure for rural policy making and administration. The party "side" of the chart illustrates the hierarchy of

[14] The communiqué of the Ninth Plenum of January 20, 1961, cited above (n. 10), stated that the Central Committee had decided to set up six regional bureaus and thus restore a condition which had existed from 1949 to 1953. See above, Chart 3, p. 129.

[15] The most important "intermediate level" is the special district (*chuan-ch'ü*), which groups together several *hsien*.

[16] For example, in some rural areas there are nationality autonomous districts or *hsien*, leagues (*meng*), and special types of communes. Moreover, the departments in the various levels of government are given variant titles. Especially confusing have been the different Chinese names for the production brigade (now standardized as *sheng-ch'an ta-tui*, though in some 1959–1960 directives and articles called *sheng-ch'an tui*) and the production team (now standardized as *sheng-ch'an tui*, though in some 1959–1960 directives and articles called *sheng-ch'an hsiao-tui*).

Level	Party apparatus		Governmental apparatus	
	Policy making	Policy supervision	Policy implementation	General administration
National	Standing Committee of Political Bureau Political Bureau	Secretariat Rural Work Department	Agriculture and Forestry Office Ministries and commissions	State Council
Provincial	Standing committee of provincial party committee	Secretariat Rural Work Department	Agriculture and Forestry Department	People's Council
Hsien	Standing committee of hsien party committee	Secretariat Rural Work Department	Agriculture and Forestry Department	People's Council
Commune	Commune committee	Functional departments	Functional departments (some merged)	Commune administrative committee
Production brigade	General branch committe			Brigade administrative committee
Production team	Branch committee			Team administrative committee
Work group	Party group		Section and work group chiefs	

Sources: 1956 party Constitution, 1954 state Constitution and various organic laws, and documents on the people's communes. The terminology used is based on Hsü Pi-hsin, "On the Basic System of Rural People's Communes at the Present Stage" (in Chinese), *Hung-ch'i*, no. 15–16, August 10, 1961, pp. 27–38.

policy and staff bodies organized to formulate and supervise guiding political tasks. As defined, the mass line method requires a mutual interaction between levels and a movement of information up the channels and across from government bodies to the party departments and standing committees. According to *Red Flag*, "party organizations in the rural people's communes (the party committees of the communes and the party general branches and branches below) are the rural basic-level organizations of the party and the cores of leadership over rural work," [17] and these commune-level party organizations have the central mission of detailing and guiding the tasks set by the higher leadership. Their dictum is Mao's 1948 statement: "To be good at translating the Party's policy into action of the masses, to be good at getting not only the leading cadres but also the broad masses to understand and master every movement and every struggle we launch—this is an art of Marxist-Leninist leadership." [18] Policy determined at higher levels, however, sets limits on that leadership art. "Basic-level party organizations may not edit or revise policies of the party center at will," *Red Flag* warns, "but they may, according to concrete local conditions, adopt suitable measures for ensuring their implementation." [19] The working cadre takes the risk of balancing central policy with local situations.

The party develops its leadership role within the communes through the commune administrative committees, the Young Communist League, and the women's and militia organizations. Particularly important are the commune's three levels of administrative apparatus detailed in Chart 4. Party cadres must "not try to take over the work of the administrative committees at

[17] Hsü Pang-i, *op. cit.*, p. 22.
[18] Mao Tse-tung, "A Talk to the Editorial Staff of the *Shansi-Suiyuan Daily*," *Selected Works* (Peking: Foreign Languages Press, 1961), IV, 242–243.
[19] Hsü Pang-i, *op. cit.*, p. 23.

these levels . . . [but] should regularly discuss and inspect the work of the congresses or conferences of communes, the administrative committees, and the supervisory committees at the corresponding levels." [20] The party in conjunction with commune members and nonparty cadres studies matters of joint importance such as "production, the livelihood of the masses, the enforcement of state policy and law, and the execution of state plans." [21] The party then formulates policy opinions for consideration and approval by the commune congresses or conferences, the administrative committees, and the supervisory committees.

The textbook separation of party and state should not be misleading, however. The high percentage of government cadres who are party members or at least "activists" prevents the government hierarchical chain from being considered simply "technical administration and implementation." In reality, of course, policy making and administration are an interwoven process, and technical matters are also considered by the party while policy questions are discussed in government organs. In general, however, the Chinese Communists strive to maintain the party committees as "political planning boards" charged with the investigation and study of major problems of policy and with general supervision while the government organizations are responsible for the "routine and concrete financial and administrative matters." [22] At each level, leading cadres supervise the work of counterpart government councils, committees, or departments, with the governmental bodies in charge of technical policies and planning estimates and routine clerical matters according to state laws and economic plans.

[20] *Ibid.*, p. 24.   [21] *Ibid.*

[22] See *Jen-min jih-pao,* December 24, 1958, and Liu Lan-t'ao, "The Communist Party of China Is the High Command of the Chinese People in Building Socialism," *Ten Glorious Years* (Peking: Foreign Languages Press, 1960), pp. 283–297.

People's Daily in December, 1961, carried a typical story exemplifying the pattern of techniques for commune party committees.[23] The story lauded the committee for Chihsieh commune in Kiangsu Province, a commune committee which had first solved the internal relations of the committee itself. The committee cadres initially determined the individual responsibilities of committee members. Of first priority was who would be responsible for what level of problems so that no one could "pass the buck." The members decided that only the most important questions would require plenary meetings for decision and that both the party committee secretary and the members should bring up important problems. One committee member, who held the concurrent post of commune leader, contended that collective leadership required each committee member to become personally familiar with topics to be discussed and to form his own opinions by consulting commune agencies and the masses prior to the scheduled meeting. Only through the "hot debate" of adequately prepared members could the proper decision be reached. After the decision had been approved by the proper commune bodies, then the party committee members would supervise implementation and control performance and reporting through their lower cadres and through the administrative arms of the commune.

As evidenced by this example, party supervision is camouflaged by the fact that party and government personnel frequently are the same people or have been merged into a single department. Although the overlapping of personnel is most evident at the highest and lowest levels, as illustrated by Charts 5 and 6, there is no reason to doubt a consistent overlapping of cadres at all levels. For example, at the provincial level (or the equivalent) 23 out of 27 known governors (or the equivalent) are Communist Party members, and of those, 13 are members or alternate members of the Central Committee.[24] In a typical report

[23] *Jen-min jih-pao*, December 14, 1961.
[24] Figures are compiled from *Biographic Information*, no. 2, May 9,

Chart 5. Overlapping of leading personnel concerned with agriculture at the national level, 1962

Party	Government
Rural Work Department.	*State Council Agriculture and Forestry Office*
Teng Tzu-hui, director *	Teng Tzu-hui, director *
Liao Lu-yen *	Liao Lu-yen *
Ch'en Cheng-jen *	Ch'en Cheng-jen *
Wang Kuan-lan †	
	T'ao Huan-fu†
	Wang Kuang-wei †

	Ministry of Agricultural Machinery	*Ministry of Agriculture*	*Other ministries concerned with agriculture*	*State Planning Commission*
	Ch'en Cheng-jen, minister *	Liao Lu-yen, minister *		Wang Kuang-wei, vice-chairman †

* Indicates member or alternate member of the Central Committee.
† Indicates member of the Chinese Communist Party.
Source: Biographic Information, no. 2, May 9, 1962.

of a production brigade in Shensi Province, "25 of the 28 party members hold such posts as the chief of the brigade, chief of a production team, accountant, or custodian." [25]

The merging of party and government organs is prohibited at all levels except for the departments at the commune level and below.[26] It is only in certain departments concerned with tech-

1962. The governor of Fukien Province is unknown.

[25] *Jen-min jih-pao,* January 11, 1962.

[26] *Sixth Plenary Session of the Eighth Central Committee of the Communist Party of China* [November 28–December 10, 1958] (Peking: Foreign Languages Press, 1958), p. 44. For an authoritative description of the merging of the governmental and commune organizations, see *Kung-jen jih-pao,* November 24, 1961, in *Current Background,* no. 677 (1962), pp. 17–20. The way in which the *Kung-jen jih-pao* article is worded suggests that the merger of government and commune had not been completed in many areas by late 1961.

nical matters that the criterion of the merger, the strengthening of the party's leading role, allows the unification of party and government departments. According to *People's Daily*, "party committees and commune administrative committees have not been united as one. Only certain departments of party committees and the corresponding departments of communes are united under the unified leadership of the party." [27] The responsibility for deciding on any merger rests with the party committee of the commune. Although the *People's Daily* article approved of mergers to strengthen direct party leadership over economic and cultural undertakings, it stipulated that such mergers were to be selective and of course excluded "departments concerned merely with the work of the party."

At the second Chengchow Conference of February, 1959, the party designated the production brigade (sometimes called "administrative district") as the basic level of ownership and accounting.[28] In a quiet retreat of late 1961 and early 1962, the production teams became the basic level of ownership, accounting, and distribution, as well as the basic production level. De-

[27] *Jen-min jih-pao*, December 24, 1958.

[28] For a description of the various conferences on the communes, see *Hung-ch'i*, no. 5, March 1, 1960, pp. 1–15. The Resolution on Some Questions concerning the People's Communes (December 10, 1958) identified the commune, brigade, and team levels as the basic administrative levels. See *Sixth Plenary Session of the Eighth Central Committee*, p. 40. During the last three months of 1960, the importance of the "three-level system of ownership" with the brigades as the foundation was emphasized in scores of articles which also underlined the need for incentives and mass activism. For examples of the 1960 changes, see *Nan-fang jih-pao* [Southern Daily], September 16, 1960, in *SCMP*, no. 2365 (1960), pp. 12–15; *Jen-min jih-pao*, December 3 and 21, 1960; *Chung-kuo ch'ing-nien pao* [China Youth News], December 1, 1960, in *SCMP*, no. 2423 (1961), pp. 1–5; and *Kung-jen jih-pao*, December 20, 1960, in *SCMP*, no. 2423 (1961), pp. 5–8. On the shift in emphasis from the brigade to the team in December, 1961, see *Hung-ch'i*, no. 23, December 1, 1961, p. 30, and the discussion below on party leadership in production teams.

spite these critical substantive changes in rural organization, however, the three key levels in the communes remain the production team, the production brigade, and the commune.[29] For cadre purposes, the work group level under the production team has also been identified as a fundamental level for policy implementation and production. Above the four commune levels of cadres, there are five senior cadre levels: *hsien*, special district (not shown on Chart 4), provincial, regional (not shown on Chart 4), and national. For rural policy, these nine levels constitute the cadre chain of command and are basic to conferences of cadres which are commonly identified by the number of levels of cadres participating.[30]

At the commune, production brigade, and production team levels, the apparatus of party leadership varies sharply according to the size and type of commune. This structural variety is to be expected when a fishing village commune on Mayi Island in Chekiang Province has only 586 families, while others may have tens of thousands of member households.[31] In general, Vice-Premier Li Hsien-nien in 1958 noted two basic structural differences in the communes: (1) a single commune for a whole *hsien* or (2) several communes in one *hsien*.[32] To adjust to the variations in size and scope of the communes, the keynote has been organizational flexibility, though generally for party purposes the commune has been considered the "primary party organiza-

[29] For a discussion of the specific functions of the administrative bodies at each of these levels, see Hsü Pi-hsin, *op. cit.*, pp. 31–34.

[30] For examples of such conferences, see *Kuang-hsi jih-pao* [Kwangsi Daily], September 30, 1959, in *SCMP*, no. 2158 (1959), pp. 32–36; *Kan-su jih-pao* [Kansu Daily], November 15, 1959, in *SCMP*, no. 2184 (1960), pp. 22–28; and *Jen-min jih-pao*, April 22, 1960.

[31] The original commune resolution of August 29, 1958, stated that communes could range from "less than 2,000 households," to "more than 20,000 households." On the Mayi Island commune, see Hsinhua News Agency release of April 28, 1960, in *SCMP*, no. 2260 (1960), pp. 18–20.

[32] *Peking Review*, no. 37, 1958, p. 12.

tion" [33] with a party committee in command of a hierarchy of general branches, branches, and party groups (see above, pp. 136–139).[34]

In one model commune in Honan Province, the party committee at the commune level had one secretary, one to three deputy secretaries, and thirty-seven members.[35] From this commune party committee, a standing committee of fifteen members was created to handle the daily work of the commune. In production brigades general party branches were established with a leading cadre, one to three deputies, and seven to nine members in each. The deputies were placed in charge of various production activities run by functional departments. Such departments included trade and finance, organization, propaganda, women's work, and rural work. Party branches or party groups were set up at the production team levels if the size of the party organization justified it.

Redistribution of Rural Cadres

The mass line working style places a premium on the points of direct contact between the cadres and the Chinese people. To combat bureaucratism, Liu Shao-ch'i at the Eighth Party Congress on September 15, 1956, advocated efforts to "help functionaries to change such ways of work as busying themselves exclusively with holding meetings and signing documents with-

[33] On primary party organizations, see the 1956 party Constitution, chap. VI.

[34] See, as an example of this, sec. 3 of the Chinese Communist Party Provincial Committee of Hopei Province directive on building people's communes (August 29, 1958) in *Hung-ch'i*, no. 8, September 16, 1958, pp. 14–16.

[35] Tseng Hou-jen and Feng Hsing-hua, "The Birth of Ch'ao-ying People's Commune," *Chung-kuo nung-pao* [Chinese Agriculture], no. 17, 1958, in *ECMM*, no. 149 (1958), p. 47.

out contacting the people or studying the relevant policies and the actual situation." [36] Liu's proposals for visits by responsible government personnel to subordinate levels as an antibureaucratic measure may be considered the beginning of the *hsia-fang* (lit.: to go to the lower levels) movement which has reshaped organizations and leadership techniques since 1957. In the directive issued on April 27 ,1957, to rectify the working style of the party,[37] the Central Committee of the Chinese Communist Party instructed leading personnel at all levels in the party, government, and military service to "devote part of their time to engaging in physical labour with the workers and peasants." [38] In a separate directive on physical labor (May 14, 1957), the Central Committee further stated that "in principle, all the Communists, irrespective of their position and seniority, should assume similar and equal work as ordinary labourers." [39] The same directive struck at superfluous staff personnel "not engaged in actual production in production units, in Party committees, governments and people's organisations, at basic levels," and called for reduction with the object of "having no staff member who is completely removed from production." [40] Above the basic level all superfluous members in organizations were directed to "return to production." [41]

The number of cadres required at the cooperative level or the commune levels (after August, 1958) alone would probably have necessitated redistribution of cadres such as occurred under the 1957 directives in order to prevent the critical production-level organizations which were then proliferating and undergoing

[36] Liu Shao-ch'i, "The Political Report," *Eighth National Congress of the Communist Party of China* (Peking: Foreign Languages Press, 1956), I, 75.

[37] Text in *Hsinhua News Agency Release*, May, 1957, item 043055, pp. 10–12.

[38] *Ibid.*, p. 11.

[39] *Ibid.*, item 051421, pp. 120–121; quotation from p. 121.

[40] *Ibid.*   [41] *Ibid.*

collectivization from becoming staffed by the least-experienced cadres or from being not staffed at all. As an example of the numbers of cadres involved at the three commune levels (commune, brigade, and team), Kwangtung Province in 1960 reportedly had 100,000 commune cadres, 300,000 production brigade cadres, and 600,000 production team cadres for 30,000,000 peasants.[42] If these same proportions of cadres to peasants (1 to 30) hold for all of China's 500,000,000 peasants, then there should be approximately 17,000,000 cadres in China at the three levels of the rural people's communes. To fill such lower-level cadre requirements as well as to supervise production and train cadres, two major systems for the distribution of cadres, both called *hsia-fang*, have been utilized since 1957. The first system constitutes a permanent reorganization based on reductions of higher-level staffs by transfers to the lower levels; the second is a temporary *hsia-fang* during which cadres are expected to receive production training, to solve concrete problems, and to supervise production.

The permanent *hsia-fang* involves the transfer of higher-level cadres and functionaries to the *hsien* and commune (or factory) levels. Those transferred usually are assigned to deputy leadership posts or to posts of leadership in organizations without cadres. An example of this permanent transfer to the lower levels took place in 1960 in Tsinnan district, Shansi Province, from which "over 40,000 leadership cadres . . . joined forces in the production teams, and over 16,000 leadership cadres served as deputy team leaders and business managers of mess halls." [43] Transfers for permanent, "long term," or indefinite periods have affected all organizations in China. For example, in Honan all levels of the province transferred cadres to the *hsien* levels and below,[44] and in three areas of Hunan 25,251 cadres were sent

[42] *Nan-fang jih-pao*, November 30, 1960, in *SCMP*, no. 2415 (1961), p. 3.
[43] *Jen-min jih-pao*, August 24, 1960.   [44] *Ibid.*, November 18, 1960.

from the communes and brigades to production teams.[45] The Canton party committee and people's councils in 1958 dispatched over 20,000 cadres or about one-third of the cadres in the city to industrial and rural production, though it is not clear how many of these were scheduled to return to their former posts.[46] In general, most provinces have reported "the transfer of large numbers of Party members and cadres from leadership posts at higher levels to leadership posts at the basic level." [47] It has usually been the "backward" brigades or teams to which cadres from the *hsien* or above have been assigned to fill such posts as production team leaders or party branch secretaries, although most of the transfers have been for specified lengths of time and thus fall into the second category of temporary *hsia-fang*.

The temporary transfer usually involves one year or less of the cadre's time. Although the permanent *hsia-fang* appears to have been revived in 1962 as part of a general organizational retrenchment in China,[48] the temporary form of *hsia-fang* probably remains the most significant type of cadre redistribution. Lacking a perspective on the 1962 changes, on balance the major proportion of permanent transfers still apparently occurred in the years from 1957 to 1960. The "excessive number of personnel in the Party and government organs" were then substantially reduced in what Teng Hsiao-p'ing called "the simplification of organization and reduction of non-productive personnel." [49] As a current leadership technique, the temporary *hsia-fang* for train-

[45] *Hsin Hu-nan pao* [New Hunan], March 21, 1959, in *SCMP*, no. 2036 (1959), pp. 13–18.

[46] *Kuang-chou jih-pao* [Canton Daily], September 27, 1959, in *SCMP*, no. 2152 (1959), p. 26.

[47] *An-hui jih-pao* [Anhwei Daily], October 30, 1959, in *SCMP*, no. 2152 (1959), p. 20.

[48] *Jen-min jih-pao*, July 21, 1962.

[49] Teng Hsiao-p'ing, *Report on the Rectification Campaign* [September 23, 1957] (Peking: Foreign Languages Press, 1957), pp. 55–56.

ing and production supervision is not only more important per se but also has had wide ramifications in the systematization of leadership techniques since 1960.

Quantitatively, the extent of the temporary *hsia-fang* is impressive. *Red Flag* on January 16, 1960, reported that "in the past two years [1958–1959], almost 1,300,000 cadres have been sent down for participation in physical labor by rotation." [50] In addition, the party dispatched 257,700 cadres in 1959 alone to engage in physical labor for an entire year.[51] At the "production levels," the cadres have participated in construction, farm labor, and political work in order "to strengthen the contact between the cadres and the masses . . . [and] to raise the mass and labor viewpoints of the cadres." [52] The *hsia-fang* cadres must supervise production by giving "encouragement to the workers" and facilitating "the timely discovery and solution of problems." [53] While superintending production, moreover, cadres are expected to look after the livelihood of the masses and assist in setting up schools, medical clinics, and well-run mess halls.[54] Generally speaking, cadres are first directed to "change their ideological aspects, strengthen their labor viewpoint, mass viewpoint, collective viewpoint and class viewpoint" [55] and then are considered capable of attaining "successes which otherwise would not have been possible." [56]

In the assignment of organizational targets for the *hsia-fang*, the Chinese Communist Party has placed a high priority on areas without cadres or organizations which have failed to meet production standards. In a *hsien* in Anhwei Province a more sys-

[50] *Hung-ch'i*, no. 2, January 16, 1960, p. 36.
[51] Hsinhua News Agency release, January 17, 1960, in *SCMP*, no. 2184 (1960), p. 9.
[52] *Hung-ch'i*, no. 2, January 16, 1960, p. 33.
[53] *Jen-min jih-pao*, January 14, 1961.
[54] Hsinhua News Agency release, January 17, 1960, in *SCMP*, no. 2184 (1960), p. 11.
[55] *Ibid.*, p. 10.   [56] *Ibid.*

tematic coverage is indicated, however, since every commune in this *hsien* reportedly has at least two party *hsien* committee members, every production brigade has a minimum of two commune committee members or cadres of equivalent standing, and every team has a production brigade party general branch member or a government cadre of equivalent rank.[57] These cadres are required to remain at the lower levels for "comparatively long periods," and they must conduct investigations in person, circulate higher-level directives in person, "take part in their enforcement in person, and solve in time whatever problems might arise." [58] The advantages seen in this method of direct, personal supervision of production by higher-level cadres are the rapid, practical implementation of policies, the training of cadres in the importance of policies, and the correct enforcement of party policies according to the "time and local conditions." [59] This direct supervision is designed to arouse the enthusiasm of the peasants and to educate the cadres in the meaning of leading the Chinese people in a concrete way, rather than by abstract edicts.[60]

To demonstrate the effectiveness of party leadership and the party's policies during their stay at the production levels, cadres utilize two important methods, both of which are also available to cadres permanently stationed in the production teams. These two methods are the experimental farm and the on-the-spot conference. The experimental farms were first devised in Hupei Province in 1957–1958,[61] and by the spring of 1958, some 1,151 out of 1,470 cadres at all levels of Hungan *hsien* in Hupei were

[57] *Jen-min jih-pao*, January 14, 1961.   [58] *Ibid.*   [59] *Ibid.*
[60] *Ibid.*

[61] This discussion of experimental farms is based on *Jen-min jih-pao*, February 15, 1958, and An Jo, "T'an shih-yen t'ien" [Talk about Experimental Farms], in Chang Yu-yü *et al.*, *Hsüeh-hsi Mao Tse-tung ti szu-hsiang fang-fa ho kung-tso fang-fa* [Study Mao Tse-tung's Thought Method and Work Method] (Peking: Chung-kuo ch'ing-nien ch'u-pan she, 1958), pp. 126–131.

cultivating these special plots of land. In one area of Hunan Province in 1959, there were 98 per cent of the party members engaged in cultivating either "high-yield fields" or experimental plots.[62] In these special plots reserved for the cadres, training and leadership are clearly dramatized for the benefit of the masses. Cadres must experiment with modern techniques and by the visible evidence of their high yields can thus induce the peasants to adopt more progressive farming methods. On one experimental farm in Liaoning, for example, the plots held by cadres produced from one to seven times the yield of "ordinary" plots of land.[63]

As a combination of the mass line method and the *hsia-fang*, the experimental farms are designed to promote the highest possible cooperation among leading cadres, technical personnel, and the peasants. The experimental farms provide "red and expert" training through the combination of theory and practice [64] and conform to Mao Tse-tung's system of creating typical experiences and linking the general to the specific.[65] In commenting on the 1,300,000 cadres who had undergone *hsia-fang* by rotation in 1958 and 1959, *Red Flag* noted that

the commonest form [of physical labor] is to direct production while participating in it. Many cadres are working shoulder to shoulder with peasants and agricultural personnel on experimental farms. This is one way of coordinating techniques with practice in labor, and experimentation with the experience gained in abundant agricultural production.[66]

[62] *Hsin Hu-nan pao*, March 21, 1959, in *SCMP*, no. 2036 (1959), p. 13.

[63] Hsinhua News Agency release, January 17, 1960, in *SCMP*, no. 2184 (1960), p. 10.

[64] *Jen-min jih-pao*, February 15, 1958; Liu Shao-ch'i, "Report on the Work of the Central Committee," *Second Session of the Eighth National Congress of the Communist Party of China* (Peking: Foreign Languages Press, 1958), p. 62.

[65] Mao Tse-tung, "On Methods of Leadership," *Selected Works*, (New York: International Publishers, 1954-1956), IV, 111-117. See above, pp. 178-183.

[66] *Hung-ch'i*, no. 2, January 16, 1960, p. 36.

In 1960 and 1961, the experimental farm was superseded in many (but not in all) areas by the use of the so-called "work models" (*kung-tso chung ti tien-hsing*) [67] as supplemented by the revitalized emphasis on mass line techniques [68] and on a "holistic" approach [69] to problems under two earlier slogans, "grasping both ends to lead the middle" and "dissecting the sparrow." [70] As reported in *Red Flag* some areas in 1960 developed the "bumper-production fields" (*feng-ch'an fang*) system "on the basis of experimental plots and the commune movement." [71] These fields were typically run by "cadres, technical personnel, and experienced farmers" and were larger than the experimental farms. By the summer of 1960, for example, one-third of the total farm-land acreage in Shansi Province was allocated to these fields which had become large enough to be treated as integrated farms.[72] Promotion of these fields was combined with a general 1961 campaign to propagandize "work models." The spate of articles on the "paupers' co-op" was part of the general campaign to grasp the universal principles of representative advanced models. According to *People's Daily:*

[67] Two important articles on "work models" are in *Jen-min jih-pao*, April 8, 1961. See also *ibid.*, April 29, 1961. These "work models" are also associated with the well-known Communist Stakhanovite principle of promoting advanced persons. See, for example, *The National Conference of Outstanding Groups and Workers in Socialist Construction in Industry, Communications and Transport, Capital Construction, Finance and Trade* (Peking: Foreign Languages Press, 1960).

[68] On the mass line, eight out of the last twelve issues of *Hung-ch'i* in 1961 carried at least one major article on the mass line. See *Hung-ch'i*, no. 24, December 16, 1961, index, p. 1. For a more recent article emphasizing the mass line, see the lead editorial in *Jen-min jih-pao*, May 23, 1962, which was written to commemorate the twentieth anniversary of Mao Tse-tung's "Talks at the Yenan Forum on Art and Literature."

[69] See the major article on the "general viewpoint" by Sha Ying in *Jen-min jih-pao*, January 3, 1962. See also above, p. 61, n. 82.

[70] These two slogans are authoritatively discussed in Chang Yu-yü et al., *op. cit.*, pp. 121–125, 138–141.

[71] *Hung-ch'i*, no. 12, June 16, 1960, pp. 22–25.

[72] *Ibid.*, p. 22.

A model thing has an objective existence. However . . . we must not only penetrate the masses to discover it . . . but also must foster it properly. . . . The fostering of a model is absolutely not the production of a man-made model [but] . . . means helping a thing which has already a model significance to develop further so that it may become more representative. [With proper fostering and popularization] . . . a model can [then] serve as a general guide.[73]

The same article inferred that experimentation was no longer sufficient to create a model. As a growth from the experimental farm technique, work models add the dimensions of continuous experimentation on a large scale and general applicability. Only thus could the experimental farm technique become part of the general mass line process of "experiment, summation, popularization, further summation, and further popularization."

The on-the-spot conference is linked both to the cadre *hsia-fang* and to experimental or model farms. After the achievement of a production success in the experimental farms, for example, "meetings were held on the spot to inspect the work, compare the results, and debate and summarize the experiences." [74] In 1959, in one area of Liaoning Province, "responsible cadres . . . held 152 on-the-spot conferences while working on experimental farms . . . and succeeded in teaching the broad masses the true meaning of close planting." [75] Party cadres advocate holding on-the-spot conferences to promote advanced "work models." [76] The on-the-spot conference, popularized in the summer of 1958, is a working conference that has been moved "from the capital to localities, from cities to the countryside and from offices to on the spot." [77] These meetings have been convened at the location of production difficulties, and their aim has been to present the crucial points at issue to those who can make immediate authoritative decisions.

[73] *Jen-min jih-pao*, April 8, 1961.   [74] *Ibid.*, February 15, 1958.
[75] Hsinhua News Agency release, January 17, 1960, in *SCMP*, no. 2184 (1960), p. 10.   [76] *Jen-min jih-pao*, April 8, 1961.
[77] *Ibid.*, June 23, 1958. This issue of *Jen-min jih-pao* carries the basic

What one hears and sees here are living facts. One can hear, see, do, and discuss things at the same time. Using their eyes, ears, hands, and minds at the same time, the conferees are animated and contented. In a few days they solve problems, including ideological problems, practical problems, and technical problems.[78]

Such was the Communist answer to paper work and red tape until 1961, when a general campaign to reduce the number of meetings, reports, and organizations forced a reduction in all on-the-spot conferences except those called to promote "advanced experiences." [79]

Until 1960, the principal form of the temporary *hsia-fang* was physical labor for one month each year, though for a limited number of cadres periods up to a year at the production levels were not uncommon.[80] Then, in 1960, the forms of the *hsia-fang* were dramatically proliferated. For example, *hsia-fang* periods became longer,[81] whole offices were moved from the *hsien* to the production levels,[82] and there was renewed emphasis on the livelihood of the masses and on cadre mass solidarity with slogans of "togetherness," [83] "sameness," [84] and "special liveli-

document concerning on-the-spot conferences.

[78] *Ibid.*   [79] *Ibid.*, May 16, 1962.

[80] Hsinhua News Agency release, January 17, 1960, in *SCMP*, no. 2184 (1960), pp. 9–11.

[81] For example, see *Jen-min jih-pao*, June 13, 1960.

[82] Hsinhua News Agency release, June 21, 1960, in *SCMP*, no. 2287 (1960), pp. 22–23; *Jen-min jih-pao*, November 26, 1960.

[83] Under the "four togetherness" system, the cadres must eat, live, labor, and consult with the masses. For examples, see Hsinhua News Agency release, July 4, 1960, in *SCMP*, no. 2294 (1960), pp. 10–11, and *Jen-min jih-pao*, November 22, 1960. Frequently this system is expanded to the system of "four togetherness and five love" which combines the "four togetherness" with an earlier "three love" (love of country, commune, and labor) slogan and two new "loves," study and research. See, for example, *Jen-min jih-pao*, November 20, 1960.

[84] For example, there is the "five sameness" movement. Under this system, cadres eat the same meals as ordinary commune members, they engage in the same kind of physical labor, their work points are assessed

hood days." [85] But the real breakthrough in the multiplication of *hsia-fang* forms came in the summer of 1960 with the so-called "2-5 system," began in Wuch'iao *hsien*, Hopei.

The "2-5 system" allots two days each week for cadre administrative work and study and five days for participation in and supervision of production.[86] The days of the week are arranged as follows:

Monday. *Hsien*-level cadres develop work schedules for the week while the commune and brigade cadres study.

Tuesday. Commune and brigade cadres examine the weekly schedules and arrange the production work. *Hsien* cadres study.

Wednesday through Sunday. All cadres go to the production teams with three or four days at "fixed points" and one day in general supervision. Schedules are arranged so that *mornings* are spent in the examination of production, *daytime* is used for manual labor with commune members, and *evenings* are spent assisting production team cadres in their study.

The fulfillment of this system is the responsibility of the *hsien* party committee secretary. The immediate product of the system is the reduction in the number of conferences, documents, and bulletins, but the reduction of cadre office time has simultaneously created secondary administrative difficulties which require solution. For example, to prevent the cadres from running back and forth to their offices, staff personnel are warned not to recall their cadres, and if emergencies arise, these personnel are directed to telephone the cadres or go themselves to the lower levels. Administrative simplification is also achieved

---

and recorded in the same manner, they receive the same wages, and their dependents are accorded the same treatment. See, for example, *Jen-min jih-pao*, November 16, 1960.

[85] For example, there is the "secretaries' livelihood work day." See *ibid.*, November 4, 1960.

[86] The basic documents on the "2-5 system" are found in *ibid.*, June 16, 1960. These documents are the basis of the discussion here. See also above, p. 163.

by cadres from different departments who "do work together at the lower levels" and cooperate on projects of mutual interest.

The "2-5 system" is the epitome of the systematic mass line. "This system combines the experience of the 'experimental plot,' the 'on-the-spot conference,' and cadres taking part in productive labour, etc.; it enriches, elaborates and systematizes this experience; it makes possible for the cadres to be at the front line most of the time." [87] At the "front line" of production, the cadres have four key tasks: (1) to become "efficient chiefs of staff for the production teams and help train basic-level cadres"; (2) to carry out crucial "projects properly, set up examples, sum up and popularize advanced experiences, and bring about a double leap forward in central work and functional work"; (3) to serve as examples; and (4) to publicize and report on party policies. In fulfilling these four major tasks, cadres are exhorted to become "five good" cadres with good personalities, good working style, good production work, good results in study, and a "good" concern for the masses. [88]

Although the "2-5 system" can be varied to account for differences in communes, the method basically applies only to non-mountainous communes for the *hsien*-level cadres and below. Because of the difficulties in traveling to the mountainous regions, the "3-7 system" (three days in administrative work and study and seven days at the basic levels) has been adopted in these areas. [89] At the levels above the *hsien*, particularly for cadres at the provincial and administrative district levels, the so-called "3-3 system" is used. [90] The requirements of this system are as follows:

One third of the cadres of a public organ are stationed at basic-level production units and participate in and supervise production. . . .

[87] *Peking Review*, no. 31, 1960, p. 16.
[88] *Jen-min jih-pao*, June 16, 1960.
[89] *Ibid.*, June 16 and July 5, 1960.
[90] See, for example, *ibid.*, November 19, 1960.

Another one-third of the personnel are required to go deep into the lower level to conduct mobile inspections, while the remaining one-third of the personnel remain in the office to handle daily routine.[91]

These three fundamental systems ("2-5," "3-7," and "3-3") have been further modified in numerous localities to form a vast diversity of subsystems. Examples of such subsystems, which need not be detailed here, might be the "one-responsibility, one-specialization, one-learning, one-meeting, three-investigation, two-examination systems" (which would be referred to as the "1-1-1-1-3-2 system"); "1-1-3-2 system" ("one day for conferences, one day for study, three days for experimentation at selected sites, and two days for universal promotion"); "one-quota and one-specialization system"; "ten-in-the-fields system"; "three-coordination system"; "1-2-3 system"; "1-3-2 system"; and "1-4-7 system." [92] A patient student could compile more than 100 such variations of and additions to the three basic systems for redistributing rural cadres for maximum leadership effectiveness. Moreover, the current inventory of systems continuously changes, and even the three fundamental systems dropped out of the news in 1961. Eventually, however, party leaders expect to discover the magic combination of mass line systems and techniques which will permit cadres to solve their rural tasks properly and efficiently.

Party Leadership in Production Teams

Party leadership in the rural areas succeeds or fails by the way production cadres, both those who are permanently assigned and those rotated from the higher levels, attend to the daily business of mass guidance and farming. Production teams became the basic level of rural accounting and production in the

[91] *Ibid.*   [92] *Ibid.*, June 16 and July 13, 1960.

winter of 1961–1962 and in 1962 were further designated as the basic distribution and ownership units. Both ownership and accounting formerly centered on the production brigade, while the team shared the responsibility for distribution and production with the brigade. The consequent shift of power to team cadres met serious resentment among brigade and commune cadres who were left with vague powers to coordinate plans, to urge cooperation among teams, and to organize ideological indoctrination. In the words of one brigade cadre in Kwangtung Province, brigade cadres became mere "propagandists and collectors." [93] Voicing the frustration of many brigade cadres deprived of the power to control accounts and food distribution, this cadre added: "When there is no rice in your hands, even the chickens will not come to you." [94] Despite these objections, the production team will continue to exercise the key powers in rural China. Thus it will perhaps be easiest to understand the nature of rural leadership techniques by turning to individual production teams where cadres experience the mundane frustrations and earthy tasks of the Chinese peasant.

The No. 6 Production Team, Huangyang Production Brigade, Erhpa People's Commune in Kansu, for example, is composed of twenty households with 108 persons and 510 *mou* (about 84 acres) of land.[95] According to the Communist categories of social class, the twenty households are divided as follows: one ex-landlord, two rich peasant, four middle peasant, and thirteen former hired hand or beggar households. In this group, 14 out of the 108 team members are classified as cadres, while 36 are qualified as "able-bodied producers." Of the 36,

[93] *Nan-fang jih-pao*, April 8, 1962, in *SCMP*, no. 2733 (1962), p. 16.
[94] *Ibid.*, p. 17. *Nan-fang jih-pao* responded to this cadre with a series of letters and articles, some of which are found in *SCMP*, nos. 2733 (1962), 2758 (1962), 2771 (1962), 2772 (1962), 2774 (1962), and 2782 (1962).
[95] This discussion is based on *Jen-min jih-pao*, November 10 and 19, 1960.

15 men and 12 women are "fully able-bodied," and 9 men and women are "semi-able-bodied." In addition, there are 20 people over 60 years of age, 13 of whom are over 65. This production team was chosen in late 1960 as a model organization for the production teams of China.

Chart 6 presents the basic organizational structure of the No. 6 Production Team. The leadership nucleus of the team particularly stands out in the chart. The five party members and one youth league member have three of the five positions on the production team committee and constitute the central core which rallies the three groups of activists (the "four advisers," "three rear-service officers," and "five vanguards") and controls all areas of team life, including the crucial mess hall control committee and the trade and finance office. Chart 6 further illustrates the lines of direction and control from the team party members, Young Communist League, and Young Pioneers through overlapping membership in the various committees and groups to every person in the No. 6 Production Team.

In theory, the general membership meetings of the commune, brigade, and team levels elect their own cadres through secret voting procedures.[96] The party press—in contrast to a considerable amount of refugee information—reports that voting is lively and that after active discussion the participants choose those most qualified rather than individual favorites. In the eyes of party leaders, this election process constitutes a mutual pledging of support between elector and elected.

Knowing that the masses had placed the burden of the family on their shoulders, the cadres worked harder than before to guide the production of the commune members. The commune members, while recognizing the fact that it was they who had elected the cadres, actively extended their support and assistance to the cadres.[97]

[96] *Kung-jen jih-pao,* July 8, 1961, in *U.S. Joint Publications Research Service,* no. 10237 (1961), pp. 74–76.
[97] *Ibid.,* p. 76.

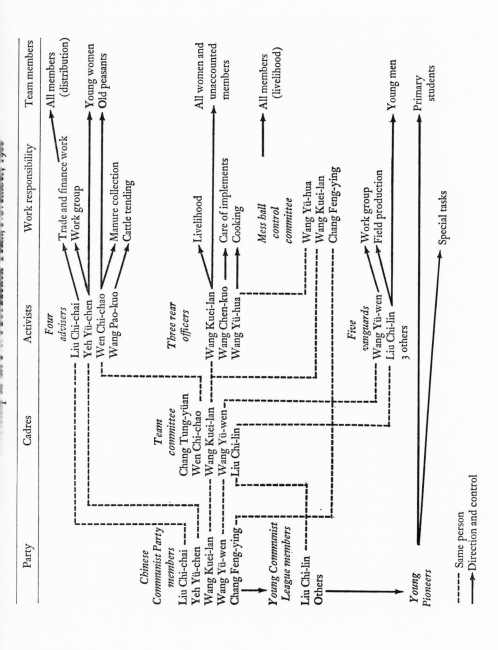

Party	Cadres	Activists	Work responsibility	Team members
Chinese Communist Party members Liu Chi-chai Yeh Yü-chen Wang Kuei-lan Wang Yü-wen Chang Feng-ying	*Team committee* Chang Tung-yüan Wen Chi-chao Wang Kuei-lan Wang Yü-wen Liu Chi-lin	*Four advisers* Liu Chi-chai Yeh Yü-chen Wen Chi-chao Wang Pao-kuo	Trade and finance work Work group Manure collection Cattle tending	All members (distribution) Young women Old peasants
Young Communist League members Liu Chi-lin Others		*Three rear officers* Wang Kuei-lan Wang Chen-kuo Wang Yü-hua	Livelihood Care of implements Cooking *Mess hall control committee* Wang Yü-hua Wang Kuei-lan Chang Feng-ying	All women and unaccounted members All members (livelihood)
Young Pioneers		*Five vanguards* Wang Yü-wen Liu Chi-lin 3 others	Work group Field production Special tasks	Young men Primary students

- - - - - Same person

———▶ Direction and control

The election of team cadres theoretically epitomizes the successful operation of democratic centralism and is a key mass line function. Because of an election's central role in maintaining the leadership line, *People's Daily* in 1961 equated this election process to the importance for the family of selecting a good son-in-law.[98]

Despite this grandiose self-appraisal, Communists insist that the party must rigidly control the actual election machinery. The team committee given in Chart 6 is composed of "representatives" reportedly elected from the three groups of activists with the approval of the party. Chang Tung-yüan, the team leader, is neither a party member nor an activist but is a respected "old peasant" who has been nominal leader since the formation of a mutual aid team in 1952. The team committee convenes daily at lunch to discuss the implementation of new instructions. Every five or seven days, it meets again and frequently invites the activists to help study directives, work out operation plans, examine production problems, and promote new techniques. Through these activists, the leadership transmits the weekly production plans to the work groups and the masses.

Chart 7 presents additional detail on team organization, particularly the work group divisions under the field management and production sections. This chart of the Tengchiatienchungtien Production Team, Lutou People's Commune in Hupei Province, incorporates information from basic party directives and demonstrates the assignment of party and Young Communist League members to the key points in the team organization. Of significance is the fact that the only known party member of the team takes charge of technical innovations which are prerequisites for revolutionizing China's agriculture.[99] An aspect

[98] *Jen-min jih-pao*, May 20, 1961.

[99] As an example of the emphasis on techniques, see *ibid.*, September 21, 1960.

Chart 7. Team organization of the Tengchiatienchungtien Production Team

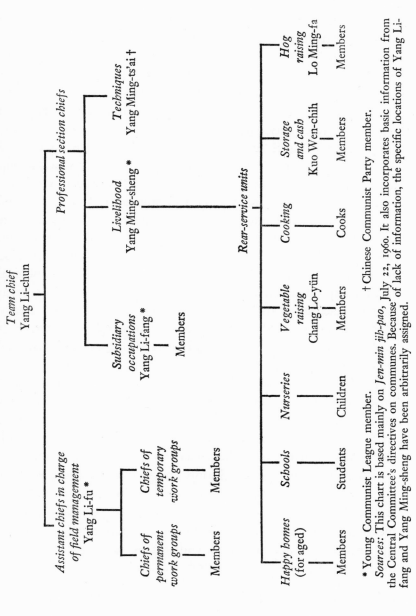

Team chief
Yang Li-chun

Assistant chiefs in charge of field management
Yang Li-fu *

Chiefs of permanent work groups

Members

Chiefs of temporary work groups

Members

Professional section chiefs

Subsidiary occupations
Yang Li-fang *

Members

Livelihood
Yang Ming-sheng *

Techniques
Yang Ming-ts'ai †

Rear-service units

Happy homes (for aged)

Members

Schools

Students

Nurseries

Children

Vegetable raising
Chang Lo-yün

Members

Cooking

Cooks

Storage and cash
Kuo Wen-chih

Members

Hog raising
Lo Ming-fa

Members

* Young Communist League member.   † Chinese Communist Party member.

Sources: This chart is based mainly on *Jen-min jih-pao*, July 22, 1960. It also incorporates basic information from the Central Committee's directives on communes. Because of lack of information, the specific locations of Yang Li-fang and Yang Ming-sheng have been arbitrarily assigned.

of production team organization evidenced by Charts 6 and 7 is the strategic location of single families. In the No. 6 Production Team, related members of the Wang family (not just individuals with the surname "Wang") appear in all parts of the hierarchy, while in the second team (Chart 7) the Yang family predominates. In still another production team in Kiangsu which received national recognition in 1960,[100] moreover, the team leader is Liu So-chin. His first elder brother is a secretary of the party branch, his second elder brother is a work group leader, his fourth younger brother is an "advanced worker," and his two sisters are Young Communist League members. For a team of 105 households, it is highly revealing that this single family has attained such a pervasive leadership position. The "proletarian" relationships among family members must be assumed to be of an order different from the strictly neutral relationships dictated by Communist ethics. Although a great deal of research is still required to demonstrate the prevalence of family-dominated leadership at the production levels, it is probable that at this level Confucian concepts of "relational leadership" have found considerable tacit support.

The interlocking lines of leadership illustrated by the No. 6 Production Team augment the flexibility of the team management. In theory, however, this management must be conducted with the approval of the commune members' meeting which the leaders usually convoke twice each month. The meeting, which may be postponed during heavy work seasons, reviews work accounts, sums up production results, confers rewards, and makes arrangements for the work groups. This general meeting also selects a mess hall control committee which governs the distribution, accumulation, and storage of food, the disposal of team pigs, chickens, and rabbits, and the use of kitchen gardens.

[100] *Ibid.*, July 19, 1960. For information on other typical teams run by single families, see *ibid.*, April 28, 1961, and January 11, 1962.

The utilization of all productive labor in the team theoretically requires adherence to such "Communist" management principles as using special skills, tapping all available sources of manpower including the aged and primary school students, and allocating men and tools to given tasks with special priorities and time limits. Arrangements are reportedly made for rest periods, which may be used to earn extra wage points. Team organization must be "rationally" devised rather than developed from the "free association" of the members.[101] "Free association" allegedly denies party leadership, threatens discipline, and "may produce loopholes."[102]

In the management of personnel, team cadres must abide by the principles of "three guarantees and one reward"[103] and "four fixed."[104] Under the first of these two principles, the teams guarantee the amount of work done (labor efficiency), the production output, and the production cost and are rewarded by additional wage points for the overfulfillment of their quotas. The "four fixed," on the other hand, means that each production team will have a fixed share of farm land, manpower, draft animals, and farm tools in order to meet the quotas. The "three guarantees" and "four fixed" therefore constitute a kind of contract in Communist terms whereby each side stipulates certain assurances which may then be taken for planning purposes by the other side. The labor regulations of each team allot quotas of work points based on a generalized assessment of each person's ability, and workers earn these points according to the quantity and quality of the work accomplished. For example, in the No. 6 Production Team, the able-bodied men

[101] *Ibid.*, July 22, 1960. In 1962, increased emphasis was placed on the rational use of manpower. See *ibid.*, April 10 and May 26, 1962.

[102] *Ibid.*, July 22, 1960.

[103] For example, see the series of articles in *SCMP*, no. 2413 (1961), pp. 1–17.

[104] For example, see *Nan-fang jih-pao*, October 28, 1960, in *SCMP*, no. 2401 (1960), p. 8.

must receive 270 work points per month, semi-able-bodied men 180 work points, able-bodied women 230 points, and semi-able-bodied women 150 work points. Under some plans,[105] the laborer must work a certain number of days each month at a specified rate of output in order to fulfill his wage-point norm. In some teams,[106] wage points are assigned and earned on a team basis alone which maximizes group effort and collective responsibility. The work of each team receives a close inspection once in ten or fifteen days. With the 1959–1962 economic—particularly farm—crisis has come ever-increased preoccupation with frequent examinatons of product quality, labor norms, and wage-point registration.[107] According to *People's Daily*, strict examination and routine control procedures represent "the practical operation of the mass line" and must therefore involve mass self-examination as well as the scrutiny of specialists.[108] In addition, shock groups are frequently organized, and cadres exhort members to overfulfill quotas voluntarily.[109]

Although movements to emulate the production performance and personal characteristics of "model" cadres and workers[110] and to overfulfill quotas[111] have had a key part in team leadership, the Communist Party currently advocates financial arrangements to accelerate production.[112] Unlike most state-owned

[105] *Jen-min jih-pao*, January 18, 1961; *Nan-fang jih-pao*, December 16, 1960, in *SCMP*, no. 2414 (1961), p. 9.

[106] *Jen-min jih-pao*, January 18, 1961.

[107] For typical articles on commune examination and control, see *ibid.*, July 20, August 11 and 19, and September 6, 1961.

[108] *Ibid.*, September 6, 1961.

[109] *Ibid.*, July 22 and November 10, 1960.

[110] For a typical series on the emulation of model cadres, see *SCMP*, no. 2285 (1960), pp. 21–29. See also above, n. 67.

[111] See n. 109.

[112] This discussion is based on *Jen-min jih-pao*, August 8, 1960, and January 18, 1961; a series of articles on "differential distribution" in *SCMP*, no. 2405 (1960), pp. 1–15; and an important collection of articles on commune finances (wages, costs, taxation, banking, and accounting) in *U.S. Joint Publications Research Service*, no. 11957 (1962), pp. 103–141.

factories, commune wages, which are at the heart of the financial system, are not fixed or distributed on a regular monthly basis but are drawn from a variable consumption fund. This fund, from which each peasant derives his income (distributed according to labor accomplished), constitutes the amount of money left "after deducting the agricultural tax, the essential production expenses, the administrative expenses, the reserve fund, and the welfare fund." [113] Commune cadres may manipulate wages and funds, varying peasant income within each year, among communes, and within communes and commune levels. Briefly, the cadres pay each member in advance for work to be completed during the coming month or two-month periods. For overfulfillment of quotas additional wage points are earned, though movements for turning "extra" points over to the mess halls and for depositing "additional" wages in the commune banks are frequent. Moreover, the sale of produce and animals grown on "private plots" is rigidly controlled by the system of "trade fairs" at which the list of marketable goods and prices is regulated in favor of the state.[114] Failure to meet assigned

[113] *U.S. Joint Publications Research Service*, no. 11957 (1962), p. 108. One exasperating aspect of Chinese Communist propaganda is its condemnation of the United States or unnamed "capitalists" for actions or statements which become honorable and proper when incorporated in Communist programs. For example, *Hung-ch'i*, no. 5, March 1, 1960, pp. 19–27, denounced the old family system in which the peasants "first had to guarantee payment of rent and taxes and only afterward could calculate what is needed for one's family's daily life." The variable consumption fund similarly deducts the state portion before people may withdraw their living wage. Articles in 1962 warned against excessively liberal distribution (*Jen-min jih-pao*, May 10, 1962).

[114] On private plots, see, for example, *Nan-fang jih-pao*, December 23, 1960, in *SCMP*, no. 2418 (1961), pp. 4–10, and *Nan-fang jih-pao*, December 28, 1960, in *SCMP*, no. 2429 (1961), pp. 7–11. On trade fairs, see, for example, *Jen-min jih-pao*, November 25, 1960; *Nan-fang jih-pao*, December 28, 1960, in *SCMP*, no. 2421 (1961), pp. 1–3; *Ta-kung pao* [Impartial] (Peking), February 20, 1961, in *SCMP*, no. 2460 (1961), pp. 10–14; and *Jen-min jih-pao*, March 14, 1961. A summary of the first year of trade fairs is in *Ta-kung pao*, January 19, 1962, in *SCMP*, no. 2675 (1962), pp. 12–14.

quotas, on the other hand, makes the member liable for severe group criticism and for all the wages which the commune "overpaid" him in advance—overpaid sums, that is, which have already gone to feed the delinquent member's family. The wage points earned, the investments made, and the advance pay obtained by each team member are recorded as permanent parts of the personal file for each member, and cadres periodically scrutinize these files to judge each member's contribution to the commune.[115]

The principle of "democratic" participation further extends the scope of party and cadre leadership.[116] Team members must take an active part in militia drill, mass organizations, newspaper writing and study,[117] prescribed study programs,[118] "recreation clubs," [119] and daily work group meetings. A 1961 editorial of *People's Daily* enumerated mess hall control committees, general meetings, "democratic" work assignments, "democratic control teams" (for the masses to participate in administrative work), "livelihood advisory teams," and a variety of techniques to enlist the democratic cooperation of team members.[120] Newspaper study, debates, emulation campaigns, model "standard-bearers," and "individual heart-to-heart talks to help the backward . . . catch up with the advanced" integrate ideological education with production motivation.[121] In 1960, separate mess

[115] *Jen-min jih-pao*, August 5, 1960.

[116] The organizational principle of the commune is democratic centralism. See *Sixth Plenary Session of the Eighth Central Committee of the Communist Party of China*, pp. 40–44. For a recent discussion of the working procedures required by democratic centralism in the commune, see *Kung-jen jih-pao*, August 4 and 8, 1961, in *U.S. Joint Publications Research Service*, no. 10631 (1961) pp. 1–7.

[117] See, for example, *Jen-min jih-pao*, November 10, 1960.

[118] See *ibid.*, November 10 and 18, 1960.

[119] See *Kung-jen jih-pao*, December 9, 1960, in *SCMP*, no. 2420 (1960), pp. 17–19.

[120] *Jen-min jih-pao*, January 27, 1961.

[121] *Ibid.*, November 10, 1960.

facilities for cadres were abolished to enable cadres to "fraternize with the masses extensively" and to transform the mess halls into "a position for strengthening the party's leadership over the masses." [122] The "leader" in Communist China is the man facing you across the mess table, in the study meeting, at the head of the pay line, in the hospital clinic, in the "recreation halls," in your children's school, and in the daily routine that surrounds the planning and carrying out of commune chores.

At the production team level, the leadership techniques of the Chinese Communist Party become sharply focused. Cadres go to the fields and mess halls to direct all the social processes of team life. No area of life escapes party supervision, for all of life is defined in basically political terms. "We need in our people's communes," *People's Daily* stated in 1960, "more such persons who 'like to mind others' business.' " [123] The team member who does not fulfill his quotas or ideologically conform becomes identified as among the technically and ideologically "backward," and the two (technical and ideological) may be freely interchanged for effective reeducation. Constant directed activity, manipulation of wage points which determine life and death, and a variety of collective pressures make leadership on the Chinese farm vividly real. It may not matter what Mao Tse-tung does, but it matters very much what a farmer's friends and neighbors do and think and how his family lives.

[122] *Ibid.*, September 17, 1960.   [123] *Ibid.*, July 22, 1960.

VIII

Communist Goals
and Chinese Society

The Problem of Marxist Objectives
in Confucian Society

IN response to the question "Don't you want to eliminate state power?" in 1949, Mao Tse-tung said it was necessary at that time to strengthen the instruments of state force (army, police, and courts) in order to protect the nation and people against imperialism and domestic reactionaries.[1] After the national defense had been consolidated and the interests of the people protected, Mao said, "China, under the leadership of the working class and the Communist Party, can develop steadily from an agricultural into an industrial country and from a New Democratic into a socialist and communist society."[2] Mao's

[1] Mao Tse-tung, *On People's Democratic Dictatorship* (7th ed.; Peking: Foreign Languages Press, 1959), p. 12.
[2] *Ibid.*

decision to seek first a powerful state was predicated on the urgent requirement to reorient the entire Chinese society to support the Communist program. This reorientation was to be carried out in conjunction with general economic reconstruction, and the two processes of change were to be mutually reinforcing.

In addition to the negative goal of suppression of reactionaries, Mao advocated a positive objective of "protecting the people" to allow them to "educate and remould themselves by democratic methods on a national and all-round scale." [3] By "people" Mao explicitly meant the working class, the peasantry, the petty bourgeoisie, and the national bourgeoisie and excluded the landlords, the bureaucratic bourgeoisie, and "their representative: the Kuomingtang reactionary clique and its accomplices." [4] The remolding of the people would rid them of "bad habits and ideas acquired from the old society." [5] They would no longer be "misled by the reactionaries" and would be able "to progress towards a socialist and communist society."

From the onset of the Communist revolution in China, Mao and other Communist leaders have demonstrated their concern for the remolding of the traditional society and the reorientation of the Chinese as a necessary concomitant or prelude to material reconstruction. As evidenced by Mao's 1957 statement, *On the Correct Handling of Contradictions among the People*, this concern by Communist leaders continues to be paramount.[6] This persistent concern for the remolding of the Chinese and the traditional society is founded on two basic Marxist-Leninist assumptions which are also central in Communist leadership techniques. The first assumption is that the personal and social relations of the economic base (as controlled by the mode and

[3] *Ibid.*, p. 13.   [4] *Ibid.*, p. 11.
[5] This and the following sentence are based on *ibid.*, p. 13.
[6] Mao Tse-tung, *On the Correct Handling of Contradictions among the People* (Peking: Foreign Languages Press, 1957), esp. p. 27.

ownership of the means of production) determine the organizational superstructure.[7] The second assumption is that within the working classes (and to a limited extent in China within the four classes of the "people" [8]) there exists a fundamental unity of social purpose which an active leadership can bring to fruition.[9] The latent unity "within the ranks of the people" must *first* be cultivated and heightened, because the social relations of the people are considered to be decisive in the attainment of ultimate and intermediate goals. This is seen not so much as a question of value as of priority. The leadership in its working methods, as was noted above in the discussion on the party line (pp. 87–97), must take account of this priority for cultivating proper social relationships if its leadership methods in pursuit of other objectives are to be successful.

For Mao, the essential question in the total revolutionary process has been the nature of the class forces involved. "All past revolutionary struggles in China achieved very little, basically because the revolutionaries were unable to unite their real friends to attack their real enemies," he wrote in 1926.[10] Consistently since 1921, the Chinese Communist Party has concerned itself with the identification of classes as "friendly" or "enemy," as they contribute to or resist the development of the revolution. The contemporary organizational form of this alignment of "friendly" forces is a "democratic system" which governs the "people" and a dictatorship which suppresses the

[7] *Ibid.*, pp. 22–27.

[8] The best-known statement of Mao's views on the classes allied in the revolution is Mao Tse-tung, "On New Democracy" [January, 1940], *Selected Works* (New York: International Publishers, 1954–1956), III, 116–121.

[9] Mao, for example, in "The Chinese Revolution and the Chinese Communist Party" [December, 1939], *Selected Works*, III, 72–82, infers that mass unity has been preserved throughout Chinese history by the use of revolts by the peasants.

[10] Mao, "Analysis of the Classes in Chinese Society" [March, 1926], *Selected Works*, I, 13.

"enemy." Since the 1957 rectification campaign and the establishment of the people's communes in 1958, the democratic dictatorship has functioned principally to eliminate the economic and mental distinctions between workers and peasants and to "reform" the remaining bourgeoisie, particularly the bourgeois intellectuals. These functions are performed in conjunction with other forms of economic and social planning "so as to rally the people of all nationalities in our country to wage a new battle—the battle against nature—to develop our economy and culture." [11]

Many points of the foregoing summary of certain doctrinal positions and the light they shed on policy developments have been elaborated elsewhere in different contexts. They are brought together here so that we may look beyond the Chinese Communist assessment of its own leadership techniques. The problem now raised arises from the nature of the Chinese society on which the Communists have superimposed concepts of "people" and class. In recasting the Chinese society, what traditional habits and activities have been utilized to bolster leadership techniques; and what habits or activities have been specifically rejected as opposed to the revolutionary movement? What must the Communist leaders do to obliterate or transform the traditional system of personal and social obligations in order to establish their own new system of social relationships and obligations?

Traditional Social Structure and Communist Goals

The Communist task of restructuring social obligations was a particularly delicate one in China because of the reverent at-

[11] Mao, *On the Correct Handling*, p. 27.

titude of Chinese toward their kin and other relationships within the traditional society.[12] From the individual's point of view, his bonds of kinship, friendship, common origin, and common experience (particularly *t'ung-hsüeh* or schoolmates) established a more or less permanent pattern of obligations. Obliged to immediate family members, kinsmen, and schoolmates, among others, the individual Chinese found himself in a relatively fixed place in the social order, for which the Confucian system provided moral justification, personal assurance of correctness, and a sense of continuity. Although the Chinese pattern of social relationships was not strikingly different from that in other patrilineal, agricultural societies, long continuous development and Confucian values made most Chinese believe that their society organized on patrilineal lines was not only unique but was morally the best. Reinforced by habitual obligations and Confucian values, the Chinese belief in the moral superiority of their society manifested itself in their attitude of reverence toward particularistic social relationships.

[12] A selected list of works consulted in the preparation of this section includes Fei Hsiao-t'ung, *China's Gentry: Essays in Rural-Urban Relations* (Rev. and ed.; Chicago: University of Chicago Press, 1953); Francis L. K. Hsü, *Under the Ancestor's Shadow: Chinese Culture and Personality* (New York: Columbia University Press, 1948); W. La Barre, "Some Observations on Character Structure in the Orient: II, The Chinese, Parts One and Two," *Psychiatry*, IX (1946), 215–237, 375–396; Olga Lang, *Chinese Family and Society* (New Haven: Yale University Press, 1946); Lin Tsung-yi, "A Study of the Incidence of Mental Disorder in Chinese and other Cultures," *Psychiatry*, XVI (1953), 313–336; David S. Nivison, "Communist Ethics and Chinese Tradition," *Journal of Asian Studies*, XVI, no. 1 (November, 1956), 51–74; Arthur H. Smith, *China in Convulsion* (New York: F. H. Revell Co., 1901); Arthur H. Smith, *Chinese Characteristics* (Enlarged and rev. ed.; New York: F. H. Revell Co., 1894); Arthur H. Smith, *Village Life in China* (New York: F. H. Revell Co., 1899); C. K. Yang, *The Chinese Family in the Communist Revolution* (Cambridge, Mass.: Technology Press, 1959); and C. K. Yang, *A Chinese Village in Early Communist Transition* (Cambridge, Mass.: Technology Press, 1959).

Based on the structure of social ties, an elaborate code of behavior was developed and perpetuated in China. Deference to elders, material support of the aged, reverence for ancestors, dispensing of influence among friends (*jen-ch'ing*), and loyalty to social groups were emphasized for succeeding generations of Chinese youth and were rigidly defined and enforced. Families, lineage, villages, and voluntary associations were the permanent elements of the institutional network which gave specific content, and controlled the individual's response, to his social obligations. The emphasis was on social relations which were elaborately structured and discrete; and the Chinese social obligations applicable to those relations were well known and enduring.

As was natural in a society which emphasized well-defined social relationships, the relationships of a Chinese with kinsmen, friends, classmates, colleagues, acquaintances, and the local elites —to name only some of the possibilities—were formalized and identified by a recognized system of nomenclature. The Chinese viewed this formal system in terms of the intimacy of social ties on a "scale" measuring the "social distance" from the individual. At the intimate or *li-mao* (good manners) end of the scale,[13] relationships were clear, unequivocal, direct, and based on the exercise of personal influence. At the less intimate or *k'o-ch'i* (politeness) end of the scale (new acquaintances, distant relatives, officials), relationships were apt to be relatively more equivocal and indirect. Throughout the scale of relationships, there were variations and exceptions to the general pattern of obligations actually forthcoming, and naturally all relationships were expected to manifest a balance of good manners and politeness. When the relative intimacy of the scale decreased to such an extent that the distinguishing act of personal recognition

[13] This scale of intimacy contained the values of *hsiao* (filial piety), *i* (righteousness), *jen* (benevolence), *chung* (loyalty), and *ai* (love) which complemented the prescribed Confucian relationships.

disappeared, the clear-cut obligations were reduced to a jumbled list of platitudes without moral sanction and social acceptance. Non-Chinese have described this lack of obligation to strangers in China as "the cheapness of human life in China" and "the lack of a Chinese social consciousness." More accurately, the obligations of acquaintance were so demanding that Chinese were reluctant to commence casual relationships with strangers or to establish even *ad hoc* contacts outside the close pattern.

Political relationships thus generally fell outside the range of social relationships—even *k'o-ch'i* relationships—for which there existed social obligations in practice. The "social distance" between leaders and led simply exceeded the distance in which social obligations were operative. The mutual exclusiveness of socially unrelated Chinese in general critically influenced contacts in the traditional polity. Within the bureaucracy, minimal political obligations were either frustrated by "social distance" or corrupted by bringing together in a single part of the apparatus, by accident or design, members obliged by the particularistic bonds of kinsmen, friends, fellow schoolmates, or fellow townsmen. On the one hand, the limited range of obligations prevented the bureaucracy from penetrating the intimate social groups; on the other hand, social obligations distorted the operation of "related" members within the bureaucracy. Moreover, despite a generalized acceptance of the imperial hierarchy and the classical political platitudes, which theoretically stipulated mutual obligations between the elite and general population, the hierarchy and the platitudes were insufficient to bridge the lack of obligations between society and polity. In general, the Chinese peasants felt that their own organizations should fulfill all but the most formal "national" functions in a well-ordered society.

The social structure presented the bureaucracy with opportunities as well as limits and distorting pressures. For example, Chinese officials attempted to manipulate the social structure through the family and lineage. When manipulation was not feasible, however, the officials outside the lineage enforced edicts or collected taxes with the aid of police and armies. An example of a partially effective adaptation of the social structure for police control was the *pao chia* system.[14] This system of collective responsibility made each head of a household (*hu*) responsible for the acts of the household members. In one of the most common variations of this system, similar responsibility was given to the head of ten households (*p'ai*), one hundred households (ten *p'ai* or one *chia*), and one thousand households (ten *chia* or one *pao*). Political obligations such as derive from concepts of "citizenship" or "rule of law" were for practical purposes nonexistent. Traditional political relationships, however much masked by other language, were more or less identical with applications of force when conducted on an intergroup basis and were relatively limited in scope. Those political relationships which relied on measures of force were strongly differentiated from, and in direct conflict with, social relationships.

The smaller Chinese political parties—including in some respects Kuomintang factions—that existed from 1911 to 1949 were political associations governed by the *li-mao* rules of intimate personal obligations and factional exclusiveness. Within these parties, the membership usually clustered around a former professor, a core of alumni of a particular academy or university, or a respected journalist. The inner ties of association were derived more from particularistic relationships than from common ideological programs or formal organizations. This personal quality, which can be traced to the traditional social relationships, partly explains the failure of the other political parties to offer the Chinese people an effective alternative to Communist domination during the civil war period.

[14] See the excellent study by Kung-chuan Hsiao, *Rural China: Imperial Control in the Nineteenth Century* (Seattle: University of Washington Press, 1960), esp. chaps. ii–iii.

The Marxist-Leninists were the first to provide China with a consistent ideology of national political power based on a thoroughgoing, reciprocal relationship between leaders and led. This relationship, which is particularly important at the production team level in the countryside, has created a special tone and character for the Chinese Communist Party, differentiating its working methods from those of the other Chinese political parties. The key to the Communist leadership and organization in China is the party's dedication of its primary effort to creating a new structure within the leadership (including the working cadres) and between the cadres and masses. Put differently, Chinese Communist cadres formulated operational principles which would permit them to penetrate the intimate or face-to-face social groups within the general society but which would enable them to resist succumbing to the obligational pulls from within those groups. Equally important, the party cadres endeavored to restructure the social obligations by selectively pressing certain useful habits drawn from the *li-mao* pattern. The party's mass line may be considered the prototype of the new and ideal social relationships which bind polity and society and yet allow political cadres to manipulate the society for political purposes.

To achieve the merger of polity and society, party leaders selectively utilized advantageous traditions in political thought as well as in social practice. For example, leading cadres exploited the tradition in Chinese theory that politics had been part of an undifferentiated whole, despite the fact that intergroup politics contradicted the idealized human relationships prescribed by Confucian ethics. Chinese thought exhibited a predilection for the unity of knowledge, and dominant philosophical and value theories usually linked human action to social obligation (although this linkage was not made as frequently in Taoism and Buddhism as in Confucianism). Chinese theory did not distinguish social from political obligation, and the society was thus denied conceptual limits on political power.

The society was, of course, the presumed source of political values, and the preoccupation with inviolable classics constituted a limitation on political action. By focusing on the conceptual continuum of all obligations and by denying the validity of the classics, party leaders hope to legitimatize their unlimited authority in the minds of the Chinese people. The Chinese political tradition, however, did not provide for a full equivalence between political and social obligations. This the Chinese Communists seek to achieve.

The Communist-directed transformation of China has entailed three principal changes from the viewpoint of the individual.[15] First, the social horizons of a Chinese in the new social system, having the "collectivity of the whole people" as its objective, are expanded far beyond the *li-mao k'o-ch'i* pattern to coincide with the Communist-controlled state. Second, creation of a nationwide collectivity has required the fostering of new obligations based on the prescribed mass relationships. Third, the traditional obligations and loyalties of a direct personal character are being reformed in order to create the new synthesis of leaders and the masses. The new common loyalties and obligations, which when created would make force unnecessary, fundamentally derive from one's identity as a member of the "people" and as a Chinese—not from kinship, friendship, or other particularistic relationships. In creating the new universalism, the Communists have attempted to redirect and expand the social habit of face-to-face obligations and to eliminate the habit of avoiding political leaders. Honoring mutual obligations between Communists and the broad masses is guaranteed by force, however, until obligations prescribed by ideology become habitual and force is supplanted by inner, personal compulsion. Also underlying the three major changes worked

[15] This paragraph is based on Fan Jo-yü, "Why We Abolished the Feudal Patriarchal System" (in Chinese), *Hung-ch'i* [Red Flag], no. 5, March 1, 1960, pp. 19–27.

253

by the Communists has been the replacement of the "natural" and habitual social systems by a structure of more self-consciously created relationships which are logically derived from the Marxist-Leninist dialectic. The Communist leadership has identified the key actions necessary to inculcate and activate the new relationships and has developed organizational techniques to carry those actions into operation.

The party leaders have used the political techniques of peaceful and nonpeaceful suasion to bridge the transition from old to new patterns during a period in which new obligations have not yet become habitual. In particular, party cadres establish small groups for study and production in which new types of intimate relationships are cultivated to replace the former li-mao ties. The small size of these groups permits the development of reciprocal obligations in general agreement with traditional schemes. Under party supervision, these obligations are nurtured and then closely examined and criticized in order to bring them into conformity with the requirements of the Communist collectivity and party leadership. Family members are dispersed when assigned to small groups, and this prevents family dominance within a single group from distorting the Communist aims of these groups, although evidence presented in the previous chapter would suggest the possibility of single-family dominance within some leadership cells. The party guides the participation and performance of small-group members and painstakingly motivates each member to change his attitudes and to develop new obligations.

During the transitional period, a flexible system of political control is adapted to foster the establishment of the desired obligational patterns. According to Mao Tse-tung, since the establishment of socialism (in 1955–1956) the major contradictions in China are those which are nonantagonistic.[16] To resolve these nonantagonistic contradictions, Mao advocated education

[16] Mao, *On the Correct Handling*, pp. 7–32.

(discussion, criticism, and persuasion) and administrative orders as effective and complementary techniques.[17] In accordance with dialectical materialism, administrative orders and laws are considered a part of the superstructure and must serve the economic base and the development of socialist construction.[18] All laws are initiated by the party which then "organizes discussions on the bills and has them amended repeatedly before submitting them to the National People's Congress for discussion and approval."[19] Legal organs must reject the "reactionary bourgeois" principles of "assumption of innocence" and the "judge's freedom of conviction"[20] and must adopt instead, as "weapons" for resolving contradictions and promoting socialism under party leadership, the mass line method of leadership. For the "people," the resolution of nonantagonistic contradictions follows the lead of the party and takes place during popular participation in "great leap" production, debates, rallies, and study and during such symbolic exercises as the annual "love the people month" sponsored by the public security forces.[21] Under this system the cadres of the police and other public security organs work among the people, who in turn are expected "on their own initiative" to disclose criminal acts and expose "counterrevolutionaries." Outside the "people," reform through labor, executions of "spies" and "counterrevolutionaries," and the unique Communist system of "suspended death sentences" continue the dictatorship for the flexible category of "the enemy."[22]

[17] *Ibid.*, p. 16.
[18] *Jen-min jih-pao* [People's Daily], February 18 and March 6, 1958.
[19] *Ibid.*, December 24, 1957.   [20] *Ibid.*
[21] See, for example, Hsinhua News Agency release, March 26, 1960, in *SCMP* no. 2229 (1960), pp. 2–3.
[22] Mao, *On the Correct Handling*, pp. 27–32; Lo Jui-ch'ing, "The Struggle between Revolution and Counter-Revolution in the Past Ten Years, *Ten Glorious Years* (Peking: Foreign Languages Press, 1960), pp. 357–359.

Since the Communist victory in 1949, the most conspicuous assaults on the family-based social structure have been the replacement of the family-owned land system with agricultural collectives and communes and a rigid control of social communication. Before these revolutionary changes could be achieved, however, a decade of basic training of party cadres in intensive, collective relationships in party and mass organizations had been completed. The objectives were to substitute a new "comradeship" for traditional relationships and common ideology for familial values and to instill or preserve characteristics of *li-mao* intimacy among Chinese in general and between cadres and the worker-peasant classes. Inculcated to live their own lives according to the new obligational precepts of Marxism-Leninism, thousands of Communist cadres set out in 1949 to bring to China what they had learned in study groups and work teams during the previous decade at Yenan (and the guerrilla areas) and in the People's Liberation Army.

These cadres accelerated and directed the social revolution in the Chinese family which was well under way before the Communists came to power. Party cadres exploited the disintegration of the family system by skillfully manipulating the emotions of youth alienated from their parents and of parents denied security and respect. Communist leaders held out the party comradeship and organizations as legitimate social alternatives to the once-pervasive family loyalties and organized structure. Simultaneously, party cadres sought to establish new codes of social morality. They demanded, for example, a rigid conduct with respect to women and eliminated prostitution, polygamy, the buying and selling of female children, infanticide, and arranged marriages. The party leaders endeavored to change the limited focus of the family so as to make the family "a source of progress," with "political life in first position." [23]

[23] Li Chung-ying, *Ko-ming-che ko-jen sheng-huo yü cheng-chih ti kuan-hsi* [The Relationship of a Revolutionary Individual's Life and Politics] (Peking: T'ung-su tu-wu ch'u-pan she, 1956), pp. 24–27.

The family system, the Communists hold, is the product of the social mode of production, and the new family pattern must keep pace with the Marxist-Leninist revolution.[24] In a series of articles for the guidance of youth, a Communist writer advocated the abolition of the family as a financial unit; separate eating, working, and study habits for family members; and the relegation of sex life to a minor position.[25] Given these changes, the writer concluded, the family would no longer be the basic unit which organizes society. Since women and men will become equal so far as labor is concerned,[26] the working masses will have "little time for their family activities, because they are mostly engaged in participating in the collective activities during their spare time." [27]

Major Communist Goals for Chinese Society

Mao's immediate objectives stated in *On People's Democratic Dictatorship* (1949) for strengthening the state power were basically attained with the liquidation of the landlords and other "class enemies" between 1949 and 1953. Toward the end of 1952, the party Central Committee inaugurated the second phase of its social goals with the "general line for the period of transi-

[24] See *Hsin chien-she* [New Construction], no. 4, April 7, 1960, in *SCMM*, no. 214 (1960), pp. 1–10, and *Hsin chien-she*, no. 5, May 5, 1960, in *SCMM*, no. 219 (1960), pp. 1–7.

[25] *Chung-kuo ch'ing-nien* [China Youth], no. 4, 1960, in *ECMM*, no. 210 (1960), pp. 38–39; *Shan-hsi jih-pao* [Shansi Daily], March 8, 1958, in *SCMP*, no. 1789 (1958), pp. 23–26.

[26] See "Speech by Comrade Teng Ying-chao," *Eighth National Congress of the Communist Party of China* (Peking: Foreign Languages Press, 1956), II, 225–235. A comprehensive collection on official policy toward women is *Fu-nü yün-tung wen-hsien* [Documents of the Women's Movement] (Hong Kong: Hsin min-chu ch'u-pan she, 1949).

[27] *Chung-kuo ch'ing-nien*, p. 39. The translation has been slightly altered to conform to the original.

tion to socialism." The major objectives for this transitional period were the "simultaneous development of socialist revolution and socialist construction" and the step-by-step socialist transformation of agriculture, handicraft industry, and capitalist industry. This second phase of social policy, which is still partly in effect, began in full force with the First Five-Year Plan (1953–1957), during which time rural collectivization, socialization of industry and commerce, the "hundred flowers" reform of intellectuals, and the purging of "rightist" elements in the first stages of the 1957 rectification campaign brought progress toward the socialist goal. With these major changes achieved by 1957, Mao Tse-tung in *On the Correct Handling of Contradictions among the People* restated the basic tasks set in 1949: "Our basic task is no longer to set free the productive forces but to protect and expand them in the context of the new relations of production." [28] The line for this new task was capsulized in the 1958 "general line for socialist construction"— "to build socialism by exerting our utmost efforts, and pressing ahead consistently to achieve greater, faster, better and more economical results."

The post-1957 "basic task" of the Chinese people under the leadership of the Chinese Communist Party was broken into five parts during discussions on the Second Five-Year Plan (1958–1962). These five "fundamental tasks" of the Plan were

(1) to continue industrial construction with heavy industry as its core and promote technical reconstruction of the national economy . . . ; (2) to carry through socialist transformation, and consolidate and expand the system of collective ownership and the system of ownership by the whole people; (3) to further increase the production of industry, agriculture and handicrafts and correspondingly develop transport and commerce . . . ; (4) to make vigorous efforts to train personnel . . . ; and (5) to reinforce the

[28] P. 30.

national defences and raise the level of the people's material and cultural life.[29]

These five tasks centered in socialist industrialization, which was scheduled for completion "within a period of three Five-Year Plans." [30] "In three five-year plans or perhaps a little longer," Mao Tse-tung said in 1957, "China's annual steel output can be raised to 20,000,000 tons or more." [31] Although Mao stated that "heavy industry is the core of China's economic construction," [32] the Chinese Communist Party Central Committee late in 1959 proposed the "supplementary" policy that "agriculture is the foundation of the national economy," a policy which acknowledged the devastating significance of two years of agricultural setbacks.[33]

The Chinese Communists have lauded the rapid transition in China to an industrial society. "We did in ten years more than our ancestors had done in hundreds and even thousands of years," a Communist leader (T'ao Chu) wrote in 1959.[34] In all cases, the fundamental causes of this swift transformation are given as "the correct leadership of the great Chinese Communist Party and the great leader Comrade Mao Tse-tung, the guidance of the general line applicable in our country during the period of transition, and the guidance of the general line for socialist construction." [35] In an all-encompassing way,

[29] See, for example, Chou En-lai, "Report on the Proposals for the Second Five-Year Plan," *Eighth National Congress*, I, 280–281.

[30] *Ibid.*, p. 281.   [31] Mao, *On the Correct Handling*, p. 68.

[32] *Ibid.*, p. 67.

[33] For a typical discussion of this policy, see Liao Lu-yen, *The Whole Party and the Whole People Go In for Agriculture in a Big Way* [September 1, 1960] (Peking: Foreign Languages Press, 1960), pp. 1–7.

[34] *Nan-fang jih-pao* [Southern Daily], September 30, 1959, in *SCMP*, no. 2130 (1959), pp. 23–27; *Wen-hui pao* [Cultural Exchange] (Hong Kong), October 2, 1959, in *SCMP*, no. 2118 (1959), p. 19. The quotation is found in the latter citation.

[35] *Wen-hui pao*, p. 23.

the party has done on a grand scale what Wang Kuo-fan did in the "paupers' cooperative" on a small scale, but the party also leads the total socialist transformation of China by its leadership guidance of the whole as well as of the parts.

Since the extraordinary crisis in agricultural production began in 1959–1960, the cadres of the party have been even more insistent on the leadership of the Communist Party as the "fundamental guarantee for the victory of all our undertakings." [36] Despite the increase in disciplinary and control measures during that crisis, the party leadership techniques have remained remarkably consistent and, as in the past, have even been strengthened in the crisis rather than yielding to desperation and irrationality. The party leadership has not always been successful and at times has miscalculated, but it has shown a critical attitude toward its own mistakes. "All our cadres," Vice-Premier Li Fu-ch'un said in 1960, "must improve their way of doing things in the spirit of scorning difficulties strategically and taking full account of them tactically." [37] On the same theme of difficulties, Li added that the party cadres must be "ambitious and bold in the cause of socialist construction." [38] He stated that the party cadres must be "diligent" and "down-to-earth" in addition to having a clear-cut direction toward "far-sighted goals."

The avowed objectives of industrialization [39] and commune

---

[36] Li Fu-ch'un, *Raise High the Red Flag of the General Line and Continue to March Forward* [August 16, 1960] (Peking: Foreign Languages Press, 1960), pp. 35 ff. See also Liu Shao-ch'i, "The Political Report," *Eighth National Congress,* I, 95–111.

[37] Li Fu-ch'un, *op. cit.,* p. 37; this is a paraphrase of a statement made by Mao Tse-tung in 1946 and popularized by an editorial in *Hung-ch'i,* no. 19, October 1, 1960, pp. 13–17.

[38] Li Fu-ch'un, *op. cit.,* p. 37.

[39] The few statistics released by the Central People's Government on economic production before 1961 indicated some important increases despite major setbacks in agriculture (*Peking Review,* no. 8, 1961, pp. 5–8). For example, steel production reportedly rose from 13,350,000 tons in 1959 to 18,450,000 tons in 1960. Compared with 1957, the gross

regimentation under party leadership have been to achieve "the socialist system and the concerted efforts of a united people." [40] Given these conditions of socialism and unity, a "dialectical reversal" of China's international and domestic position has been predicted by Mao Tse-tung (see above, pp. 50–51). He said in 1957: "China's situation as a poor country denied her rights in international affairs will also be changed—a poor country will be changed into a rich country, a country denied her rights into a country enjoying her rights—a transformation of things into their opposites." [41] To effect this reversal, the Communists have maintained the priority for the establishment of the socialist system of relationships which they regard as fundamental to economic construction. Party leaders have continued the rectification movements into 1962 [42] and have relentlessly advocated "radical changes in human relations" through the utilization of the rectification techniques of criticism and self-criticism.[43] Taking the broad view, Liu Shao-ch'i in 1958 stated that "the tasks of the Party at present are, on the basis of the rectification campaign, to continue to handle contradictions among the people, systematically improve the work of the state, strengthen the work of Party organizations at all levels, and work unswervingly for the implementation of the general line." [44] Liu particularly emphasized the crucial importance of rectification in a statement

---

value of industrial output in 1960 increased nearly threefold, the average annual rate being "more than 40 per cent." No comparable figures were released in 1962. (See *Peking Review*, no. 1, 1962, pp. 9–10.) By October, 1962, no plans had been announced concerning the end of the Second Five-Year Plan (1958–1962) or the inauguration of a Third Five-Year Plan.

[40] Mao, *On the Correct Handling*, p. 65.   [41] *Ibid.*, pp. 64–65.

[42] See *Peking Review*, no. 4, 1961, p. 6; *ibid.*, no. 8, 1961, p. 8; and *Jen-min jih-pao*, April 3, 1962. See also above, pp. 169–175.

[43] Liu Shao-ch'i, "Report on the Work of the Central Committee," *Second Session of the Eighth National Congress of the Communist Party of China* (Peking: Foreign Languages Press, 1958), p. 26.

[44] *Ibid.*, p. 52.

which still remained in full force in 1962: "The present task is to effect a thorough and systematic readjustment in the relationships between people, rooting out the capitalist and feudal survivals of bygone days and building completely new socialist relations." [45] Presumably the changes in social relationships, which would be along the lines suggested in the previous section, would set the stage for the "dialectical reversal." That reversal would usher in the period of "transition to communism."

The Communist society is the final goal of the Chinese Communists. Yet, from current Communist revelations on utopia, it is difficult to differentiate the Communist society from what exists currently or what will supposedly exist in the socialist society after the "dialectical reversal." For example, forums conducted on the topic of the transition to communism in China merely reiterate either the Central Committee resolution of August 29, 1958 ("commune resolution"), that "people's communes are the best form for the attainment of socialism and gradual transition to communism" or Liu Shao-ch'i's statement that under communism there will be "no exploiters, oppressors, landlords, capitalists, imperialists, fascists, oppressed, exploited, or darkness, ignorance, and backwardness." [46] However, communes exist in the China of the pre-Communist era, a China which allegedly vanquished most of the various villains on Liu's list before the establishment of the communes. Adding to the confusion, the forums on communism attempt to adhere to the vague criteria for moving to communism set forth in the August, 1958, resolution and repeated in the subsequent Central Committee resolution of December 10, 1958. These criteria or prerequisites for the Communist society were summarized as follows:

[45] *Ibid.*, p. 53.
[46] See, for example, *Hsin chien-she*, no. 4, April 7, 1959, in *ECMM*, no. 171 (1959), pp. 26–27, and Liu Shao-ch'i, "On the Cultivation of the Communist Party Member" (in Chinese), *Hung-ch'i*, no. 15–16, August 1, 1962, p. 15.

Some years after that [transition to socialism] the social product will become very abundant; the communist consciousness and morality of the entire people will be elevated to a much higher degree; universal education will be achieved . . . ; the differences between worker and peasant, between town and country, between mental and manual labour . . . and the remnants of unequal bourgeois rights . . . will gradually vanish; and the function of the state will be limited to protecting the country from external aggression; and it will play no role internally.[47]

The well-worn Marxist pronouncements that the Communist society will witness the abolition of classes, political parties, and the state (except for the "administration of things" by rotating officials) were subtly modified in 1956, when *People's Daily* stated that in a Communist society "there will still be contradictions among people . . . [and] there will still be a struggle between people, though its nature and form will be different from those in class societies." [48] Moreover, the Communist society will not be a society of ease, although it will presumably be a society of plenty. "Persons who think a Communist society will breed lazy bones always regard laziness as a common nature of mankind having nothing to do with social conditions." [49] Attributing laziness and the desire for ease to the system of private property, the Chinese Communists hold that "conscious and selfless labor as an aspect of the Communist spirit" will grow in the struggle toward communism.[50]

Not only will people struggle and work hard under com-

[47] "Resolution on Some Questions concerning the People's Communes," *Sixth Plenary Session of the Eighth Central Committee of the Communist Party of China* (Peking: Foreign Languages Press, 1958), pp. 25–26.

[48] "On the Historical Experience of the Dictatorship of the Proletariat" [April 5, 1956], *The Historical Experience of the Dictatorship of the Proletariat* (Peking: Foreign Languages Press, 1959), p. 11.

[49] *Wen-hui pao*, October 23, 1958, in *SCMP*, no. 1900 (1958), pp. 2–5.

[50] *Ibid.*, p. 5.

munism, but they will also have leaders despite the scheduled disappearance of the party organization. The importance of leadership, *Red Flag* wrote in 1959, "is a universal law of social life within the easy comprehension of all." [51] The form of leadership applicable to the future Communist society was clarified somewhat in 1957 by Lu Ting-yi.[52] The future society, Lu declared, would be organized according to the principle of democratic centralism. Democratic centralism is currently the organizational principle of the Chinese Communist Party, the Chinese state, mass organizations, industries and enterprises, the army, and the communes. All organizations under the *direct* leadership of the Communist Party are organized according to democratic centralism. The application of democratic centralism to a total scheme of leadership operation was examined in Chapter VI. Given the clues provided by Lu Ting-yi, it is probable that the Chinese Communists understand totalitarianism as the integration and systematization of Chinese society—and later all human society—within the framework of democratic centralism. This is their mechanism for comprehending the totality and adjusting current leadership techniques to promote it. In a Communist society, Lu Ting-yi said, "the question of democracy will still exist; however, it will not be democracy within the framework of 'democracy and dictatorship' but democracy within the framework of 'democracy and centralism.' " [53] He added:

[51] *Hung-ch'i*, no. 24, December 16, 1959, p. 14. The Chinese Communists, however, accept Lenin's dictum that a rotation of public offices will occur in the period of communism. As stated in a recent organizational manual: "In the period of communism, the concept of cadre will be taught with new meaning; that is, everybody can be a cadre."

[52] Lu Ting-yi, "Wo-men t'ung tzu-ch'an-chieh-chi yu-p'ai ti ken-pen fen-ch'i" [The Basic Difference between the Bourgeois Rightists and Us], speech given on July 11, 1957, at the fourth session of the First National People's Congress, in *She-hui-chu-i chiao-yü k'o-ch'eng ti yüeh-tu wen-chien hui-pien* [Collected Readings and Documents for the Curriculum in Socialist Education] (Peking: Jen-min ch'u-pan she, 1959), pp. 94–95. Cf. the discussion of "directness" in Chapter I, above.

[53] *Ibid.*

"Without centralism [i.e., leadership], just as without democracy [i.e., participation], it is unthinkable for human society to exist." [54]

To achieve the "totalization" of human society in China, leadership has been moving in the direction of the coordination of all its techniques within the conceptual framework of democratic centralism. This development is only in the incipient stages, however, and there are few clues on which to draw. *Yünnan Daily*, in a 1959 editorial, for example, stated that "many comrades . . . are still void of a complete and integrated understanding in respect [to] . . . democratic centralism, the collective leadership of the Party . . . and the unanimity of the Party coming from and going to the masses." [55] This editorial stressed the interaction between democratic centralism and the mass line along the lines suggested above in Chapters III and VI. It is also possible to find insights into the integrative aspects of democratic centralism in Liu Shao-ch'i's 1958 report to the second session of the Eighth National Congress of the Chinese Communist Party. [56]

The most significant article on democratic centralism in recent years appeared in *People's Daily* on July 18, 1959. [57] In this article by Sha Ying, the entire scope of Chinese Communist leadership activity was explained and rationalized within the framework of democratic centralism. The basis for a rethinking of democratic centralism, Sha declared, was that "during the past several years, because of the victory of the socialist revolution and especially because of the rectification movement and the great leap for-

[54] *Ibid.*, p. 95.
[55] *Yün-nan jih-pao*, July 27, 1959, in *SCMP*, no. 2092 (1959), p. 39.
[56] *Liu Shao-ch'i*, "Report on the Work," p. 27.
[57] Sha Ying, "T'an min-chu chi-chung-chih" [Talk about Democratic Centralism], reprinted in *Hsin-hua pan-yüeh k'an* [New China Semimonthly], no. 15, September 10, 1959, pp. 14–17. For a more recent series which fully endorses the organic role of democratic centralism, see the *Nan-fang jih-pao* series on democratic centralism in *SCMP*, nos. 2738 (1962), 2750 (1962), 2770 (1962), and 2772 (1962); and *Jen-min jih-pao*, July 3, 1962.

ward, fruitful experiences have been obtained, the contents of democratic centralism have become even more abundant, and new political situations have already begun to form."

Sha Ying explained the new "contents" of democratic centralism by examining first democracy and then centralism. Democracy, he wrote, is manifested in the constitutional rights of the people, the "hundred flowers" movement, the cadre meetings and the unity of cadres and masses, the autonomous regions, the policy toward democratic parties of "long-term coexistence and mutual supervision," [58] the system of collective leadership, the cadre *hsia-fang* movement and programs for living with the masses, the leadership system which promotes local initiative, experimental farms, on-the-spot conferences, competitions, emulations and comparisons, and all mass line systems to improve the "spontaneous" and mutual relationships of the cadres and the Chinese people. On the other hand, centralism was effected by the party's lines and policies, the legal and constitutional system, state planning, the integration of all local efforts under the slogan that the "whole nation is a chess game," [59] the central directives and guidance at each level of organization, the unity and obedience of the masses, and all other forms of leadership. Echoing Mao's statement that "democracy is part of the superstructure" and "only a means," [60] Sha continued that "democratic centralism is a kind of superstructure, which serves the economic base."

As a "kind" of superstructure, democratic centralism epitomizes an all-encompassing unity. But, Sha wrote, again repeating Mao, "democracy *and* centralism" are dialectically related and are in that sense contradictory.[61] When problems arise, Sha said,

[58] See Mao, *On the Correct Handling*, pp. 57–59.

[59] See *Hung-ch'i*, no. 4, February 16, 1959, pp. 9–12.

[60] Mao, *On the Correct Handling*, p. 15.

[61] Sha, *op. cit.*, pp. 15–16; Mao, *On the Correct Handling*, pp. 9, 15. Italics added.

under general circumstances the discussions originating within the masses continue through succeeding levels of cadres to a point where decision takes place and directives are communicated to the masses. In this familiar mass line process, contradictions "inevitably" occur between the masses who see the "immediate and partial interests" and the leaders who see the "long-range and total interests." Democracy and centralism also interact in a relative way, according to time and conditions; flexibility is needed to prevent excessive centralism or excessive democracy at any particular time or place. Despite the contradictions that exist between democracy *and* centralism, they are absolutely united and in Communist theory cannot exist apart. Moreover, under certain conditions, democracy and centralism will reverse ("dialectical reversal").[62] As examples of "dialectical reversal," Sha explained that in the summing up of discussions and scattered, unsystematic views into a decision ("from the masses") a "dialectical reversal" of democracy into centralism occurs. Conversely, when directives are taken to the masses who in turn find imperfections, a reversal of centralism into democracy may be seen. "This all explains," Sha continued, "that the democracy and centralism which we carry out are closely related and united and are not antagonistic things." [63] It is crucial to note that when Mao Tse-tung, Sha Ying, and other Chinese Communists explain the contradictory relationship between democracy and centralism, they use democracy *and* centralism (*min-chu ho chi-chung*) not democratic centralism (*min-chu chi-chung-chih*). Thus, Sha Ying added, switching to *min-chu chi-chung-chih:* "Our democratic centralism then is a *resolution* of the contradiction between two things which allows them to become united and complementary, with democracy guaranteeing centralism and centralism guaranteeing democracy." [64] "Resolution" is the key

[62] See above, pp. 50–51, and Mao, *On the Correct Handling,* pp. 64–65.
[63] Sha, *op. cit.,* p. 16.   [64] *Ibid.* Italics added.

word. Contradictions exist now and will exist under communism, but every time they are resolved the organized form of the resolution will be that of democratic centralism.

Such a resolution will become possible when all aspects of Chinese life allow a grand "dialectical reversal." All that is bad will become good, and the good will become immeasurably better.[65] At each stage in the development toward this critical moment, the form of resolution will be democratic centralism (as it is now, though on a reduced scale). The problem is to systematize the economic base and socialist construction with the united efforts of the people. The Chinese Communists conceptualize the general method used by leadership in resolving this problem as the mass line. Although in this sense the mass line constitutes a method and democratic centralism the goal, there is a growing indication that the mass line techniques and democratically centralized organization fully supplement one another, and, as the theory of contradictions would have it, each is the prerequisite of the other. Moreover, within the highly advanced organization of the Chinese Communist Party, democratic centralism has acquired the functions of goal and means and, as mentioned earlier, serves as the model for the extraparty mass line. Sha Ying further suggests that the integration of democratic centralism and the mass line essentially rests on the solidarity of the party cadres and the Chinese people. A united, "democratically centralized" relationship based on habit and mutual interest will gradually (and in the grand "dialectical reversal" sense, totally) replace the current coercive and self-conscious relationship. In the light of this vital core of relational unity, the key role of rectification movements in Communist China becomes apparent. In Communist eyes, rectification alone will order and motivate the cadres and people to use their subjective activity

[65] As was stated in an earlier context (p. 51), the present "good" will not be transformed into something bad because of the nonantagonistic nature of contradictions in the socialist society.

willingly and creatively in preparing, under the guidance of the party leadership, the conditions necessary for the supreme dialectical reversal and the establishment of the Communist society. The Chinese Communists have made clear that they are willing to take substantial risks, including mass hunger, to realize those conditions.

IX

Conclusion

THE principal generalizations suggested in this study pertain to the conscious and judicious use of explicit leadership techniques by ideologically alert and disciplined cadres, and they have been derived in discussions of the chief themes concerning the Chinese Communist elite. The scope of these generalizations spans the range of activity from the fields of the "paupers' cooperative" to the secret world of utopia and might seem to need no further clarification here. It would be misleading, however, to convey the impression that this broad-gauge study has in any way exhausted the diverse aspects and peculiar nuances of political leadership in China. This conclusion may therefore serve to highlight some of these additional dimensions as well as some of the essential problems concerning Chinese Communist leadership doctrine.

In the first place, the proliferation of *ad hoc* leadership techniques during recent production crises in mainland China suggests that more should be said concerning the variety of policy shifts occurring since the inauguration of the great leap forward in 1958. Particularly those policy changes in the field of industrial management have influenced the basic Communist leadership techniques when applied to urban China. Industrial leadership techniques have shown a marked tendency to imitate Soviet methods of enforced centralism and "rational" control since early 1961, as was the case from 1949 to 1953. Nevertheless, in industry the predominant methods of leadership continue to be rationalized within the mass line framework and exhibit a clear affinity for techniques first evolved in rural areas.[1] Urban industrial management closely parallels the party's system of internal operation based on the combination of collective leadership and individual responsibility. Essentially, cadres in industry must use the same techniques as their rural comrades, in spite of the fact that more recently party leaders have also urged cadres to adhere to "rational" principles of personnel management and material allocation.[2]

Throughout China, Communist leadership techniques more or less uniformly reflect the fundamental outlines of the mass line which places permanent emphasis on the production-level cadres and on the necessity of mutual respect and cooperation between levels within the party and between party cadres and the Chinese people. Lacking the opportunity for direct observations in China, however, we do not yet know the degree to which the mass line ideal has been realized and thus to what degree

[1] For typical articles linking industrial leadership techniques to the mass line, see *Jen-min jih-pao* [People's Daily], June 28, 1961, and *Hung-ch'i* [Red Flag], no. 2, January 16, 1960, pp. 1–6.

[2] See *Hung-ch'i*, no. 3–4, February 1, 1961, pp. 19–25. Despite this flexible emphasis on rational principles, Li Hsüeh-feng's 1956 speech remains the basic statement on party committee leadership in industry (*Eighth National Congress of the Communist Party of China* [Peking: Foreign Languages Press, 1956], II, 304–317). For a recent statement reaffirming the 1956 policy, see *Jen-min jih-pao*, August 4, 1961. An important analysis of industrial management in the People's Republic of China is H. F. Schurmann, "The Dialectic in Action—Vicissitudes in Industrial Management in China," *Asian Survey*, I, no. 3 (May, 1961), 3–18.

methods of suasion rather than threats and violence are employed by cadres to mobilize and indoctrinate the Chinese people. Yet this gap in our knowledge should not lead us to the erroneous assumption that the party leaders do not regard the mass line method and style of work as a practical and necessary goal. In response to recent production setbacks, the party exhorts its cadres still further to employ leadership techniques which are grounded in the realism and confidence that comes from "investigation and research" at the production levels.[3] Articles in the Communist press have suggested that party leaders blame the crisis partly on the failure of its cadres to abide by the mass line principles.[4] It is almost axiomatic that as the crisis deepens, methods become more flexible and "democratic," although we do not know at what point the mass line itself may be called into question. The party increasingly demands that its cadres use the tried systems of democratically centralized organization and the mass line.[5] Crises have spurred the adoption of regularized methods to effect the mass line, as was evident in the development of *hsia-fang* and the permanent "2-5" type of system. The mounting evidence of cadre malfeasance and passivity in violation of Marxist-Leninist ethics and mass line dicta has also led to a reassertion of the permanent style of Communist morality and work and has been used to justify the continuation of cadre rectification campaigns.

[3] In 1961, eight out of the final twelve issues of *Hung-ch'i* carried at least one article on the mass line, and as part of the emphasis on "investigation and research" a collection of Mao's sayings on the subject was published. See *Mao Tse-tung lun tiao-ch'a yen-chiu* (Hong Kong: San-lien shu-tien, 1961).

[4] *Hung-ch'i*, no. 6, March 16, 1962, pp. 1–7; *Jen-min jih-pao*, April 3, 1962. This blame was made explicit at the Tenth Plenum of the Central Committee (*Jen-min jih-pao*, September 29, 1962). To cope with the deterioration of morale and discipline among party members and cadres, the party revised and reissued Liu Shao-ch'i's *How to Be a Good Communist* on August 1, 1962 (*Hung-ch'i*, no. 15–16, August 1, 1962, pp. 1–38).

[5] See *Hung-ch'i*, no. 14, July 16, 1961, pp. 1–8.

It may be concluded, therefore, that response to ideal leadership practices has been incomplete and certainly has fallen short of the goal of automatic and self-correcting operation. Methods to instill sacrificial devotion and self-correction were formerly sustained by the spirit of revolution. It may be that "continuous revolution" without visible warfare is insufficient to compete with traditional schemes of political influence among Chinese leaders or to resist by "democratic" means the growing demands of the people for payment on as yet unfulfilled promises.

Two central contradictions are evident when assessing Communist leadership in China, although to the party elite these contradictions are "natural" manifestations. One contradiction, which has frequently appeared in the discussion, is the party's extraordinary adaptability in pursuit of rather rigid objectives. This is not merely the appearance of the hackneyed "strategy and tactics" pair in disguise. Both strategic and tactical objectives, once set, tend to persist. Although what is strategic and what is tactical in Communist China are moot points, a case could be made that tactical procedures have been less subject to modification after their determination than general plans and skills of strategy. More significantly (and more easily proved), after the general tactical and strategic decisions are made, the process of policy implementation adapts itself to local conditions and unforeseen situations with remarkable facility. This development of flexibility from rigid general decisions has achieved theoretical preeminence in the principle of democratic centralism as grounded in the dialectical philosophy of contradictions. Democratic centralism theoretically coordinates levels of organization, the scope of operation, and the stages of totalization within the Chinese society. The principle exerts a powerful influence on the actions of party cadres as they assess both their personal role in the decision-making process and the paramilitary operation of the party in guiding the Chinese people.

The other contradiction to be considered is the aura of scientific calculation and self-conscious manipulation pervading the leadership elite while it fosters mass movements and super-charged emotions. Very early, the Chinese Communists learned to penetrate face-to-face groups without falling victim to the narrow, personal obligations and emotions of those groups. In the process party cadres also determined ways to manipulate the emotions and obligations of others in the interests of party ob-jectives. Indeed, so general is this balance of leadership control and mass emotion that this second contradiction may be only another way of stating the first one, for mass rectification has been deftly integrated with the principles of democratic central-ism and the mass line. By consciously regulating collective emo-tion with a disciplined rationality, the Communist Party appears to have gained the best of two possible worlds. For example, party leaders have not permitted the expanding scope of mass rectification movements to deteriorate into superficial propa-ganda coverage but combine these movements with intensive methods of self-reform. Nevertheless, the recent lassitude of the peasants and workers and the growing sullenness of commune members as reported by refugees in Hong Kong may belie the party's capacity for activating and terminating participation and animation on signal. Fooling the Chinese people on cue may have reached the point of diminishing returns and impaired the next generation's responsiveness to Communist calls for action.

Attuned to the mass line, Communist leadership doctrine may awaken among Chinese the desire to compare slogans with real life and to resist changes detrimental to their survival or to independently conceived interests. Communist leaders have fore-seen such developments, however, and they acknowledge the possibility of popular discontent. They seek to forestall the emergence of hostility toward party goals by expressing lines and policies in ways attractive to the nonparty Chinese and by reminding the Chinese that the hardships of this generation will bring a better life to the generations of tomorrow. To frustrate hostility and enlist support, the Communists astutely exploit habits and obligations of the traditional society and appeal selectively to traditional sentiments and ethical preferences. It remains to be seen whether the affirmative acknowledgement of some traditional schemes may not provide a justification for anti-Communist tendencies and a refuge for the preservation of "corrupting" influences.

Fears, suspicions, and hostility provoked within the people by Communist cadres are subtly exorcised by transference to approved "hate" objects, both foreign and domestic. Mass line leadership has until now been an acceptable alternative to more forceful leadership techniques because of its success and its adaptability to new, even extreme, conditions. For work, study, eating, and "resting," the cadres assign individual Chinese to "small groups" where they are constantly and intimately supervised. Efforts to resist, should there be any, are difficult to conceal, and the people must maintain a pattern of activity that frustrates "passive resistance." Some frustration is, of course, siphoned off or redirected in the mass campaigns and the "tell hate" meetings, but most of it is simply exhausted in the overwhelming demands of daily routine. The balance between permanent changes in the thinking of the Chinese and sheer mental immobility caused by the punishing hours of physical work cannot yet be determined.

When all people become animated and mobilized to the same theoretical degree and to things which are similar, not only is dissension reduced but the very absence of diversity inhibits the capacity for comparison. This kind of inbreeding of selected knowledge and the rigid control of social communication dominate China. Indoctrination in schools and all adult organizations places most information in protected isolation, where it is impossible to determine independently degrees of validity and additional or alternative categories of thought. This inability to distinguish fact from fiction or, more importantly, the inability to appreciate the existence of substitute courses of action will

275

tend to intensify with the death of older generations of Chinese. Eventually, when the party cadres initiate calls for action to mobilize the Chinese people, it may become psychologically impossible to resist or defer an affirmative response or even to suggest more suitable options.[6] Although independent creativity in China will probably decline, it is equally probable that the approved areas of science and technology will become the focal points for competitive initiative and bold advance.[7]

The greatest leadership asset of the Chinese Communist Party is its explicit, practical techniques of operation tested during three decades of party history. Aside from certain vital problems noted in the adaptation of wartime techniques to economic construction, these techniques when consciously employed in a creative, nonmechanical way can still be expected to induce mass support and promote clear progress toward socialism. This is particularly true because of the party's willingness to modify earlier techniques as a result of lessons learned in new experiences. In the Communist view, deviations from these universally applicable techniques so damage mass support that numerous checks to ensure their correct employment have been devised. These checks—which have thus far failed to rally the cadres and to arouse the Chinese people in the deepening economic crisis—include a well-defined style of work, party lines and policies, and disciplined organizations controlled by strict chains of command. The explicit identification of deviations from the mass

[6] See Robert Jay Lifton, *Thought Reform and the Psychology of Totalism: A Study of "Brainwashing" in China* (New York: W. W. Norton, 1961). The subjects interviewed by Dr. Lifton contain a high percentage of non-Chinese. Moreover, his Chinese subjects were selected from those whom the Chinese Communist Party would classify as "non-people," and thus they would have been liable to the methods of dictatorship (i.e., suppression) rather than the leadership methods of the mass line.

[7] See especially Sidney H. Gould, ed., *Sciences in Communist China* (Washington, D.C.: American Association for the Advancement of Science, 1961).

line facilitates the establishment of orthodox conduct through use of criticism and self-criticism. Moreover, the checks on the mass line are supported by increasingly rigorous and detailed organizational schemes of which the "2-5 system" has become the prototype. The numbered systems theoretically leave nothing to chance. No required cadre activity is left unspecified.

Again and again the way in which the Communist elite utilizes organizations and well-structured groups has been brought out. Communist organizations are effectively coordinated on a national basis, and their cadres are prevented by a variety of means from becoming bureaucratically attached to particular organizational units which would damage the cadre's capacity for flexibility and objectivity. Organizations regulate the limits of cadre mass action and allow highly personalized leadership to conform to the Marxist-Leninist concepts of the directing vanguard. The particular form of any organization usually depends on which apparatus or institution may have been found temporarily expedient. Any given organizational arrangement will be changed with alacrity should the need arise. One advantage assumed to exist in a clearly structured framework is predictability. The ability to anticipate rests on the Communist belief that correctly resolved human relationships are governed by the laws of objective reality. In large organizations, human variables theoretically become limited by the organizational framework and reducible to principles governed by the objective laws. When combined with tested leadership techniques, these principles permit prediction. Thus party actions, including the conscious shifts in direction, are taken with deliberateness and a self-confident air of infallible leadership. Even in crises, the Communists ensure leadership authority by resorting to ambiguous explanations rationalized within consistent doctrine, though this authority may lack its original luster in the minds of the Chinese people. Party leaders keep in touch with mundane affairs, but they are still leaders with a special mission and capacity—at least in theory—

to delve beneath immediate crisis. Organizations provide the mechanism to control both crisis and response and to sustain an unpopular policy direction. Theoretically, by seeing beneath the gloss of immediacy, Communist Party leaders may ascertain correctness and capitalize on the confusion of others.

The greatest single impression received by the present writer from a review of forty years of party history concerns the genuine animation within the Communist Party's senior echelons —particularly within the militant group led by Mao Tse-tung and Liu Shao-ch'i. This study has attempted to analyze the general principles of a leadership doctrine which remains the fundamental creative design and lasting legacy of that group. Vigorous, bold leadership has dramatically appealed to the common man in China. This kind of leadership has also excited the imagination of a generation of Communists, who now face the problem of kindling the same spirit in the next generation of the elite. This rather than the problem of personality is the real issue in the succession to the Maoist leadership. Whether the kindling of revolutionary spirit is possible in the present environment also remains a critical variable underlying Communist economic success and the very survival of the present regime. Communist leadership has been willing to gamble, and in taking enormous risks it has been willing to be wrong. This experimenting, driving, activating leadership has struck hard to enliven the Chinese people. Ruthless devotion to purpose has achieved remarkable revolutionary goals. There is no assurance that ruthlessness may not become magnified and increasingly violent, but the uneasy possibility exists that nothing short of enforced motivation can bring the changes required by China in its quest for modernity. The only effective ways to attack China's massive difficulties particularly with respect to capital construction, population control, and national unification may be drastic, although the manipulating hands need not have been Communist. There is certainly no assurance that other previous alternatives to Communist leadership would have been more humane.

Revolutionary leadership in China stands at a crossroads. More clearly than ever before, the leadership itself must bear the blame for economic catastrophes at home and mounting hostilities from abroad. Party leadership on trial dramatically reveals the political realities and central dynamics of the Chinese state. By focusing on leadership, this study may thus advance our knowledge of China and permit even more critical questions concerning the Chinese polity to be asked. The significance of a deepening understanding of China can hardly be overestimated. No perceiving person can remain unmoved while one-fourth of mankind is drawn toward the brink of chaos, nor can he fail to grasp the magnitude of the forces that once swept Communist leaders forward and of the tasks that now confound their strategies and techniques.

Bibliography

THE research sources on Chinese Communist leadership are vast and largely untapped. The number of significant publications used to prepare this study far exceeds the items cited and included in the bibliography. To acquaint the reader with the extensive sources, it may be useful to review briefly the range of documents and additional works read or consulted for this study.

The materials enumerated here and in the list of sources cited are readily available at The Hoover Institution on War, Revolution, and Peace at Stanford University, government libraries in Taiwan, the Union Research Institute in Hong Kong, and several university libraries in the United States. Most of the publications are or have been available for purchase in Hong Kong. No unique or secret Communist Party documents were used, because these were found to contain in general only detailed operational orders or specific discussions of problems within the leadership and organizational framework described.

An imposing section of the relevant material on leadership techniques is available in English translation. In most cases, I have checked the items used against the original. The Press Unit of the United States Consulate General in Hong Kong publishes in mimeographed form translations of the press survey, magazines, and some pamphlets which, generally speaking, are reliably translated. There is an index of these translations. The other translation series used extensively in the preparation of this study is the *U.S. Joint Publications Research Service*, published in Washington, D.C.

The Peking Foreign Languages Press and certain other minor presses of the Central People's Government also provide English translations which are official and usually faithful to the original published Chinese versions. Major speeches and reports and works of prominent Chinese, Communist and non-Communist, are translated by the Foreign Languages Press. In some cases, such as with Liu Shao-ch'i's *On the Party*, it seemed desirable to use different editions, both Chinese and English, to support varying aspects of the argument.

Until banned for export in 1959, the indispensable guide to the press and publications of China was *Hsin-hua yüeh pao* (New China Monthly; Peking, 1949–1955) and its successor, *Hsin-hua pan-yüeh k'an* (New China Semimonthly; Peking, 1956–1959). This journal follows regular categories and is indexed. The file of *Hsin-hua pan-yüeh k'an* when combined with the major theoretical journals (*Hsüeh-hsi* [Study; at various times monthly or semimonthly; Peking, 1949–1958] and *Hung-ch'i* [Red Flag; semimonthly; Peking, 1958–1961]) provides the single most important documentary source on Communist leadership. The reading of this group of sources was supplemented by a systematic reading of the file of *Jen-min jih-pao* (People's Daily; Peking) from May, 1958, through September, 1962. These two areas of systematic reading provided the main substantive data to support the major theses of this study.

Many journals published on the China mainland relate to topical questions of leadership. Such journals include *Chung-kuo ch'ing-nien* (China Youth; semimonthly; Peking) and *Chung-kuo fu-nü* (China Women; monthly; Peking). I have used these journals selectively, relying heavily on the Hong Kong translations. On organization and leadership, such brief publications as *Cheng-chih hsüeh-hsi* (Political Study; variously monthly and semimonthly; 1955–1959) and *Shih-shih shou-ts'e* (Current Events Handbook; semimonthly; Peking, scattered issues in 1950–1959), both of which are now banned for export, provided special material on propaganda themes and methods.

The additional documents consulted for this study may be conveniently divided into three rough categories. The first category includes official publications of the Communist Party and the Central People's Government. The Chinese mainland press regularly publishes authoritative handbooks, reference guides, and biographies, the most useful of which for this study have been the annual *Jenmin shou-ts'e* (People's Handbook; Peking: Ta-kung pao she, 1956–1958) and the semiannual law series *Chung-hua jen-min kung-ho-kuo fa-kuei hui-pien* (Collected Laws of the Chinese People's Republic; Peking: Fa-lü ch'u-pan she, 1954–1959). The latter series is compiled by the State Council Legal Section and the Chinese People's Republic Law Documents Committee. I have relied on the Foreign Languages Press translation of the most important party documentary collection used, *Eighth National Congress of the Communist Party of China* (Peking, 1956), after I had established that the translation is completely adequate.

The second group of additional documents are published compilations and "study" series, many of which have been examined in the preparation of this study. Editorials from *Jen-min jih-pao* since 1957 have been collected in general editions and on special themes (such as on the Communist style of work or the general line). These are supplemented by regular study series, one of which is a thirteen-volume "Communist Youth Readers" with such titles as *Democracy and Freedom, The Road of the October Revolution,* and *On Technical Revolution* (all in Chinese). These were published in 1958 by the Chung-kuo ch'ing-nien ch'u-pan she in Peking. Of special significance for this study on party leadership have been the Chinese Communist Party study documents. I have had occasion to cite only a few of the sources of this kind actually consulted. In Chapter V, I have also enumerated many other cadre study documents, including the "cadres must read" series.

The third category of additional sources used includes works dealing with special themes usually written by a single, prominent author. These consist of essays; books on theoretical or practical topics; government, party, or mass organization leaders' reports; and specialized pamphlets. Many of these appear in more comprehensive publications or journals. The most useful of these were

Chou En-lai's reports on the work of the government which until 1959 appeared annually under variant titles. In addition to the well-known works of Mao Tse-tung, Liu Shao-ch'i, and Teng Hsiao-p'ing, those authors whose writings were particularly important in the preparation of this study were Ai Szu-ch'i (such as *Li-shih wei-wu-lun she-hui fa-chan shih* [Historical Materialism: The History of Social Development; Peking: San-lien shu-tien, 1950, 270 pp.] and *Pien-cheng wei-wu-chu-i chiang-k'o t'i-kang* [Lecture Principles on Dialectical Materialism; Peking: Jen-min ch'u-pan she, 1957, 232 pp.]), Ch'en Po-ta (such as *Notes on Mao Tse-tung's "Report of an Investigation into the Peasant Movement in Hunan"* [1954, 62 pp.], *Stalin and the Chinese Revolution* [1953, 55 pp.], *Speech before the Study Group of Research Members of Academia Sinica* [1953, 35 pp.], and *Notes on Ten Years of Civil War (1927–1936)* [1954, 108 pp.], all published in Peking by Foreign Languages Press), and Chou Yang (such as *New China's Literature and Art* [Peking: Foreign Languages Press, 156 pp.]). One book which was particularly important in the development of my thinking on the interrelationship of the various parts of the leadership ideology was Wang Chin-piao and Wu Ch'eng-keng, *T'an Chung-kuo kung-ch'an tang ti chih-tao szu-hsiang* (Talk about the Chinese Communist Party's Leadership Thought; Peking: T'ung-su tu-wu ch'u-pan she, 1957, 42 pp.).

For convenience, this bibliography is divided into three parts as follows: (1) all the Chinese-language documentary sources cited, (2) all the English-language sources cited, and (3) a list of continuations cited.

Chinese Sources Cited

Chang Chu-shih. *Tsen-yang hsieh: tzu-chuan, t'ung-hsün, tsung-chieh, shu-hsin, tu-shu pi-chi* [How to Write Autobiography, News Articles, Summing Up, Letters, and Book Notes]. 3d ed. Peking: Hsüeh-hsi shu-tien, 1951. 40 pp.

Chang Yu-yü *et al. Hsüeh-hsi Mao Tse-tung ti szu-hsiang fang-fa ho kung-tso fang-fa* [Study Mao Tse-tung's Method of Thought and Method of Work]. Peking: Chung-kuo ch'ing-nien ch'u-pan she, 1958. 164 pp.

Chao Han, ed. *T'an-t'an Chung-kuo kung-ch'an tang ti cheng-feng yün-tung* [Talk about the Rectification Campaigns of the Chinese Communist Party]. Peking: Chung-kuo ch'ing-nien ch'u-pan she, 1957. 75 pp.

Ch'en Chih-yüan. *Ko-ming jen-sheng kuan* [Revolutionary View of Life]. Shanghai: Chan-wang ts'ung k'an, 1951. 18 pp.

Ch'en Chung-ta. *Tsen-yang hsüeh-hsi shih-shih* [How to Study Current Events]. Canton: Kwangtung jen-min ch'u-pan she, 1957. 40 pp.

Ch'en Yün. *Tsen-yang tso i-ko kung-ch'an tang yüan* [How to Be a Communist Party Member; May 30, 1939]. Reprinted 2d ed. Canton: Hsin-hua shu-tien, 1950. 22 pp.

Cheng Ch'ang, Shen Chih-yüan, Li Ta, *et al. Hsüeh-hsi "Mao Tse-tung hsüan-chi" ti-i chüan* [Study the First Volume of the "Selected Works of Mao Tse-tung"]. Peking: Hsin chien-she tsa-chih she, 1952. 182 pp.

Cheng-feng wen-hsien [Rectification Documents]. Rev. ed. Shanghai: Chieh-fang she, 1950. 318 pp.

Ch'ing-nien t'uan Su-nan ch'ü kung-wei hsüan-ch'uan pu [(New Democratic) Youth League, Su-nan Work Committee, Propaganda Department], ed. *Yao i cheng-ch'üeh ti t'ai-tu tui-tai ju tang wen-t'i* [Have the Correct Attitude toward Entering the Party]. Reprint. Wu-hsi: Su-nan jen-min ch'u-pan she, 1952. 32 pp.

Chu Yü-chin *et al. Ho ch'ing-nien t'an ju tang wen-t'i* [Chat with the Youth about Questions of Entering the Party]. 3d ed. Hankow: Chung-nan ch'ing-nien ch'u-pan she, 1952. 33 pp.

Chung-hua ch'üan-kuo tsung kung-hui kan-pu hsüeh-hsiao Ma-k'o-szu-Lieh-ning-chu-i chiao-yen shih [All-China Federation of Trade Unions, Cadre School, Marxist-Leninist Institute], ed. *Lun ch'ün-chung lu-hsien* [On the Mass Line]. 1st enlarged 3d ed. Peking: Kung-jen ch'u-pan she, 1957. 345 pp.

Chung-kung chung-yang Hua-pei chü tang hsiao chiao-wu ch'u [Communist Party of China, Central Committee, North China

Regional Party School, Education Office], ed. *Chung-kuo kung-ch'an tang tang-chang chiao-ts'ai* [Teaching Materials on the Constitution of the Communist Party of China]. Rev. 3d ed. Peking: Jen-min ch'u-pan she, 1951. 141 pp.

Chung-kung Hu-nan sheng wei hsüan-ch'uan pu [Communist Party of China, Hunan Provincial Committee Propaganda Department], ed. *Chung-kuo kung-ch'an tang chang-ch'eng chiao-ts'ai* [Teaching Materials on the Constitution of the Communist Party of China]. Changsha: Hunan jen-min ch'u-pan she, 1957. 106 pp.

Chung-kuo hsin min-chu-chu-i ch'ing-nien t'uan Hua-tung kung-tso wei-yüan-hui hsüan-ch'uan pu [China New Democratic Youth League, East China Work Committee, Propaganda Department], ed. *An-chao tang yüan piao-chun tuan-lien tzu-chi* [Train Yourself According to the Standard of the Party Member]. Rev. 10th ed. Shanghai: Hua-tung ch'ing-nien ch'u-pan she, 1952. 101 pp.

——. *Hsüeh-hsi kung-ch'an tang yüan ti yu-hsiu p'in-chih* [Study the Excellent Character of the Communist Party Member]. 4th ed. Shanghai: Hua-tung ch'ing-nien ch'u-pan she, 1953. 79 pp.

——. *Kung-ch'an-chu-i jen-sheng kuan* [The Communist View of Life]. Rev. 14th ed. Shanghai: Hua-tung ch'ing-nien ch'u-pan she, 1952. 98 pp.

Chung-kuo k'o-hsüeh yüan li-shih yen-chiu so ti-san so [Chinese Academy of Sciences, Historical Research Institute, Third Office], ed. *Shan-Kan-Ning pien-ch'ü ts'an-i-hui wen-hsien hui-chi* [Collected Documents of the Shensi-Kansu-Ningsia Border Region Assemblies]. Peking: K'o-hsüeh ch'u-pan she, 1958. 379 pp.

Chung-kuo kung-ch'an tang chung-yang Chung-nan-chü hsüan-ch'uan pu [Communist Party of China, Central Committee, Central South Regional Propaganda Department], ed. *Kung-ch'an tang yüan k'o-pen* [Communist Party Member Textbook]. 4th ed. Hankow: Hsin-hua shu-tien, 1950. 72 pp.

Chung-kuo kung-ch'an tang chung-yang Hua-nan fen-chü hsüan-ch'uan pu [Communist Party of China, Central Committee, South China Regional Propaganda Department], ed. *Chung-kuo kung-ch'an tang shih hsüeh-hsi tzu-liao* [Study Materials on the History of the Communist Party of China]. 2 vols. Canton: Hua-nan jen-min ch'u-pan she, 1951.

——. *Kan-pu hsüeh-hsi tzu-liao* [Cadre Study Materials]. 51 vols. Canton: Hua-nan hsin-hua shu-tien, 1950–1952.

Chung-kuo nung-ts'un ti she-hui-chu-i kao-ch'ao [Socialist Upsurge in China's Countryside]. 3 vols. Peking: Jen-min ch'u-pan she, 1956.

Fei-wei-shih tzu-liao tiao-ch'a yen-chiu hui [(Communist) Bandit Materials Investigation and Research Committee], ed. *Fei-wei jen-shih tzu-liao hui-pien: tsu-chih piao* [Collection on (Communist) Bandit Personnel and Activities: Organization Tables]. 3 vols. Taipei: Szu-fa yüan, 1956–1958.

Fu-nü yün-tung wen-hsien [Documents of the Women's Movement]. Hong Kong: Hsin min-chu ch'u-pan she, 1949. 167 pp.

Hsin min-chu-chu-i lun hsüeh-hsi tzu-liao [Study Materials on New Democracy]. Canton: Kuang-chou-ch'ü kao-teng hsüeh-hsiao cheng-chih k'o tsung chiao-hsüeh wei-yüan-hui and Kwangtung jen-min ch'u-pan she, 1951. 323 pp.

Hu Ch'iao-mu. *Chung-kuo kung-ch'an tang ti san-shih nien* [Thirty Years of the Communist Party of China]. 3d ed. Peking: Jen-min ch'u-pan she, 1951. 94 pp.

Huang Ho, ed. *Chung-kuo kung-ch'an tang san-shih-wu nien chien shih* [A Short History of Thirty-five Years of the Communist Party of China]. Peking: T'ung-su tu-wu ch'u-pan she, 1957. 96 pp.

Hung Yen-lin. *Tsen-yang tso kung-tso tsung-chieh* [How to Sum Up Work]. Hong Kong: Hsin min-chu ch'u-pan she, 1949. 124 pp.

I-wang wu-ch'ien [Go Forward Regardless of What is Ahead]. Hong Kong: Hung-mien ch'u-pan she, [1948?]. 81 pp.

Jen-min ch'u-pan she pien-chi pu [People's Press, Editorial Office], ed. *Tsen-yang tso hsüan-ch'uan yüan* [How to Be a Propagandist]. Peking: Jen-min ch'u-pan she, 1951. 189 pp.

Jen-min ta hsien-chang hsüeh-hsi shou-ts'e [Study Handbook on the People's Great Constitution]. Shanghai: Chung-kuo k'o-hsüeh kung-szu, 1949. 140 pp.

Kung-hui hsiao-tsu chang kung-tso [The Work of the Labor Union Small-Group Leader]. Trial ed. Peking: Kung-jen ch'u-pan she, 1954. 22 pp.

287

Li Chung-ying. *Ko-ming-che ko-jen sheng-huo yü cheng-chih ti kuan-hsi* [The Relationship of a Revolutionary Individual's Life and Politics]. Peking: T'ung-su tu-wu ch'u-pan she, 1956. 34 pp.

Li Jui. *Mao Tse-tung t'ung-chih ti ch'u-ch'i ko-ming huo-tung* [The Early Revolutionary Activities of Comrade Mao Tse-tung]. Peking: Chung-kuo ch'ing-nien ch'u-pan she, 1957. 276 pp.

Li Kuang-ts'an. *Lun ch'ing-nien ti ko-ming hsiu-yang* [On the Revolutionary Cultivation of Youth]. 4th ed. Tientsin: Chih-shih shu-tien, 1950. 92 pp.

Liao Yüan. *Tsen-yang hsüeh-hsi wen-chien* [How to Study Documents]. Hong Kong: Nan-fang shu-tien, 1950. 79 pp.

Liu Shao-ch'i. *Kuan-yü hsiu-kai tang-chang ti pao-kao* [Report on the Revision of the Party Constitution]. Reprint of May 14, 1945, report. Hong Kong: Chung-kuo ch'u-pan she, 1948. 100 pp. Same work as *Lun tang* and, in English, *On the Party* listed below.

———. *Lun kung-ch'an tang yüan ti hsiu-yang* [On the Cultivation of the Communist Party Member]. Reprint of August, 1939, lectures. Hong Kong: Hsin min-chu ch'u-pan she, 1949. 111 pp. Also published in English as *How to Be a Good Communist*. A revised edition of these lectures was issued on August 1, 1962. The English and 1962 editions state that the original lectures were given in July, 1939.

———. *Lun tang* [On the Party, May 14, 1945]. Peking: Chieh-fang she, 1950. 176 pp.

———. *Lun tang-nei tou-cheng* [On Inner-Party Struggle]. Reprint of July 2, 1941, report. Hong Kong: Cheng-pao she, 1947. 49 pp.

Liu Shao-ch'i Chou En-lai Chu Te t'ung-chih tsai ch'ün-chung chung [Comrades Liu Shao-ch'i, Chou En-lai, and Chu Teh among the Masses]. Peking: Jen-min ch'u-pan she, 1958. 141 pp.

Lun kan-pu li-lun hsüeh-hsi [On Cadre Theoretical Study]. 3d ed. Shenyang: Tung-pei jen-min ch'u-pan she, 1951. 328 pp.

Lun yu hung yu chuan [On Red and Expert]. Peking: Chung-kuo ch'ing-nien ch'u-pan she, 1958. 212 pp.

Mao chu-hsi tsai jen-min ch'ün-chung chung [Chairman Mao among the Masses]. 3 vols. Peking: Wen-wu ch'u-pan she, 1958.

Mao Tse-tung. *Chung-kuo kung-ch'an tang hung chün ti-szu chün ti-chiu t'zu tai-piao ta-hui chüeh-i-an* [Resolution of the Ninth Party Representatives' Conference of the Fourth Red Army]. Hong Kong: Hsin min-chu ch'u-pan she, 1949. 49 pp.

——. *Lun hsin chieh-tuan* [The New Stage]. Hong Kong: Hsin min-chu ch'u-pan she, 1949. 93 pp.

——. *Mao Tse-tung hsüan-chi* [Selected Works of Mao Tse-tung]. 4 vols. Peking: Jen-min ch'u-pan she, 1951–1960. Contains selections of Mao's writings from 1926 to 1949. See the English section for translations used and additional works representing the period from 1950 to 1957.

——. *Mao Tse-tung lun tiao-ch'a yen-chiu* [Mao Tse-tung on Investigation and Research]. Hong Kong: San-lien shu-tien, 1961. 62 pp.

——. *Nung-min yün-tung yü nung-ts'un tiao-ch'a* [The Peasant Movement and Village Investigations]. Comp. and reprinted. Hong Kong: Hsin min-chu ch'u-pan she, 1949. 184 pp.

Mu-ch'ien hsing-shih ho wo-men ti jen-wu [The Present Situation and Our Tasks]. Hong Kong: Hsin min-chu ch'u-pan she, 1949. 202 pp.

Po Ching. *T'an-t'an "ts'o-wu"* [Talk about "Mistakes"]. Peking: Hsüeh-hsi tsa-chih she, 1957. 70 pp.

She-hui-chu-i chiao-yü k'o-ch'eng ti yüeh-tu wen-chien hui-pien [Collected Readings and Documents for the Curriculum in Socialist Education]. 3 vols. Peking: Jen-min ch'u-pan she, 1957–1958.

Shih Yün, ed. *Chung-kuo kung-ch'an tang ti ch'eng-li* [The Establishment of the Chinese Communist Party]. Peking: T'ung-su tu-wu ch'u-pan she, 1957. 28 pp.

Szu-hsiang kai-tsao wen-hsüan [Essays on Ideological Reform]. 5 vols. Peking: Kuang-ming jih-pao she, 1951–1952.

Ta-kung pao [Impartial], ed. *Szu-hsiang tsung-chieh* [Ideological Summing Up]. Shanghai: T'ang-ti ch'u-pan she, 1950. 136 pp. This is a collection of articles from the *Ch'ing-nien ch'ün* (Youth Masses) series edited by *Ta-kung pao*.

Tsen-yang ting-li ho chih-hsing ai-kuo kung-yüeh [How to Draw Up and Carry into Effect Patriotic Declarations]. Hankow: Chung-nan jen-min ch'u-pan she, 1951. 67 pp.

Tso Mao chu-hsi ti hao hsüeh-sheng [Be a Good Student of Chairman Mao]. Peking: Chung-kuo ch'ing-nien ch'u-pan she, 1960. 204 pp.

T'u-kai cheng-tang tien-hsing ching-yen [Model Experiences of Agrarian Reform and Party Rectification]. Hong Kong: Chung-kuo ch'u-pan she, 1948. 58 pp.

T'u-ti kai-ko shou-ts'e [Land Reform Handbook]. Hankow: Hsin-hua shu-tien, 1950. 118 pp.

Wo tsen-yang ch'eng-wei kuang-jung ti kung-ch'an tang yüan [How I Became a Glorious Communist Party Member]. Hankow: Chung-nan jen-min ch'u-pan she, 1953. 59 pp.

Wu Yün-to. *Pa i-ch'ieh hsien-kei tang* [Give Everything to the Party]. 3d ed. Peking: Kung-jen ch'u-pan she, 1954. 206 pp.

Yang Yu-chiung. *Chung-kuo cheng-tang shih* [History of China's Political Parties]. Shanghai: Shang-wu yin-shu kuan, [1936?]. 225 pp.

Yü Kuang-yüan. *Tsen-yang tso tiao-ch'a yen-chiu ho t'ung-chi* [How to Do Investigation, Research, and Statistical (Work)]. Rev. 4th ed. Peking: Jen-min ch'u-pan she, 1951. 76 pp.

Yü Ming-huang. *Hsin jen-sheng kuan* [The New View of Life]. Hong Kong: Hsin chih-shih shu-tien, 1948. 94 pp.

English Sources Cited

The Agrarian Reform Law of the People's Republic of China. Peking: Foreign Languages Press, 1950. 85 pp.

Brandt, Conrad, Benjamin Schwartz, and John K. Fairbank. *A Documentary History of Chinese Communism.* Cambridge: Harvard University Press, 1952. 552 pp.

Chao Kuo-chün. "Leadership in the Chinese Communist Party," *Annals of the American Academy of Political and Social Science,* CCCXXI (January, 1959), 40–50.

Chinese People's Republic. State Statistical Bureau, comp. *Ten Great Years.* Peking: Foreign Languages Press, 1960. 223 pp.

Chou En-lai. *Report on the Question of Intellectuals* [January 14, 1956]. Peking: Foreign Languages Press, 1956. 45 pp.

Cohen, Arthur A. "How Original Is 'Maoism'?" *Problems of Communism,* X, no. 6 (November–December, 1961), 34–42.

Compton, Boyd, trans. *Mao's China: Party Reform Documents, 1942–1944.* Seattle: University of Washington Press, 1952. 278 pp. This is a translation of the major Chinese documents in *Chengfeng wen-hsien, q.v.*

Co-operative Farming in China [December 16, 1953]. Peking: Foreign Languages Press, 1954. 34 pp.

Decisions on Agricultural Co-operation [October 11, 1955]. Peking: Foreign Languages Press, 1956. 55 pp.

Documents of the First Session of the First National People's Congress of the People's Republic of China. Peking: Foreign Languages Press, 1955. 231 pp. The first session was held September 15–28, 1954.

Documents of the National Conference of the Communist Party of China (March 1955). Peking: Foreign Languages Press, 1955. 64 pp.

The Draft Programme for Agricultural Development in the People's Republic of China 1956–1967 [January 23, 1956]. Peking: Foreign Languages Press, 1956. 44 pp.

Eighth National Congress of the Communist Party of China. 3 vols. Peking: Foreign Languages Press, 1956.

Fei Hsiao-t'ung. *China's Gentry: Essays in Rural-Urban Relations.* Rev. and ed. Chicago: University of Chicago Press, 1953. 289 pp.

Gould, Sidney H., ed. *Sciences in Communist China.* Washington, D.C.: American Association for the Advancement of Science, 1961. 872 pp.

Gourlay, Walter E. *Chinese Communist Cadre: Key to Political Power.* Cambridge, Mass.: Russian Research Center, Harvard University, 1952. 122 pp.

The Historical Experience of the Dictatorship of the Proletariat. Peking: Foreign Languages Press, 1959. 64 pp. This contains two *People's Daily* editorials from the issues of April 5 and December 29, 1956.

Ho Kan-chih. *A History of the Modern Chinese Revolution.* Peking: Foreign Languages Press, 1959. 627 pp.

Houn, Franklin W. *To Change a Nation: Propaganda and Indoctrination in Communist China* (New York: Free Press, 1962). 250 pp.

Hsiao, Kung-chuan. *Rural China: Imperial Control in the Nineteenth Century.* Seattle: University of Washington Press, 1960. 783 pp.

Hsiao, Tso-liang. *Power Relations within the Chinese Communist Movement, 1930–1934: A Study of Documents* (Seattle: University of Washington Press, 1961). 404 pp.

Hsü, Francis L. K. *Under the Ancestor's Shadow: Chinese Culture and Personality.* New York: Columbia University Press, 1948. 317 pp.

Hu Ch'iao-mu. *Thirty Years of the Communist Party of China.* 4th ed. Peking: Foreign Languages Press, 1959. 114 pp.

Isaacs, Harold R. *The Tragedy of the Chinese Revolution.* 2d rev. ed. Stanford: Stanford University Press, 1961. 392 pp.

La Barre, W. "Some Observations on Character Structure in the Orient: II, The Chinese, Parts One and Two," *Psychiatry,* IX (1946), 215–237, 375–395.

Lang, Olga. *Chinese Family and Society.* New Haven: Yale University Press, 1946. 395 pp.

Lenin, V. I. *Selected Works.* 4 vols. Moscow: Foreign Languages Press, 1952.

Li Fu-ch'un. *Raise High the Red Flag of the General Line and Continue to March Forward* [August 16, 1960]. Peking: Foreign Languages Press, 1960. 41 pp.

Liao Lu-yen. *The Whole Party and the Whole People Go In for Agriculture in a Big Way* [September 1, 1960]. Peking: Foreign Languages Press, 1960. 20 pp.

Lifton, Robert Jay. *Thought Reform and the Psychology of Totalism: A Study of "Brainwashing" in China.* New York: W. W. Norton, 1961. 510 pp.

Lin Tsung-yi. "A Study of the Incidence of Mental Disorder in Chinese and Other Cultures," *Psychiatry,* XVI (1953), 313–336.

Liu Shao-ch'i. *On the Party* [May 14, 1945]. 2d ed. Peking: Foreign Languages Press, 1950. 206 pp.

Lu Ting-yi. *Education Must Be Combined with Productive Labour* [September 1, 1958]. Peking: Foreign Languages Press, 1958. 33 pp.

——. *"Let Flowers of Many Kinds Blossom, Diverse Schools of*

Thought Contend!" [May 26, 1956]. Peking: Foreign Languages Press, 1957. 40 pp.

Mao Tse-tung. *Combat Liberalism* [September 7, 1937]. Peking: Foreign Languages Press, 1954. 6 pp.

——. *On Contradiction* [August, 1937]. Rev. trans. Peking: Foreign Languages Press, 1958. 55 pp.

——. *On People's Democratic Dictatorship* [June 30, 1949]. 7th ed. Peking: Foreign Languages Press, 1959. 19 pp.

——. *On Practice* [July, 1937]. Rev. trans. Peking: Foreign Languages Press, 1958. 22 pp.

——. *On the Correct Handling of Contradictions among the People* [February 27, 1957]. Peking: Foreign Languages Press, 1957. 70 pp.

——. *On the Rectification of Incorrect Ideas in the Party* [December, 1929]. Peking: Foreign Languages Press, 1953. 19 pp.

——. *The Question of Agricultural Co-operation* [July 31, 1955]. Peking: Foreign Languages Press, 1956. 39 pp.

——. *Report of an Investigation into the Peasant Movement in Hunan* [March, 1927]. Peking: Foreign Languages Press, 1953. 64 pp.

——. *The Role of the Chinese Communist Party in the National War* [October, 1938]. Peking: Foreign Languages Press, 1956. 33 pp.

——. *Selected Works of Mao Tse-tung.* 4 vols. New York: International Publishers, 1954–1956.

These four volumes correspond to the first three volumes in Chinese.

——. *Selected Works of Mao Tse-tung.* Peking: Foreign Languages Press, 1961. Vol. IV.

This volume, the only one thus far translated by Foreign Languages Press, corresponds to the fourth Chinese volume.

Model Regulations for Advanced Agricultural Producers' Co-operatives [June 30, 1956]. Peking: Foreign Languages Press, 1956. 34 pp.

Model Regulations for an Agricultural Producers' Co-operative [March 17, 1956]. Peking: Foreign Languages Press, 1956. 52 pp.

Mutual Aid and Co-operation in China's Agricultural Production [February 15, 1953]. Peking: Foreign Languages Press, 1953. 38 pp.

The National Conference of Outstanding Groups and Workers in Socialist Construction in Industry, Communications and Transport, Capital Construction, Finance and Trade. Peking: Foreign Languages Press, 1960. 143 pp.

Nivison, David S. "Communist Ethics and Chinese Tradition," *Journal of Asian Studies*, XVI, no. 1 (November, 1956), 51–74.

Orleans, Leo A. *Professional Manpower and Education in Communist China.* Washington, D.C.: National Science Foundation, 1961. 260 pp.

Scalapino, Robert A., and George T. Yu. *The Chinese Anarchist Movement.* Berkeley: Center for Chinese Studies, University of California, 1961. 81 pp.

Schein, Edgar H., *et al. Coercive Persuasion: A Socio-psychological Analysis of the "Brainwashing" of American Civilian Prisoners by the Chinese Communists.* New York: W. W. Norton, 1961. 320 pp.

Schwartz, Benjamin I. *Chinese Communism and the Rise of Mao.* Cambridge: Harvard University Press, 1951. 258 pp.

Second Session of the Eighth National Congress of the Communist Party of China. Peking: Foreign Languages Press, 1958. 95 pp.

Sixth Plenary Session of the Eighth Central Committee of the Communist Party of China. Peking: Foreign Languages Press, 1958. 51 pp.

Smith, Arthur H. *China in Convulsion.* 2 vols. New York: F. H. Revell Co., 1901.

———. *Chinese Characteristics.* New York: F. H. Revell Co., 1894. 342 pp.

———. *Village Life in China.* New York: F. H. Revell Co., 1899. 360 pp.

Snow, Edgar. *Red Star over China.* New York: Modern Library, 1944. 529 pp.

Spencer, J. E. "Agriculture and Population in Relation to Economic Planning," *Annals of the American Academy of Political and Social Science*, CCCXXI (January, 1959), 62–70.

Stalin, Joseph. *Defects in Party Work and Measures for Liquidating Trotskyite and Other Double-Dealers* [March 3–5, 1937]. Moscow: Cooperative Publishing Society of Foreign Workers in the U.S.S.R., 1937. 44 pp.

———. *Problems of Leninism.* Moscow: Foreign Languages Publishing House, 1954. 803 pp.

Steiner, H. Arthur. "Constitutionalism in Communist China," *American Political Science Review*, XLIX (March, 1955), 1–21.

———. "Current 'Mass Line' Tactics in Communist China," *American Political Science Review*, XLV (June, 1951), 422–436.

———. "Ideology and Politics in Communist China," *Annals of the American Academy of Political and Social Science*, CCCXXI (January, 1959), 29–39.

———. " 'On the Record' with Mao and His Regime," *Journal of Asian Studies*, XVII, no. 2 (February, 1958), 215–223.

Ten Glorious Years. Peking: Foreign Languages Press, 1960. 368 pp.

Teng Hsiao-p'ing. *Report on the Rectification Campaign* [September 23, 1957]. Peking: Foreign Languages Press, 1957. 59 pp.

Teng Tze [Tzu]-hui. *The Outstanding Success of the Agrarian Reform Movement in China.* Peking: Foreign Languages Press. 1954. 20 pp.

U.S. Department of State, Bureau of Intelligence and Research. *Directory of Party and Government Officials of Communist China.* (B.D. no. 271; unclassified.) 2 vols. Washington: U.S. Government Printing Office, 1960.

Wilbur, C. Martin, and Julie Lien-ying How. *Documents on Communism, Nationalism, and Soviet Advisers in China 1918–1927: Papers Seized in the 1927 Peking Raid.* New York: Columbia University Press, 1956. 617 pp.

Yakhontoff, Victor A. *The Chinese Soviets.* New York: Coward-McCann, 1934. 296 pp.

Yang, C. K. *The Chinese Family in the Communist Revolution.* Cambridge, Mass.: Technology Press, 1959. 296 pp.

———. *A Chinese Village in Early Communist Transition.* Cambridge, Mass.: Technology Press, 1959. 284 pp.

Continuations Cited

Asian Survey. Monthly. Berkeley, 1961–1962.

Biographic Information. Irregular. Hong Kong: American Consulate General, 1960–1962.

China Quarterly. Quarterly. London, 1960–1962.

Current Background. Irregular. Hong Kong: American Consulate General, 1950–1962.

Daily News Release. Daily; compiled monthly. Peking, 1954–1955. Name changed to *Hsinhua News Agency Release, q.v.,* beginning in 1956.

Extracts from China Mainland Magazines. Weekly. Hong Kong: American Consulate General, 1955–1960.

Name changed to *Selections from China Mainland Magazines, q.v.,* in June, 1960.

Hsinhua News Agency Release. Daily; compiled monthly. Peking, 1956–1957.

Terminated in this form with the August, 1957, issue.

Hsin-hua pan-yüeh k'an [New China Semimonthly]. Semimonthly. Peking, 1956–1959.

Superseded *Hsin-hua yüeh pao, q.v.,* in 1956. Banned for export after September, 1959.

Hsin-hua yüeh pao [New China Monthly]. Monthly. Peking, 1949–1955.

Hsüeh-hsi [Study]. Monthly or semimonthly. Peking, 1949–1958. Ceased publication in October, 1958.

Hung-ch'i [Red Flag]. Semimonthly. Peking, 1958–1962.

This journal, which began in June, 1958, is the official organ of the Central Committee of the Chinese Communist Party and is identified according to the new Chinese orthography as *Hongqi.*

Jen-min jih-pao [People's Daily]. Daily. Peking, scattered issues 1949–1957 and 1958–1962.

Jen-min shou-ts'e [People's Handbook]. Annual. Peking, 1956–1958, 1961.

Kuang-ming jih-pao [Bright Daily]. Daily. Peking, 1961–1962.

Peking Review. Weekly. Peking, 1958–1962.
   Began publication in March, 1958.
People's China. Semimonthly. Peking, 1950–1957.
   Ceased publication in December, 1957.
Selections from China Mainland Magazines. Weekly. Hong Kong:
   American Consulate General, 1960–1962.
Shih-shih shou-ts'e [Current Events Handbook]. Semimonthly.
   Peking, scattered issues 1950–1959.
   Banned for export in September, 1959.
Survey of China Mainland Press. Daily, Monday-Friday. Hong
   Kong: American Consulate General, 1957–1962.
U.S. Joint Publications Research Service. Various series with regular
   and irregular issue. New York and Washington, 1958–1962.
World Marxist Review. Monthly. Prague, 1958–1962.
   This journal of international communism has not carried an
   article by a Chinese since August, 1960.

Index

INDEX

305